Genteel Barbarism

". . . ideal against reality in Mármol, civilization against barbarism in Sarmiento, European against creole, immigrant in place of gaucho, city at war with country, capital versus provinces . . ."

—DAVID VIÑAS

JOHN S. BRUSHWOOD

Genteel Barbarism

EXPERIMENTS IN ANALYSIS OF NINETEENTH-CENTURY
SPANISH-AMERICAN NOVELS

University of Nebraska Press   *Lincoln and London*

Chapter 8 previously appeared, in a somewhat different form, as "Message and Meaning in Federico Gamboa's *Suprema Ley,*" in *Homenaje a Luis Leal: Estudios sobre literatura hispanoamericana,* edited by Donald W. Bleznick and Juan O. Valencia (Madrid: Insula, 1978), pp. 27–41.

Publication of this book was aided by a grant
from the National Endowment for the Humanities.

The paper in this book meets the guidelines for permanence and durability of the Committee on Production Guidelines for Book Longevity of the Council on Library Resources.

Library of Congress Cataloging in Publication Data

Brushwood, John Stubbs, 1920–
    Genteel barbarism.

    Bibliography: p.
    Includes index.
    1. Spanish American fiction—19th century—History
and criticism. I. Title.
PQ7082.N7B68   863   80-27722
ISBN 0-8032-1165-1

To
Pedro Frank de Andrea—
loyal friend,
gracious man of books

Contents

Preface

The relationship between literary text and literary analysis is symbiotic. Although each can be read separately, there is no question that greater meaning emanates from an association of the two. There is variety in literary texts and also in analytical procedures, and it is tempting to think that within this variety ideal associations exist. It is doubtful, however, that there is a perfect analytical procedure for a given text. On the other hand, one may reasonably assume that some particular critical approach can best illuminate a certain aspect of a given work or answer a specific question raised by the critic. The present study, following an introductory chapter on literary movements in nineteenth-century Spanish America, undertakes the analysis of eight novels, using a different analytical procedure in each case. The critical approach used for each novel was selected because it promised to answer a question that interested me with respect to the meaning of the text. A concluding chapter speculates on the usefulness of each critical procedure as applied to the other seven novels.

The project has a dual purpose: to experiment with various critical methods and to study the nineteenth-century novel in Spanish America. Choice of the nineteenth-century novel as an object of study does not indicate that the material has been ignored. The bibliography offered in this volume clearly indicates otherwise, and it is appropriate to add that many of the works listed are very good. I do hope that the present study will emphasize qualities that have often been ignored in earlier studies. If those of us who have written earlier about these books deserve criticism of any particular aspect of our work, it is probably that we have emphasized unduly the value of the novels as semi-anthropological portrayals of customs. The present study pays little attention to this phenomenon, and tends to emphasize the novels' value as experiences in fiction.

I can offer no satisfactory explanation of why I chose these eight novels beyond saying that each one interests me for a particular reason that I trust will be apparent in the corresponding chapter. Obviously there are many more novels that could just as reasonably be included. Faced with a similarly impossible justification in his *La novela chilena,* Cedomil Goic expresses the hope that other critics will undertake detailed analyses of other novels. I feel the same way, and hope also that others will continue to approach novels in different ways. The eight novels studied here are not representative of countries or regions. They are fairly representative of different kinds of fiction written during the last century.

In the very early stages of the study, I thought it might be possible to use the ideas of one particular theorist in each chapter, but it soon became apparent that such exclusiveness would not work. Emphasis on one or another theorist, however, will be quite apparent. Some of the chapters follow a model more closely than others—for example, Brooks and Warren for *Amalia,* Arnold Kettle's essay on *Bleak House* for *Aves sin nido,* Floyd Merrell for *Martín Rivas.* Roman Jakobson's scheme of the communication act is the basis for the study of *Suprema ley,* but this chapter is not an exposition of Jakobson's ideas. The chapter on *El sargento Felipe* is based on two essays by Tzvetan Todorov. Roland Barthes is a major influence in the analyses of *María* and *Mi tío el empleado.* The latter study follows very closely a Barthesian reading; the former is suggested by Barthes's work, but takes a different tack and brings in some considerations set forth by speech act theorists. Wayne Booth and Gérard Genette are especially apparent in the chapter on *Guatimozín,* but they are really present throughout the book. Although no single chapter depends exclusively on the ideas of either one, they are probably the most influential of all the theorists whose work I have used.

The analyses are presented here in chronological order according to the publication dates of the novels. The chapters were not written in the order presented; therefore, it is not possible to find any kind of progression in the application of different analytical procedures. Insofar as possible, I have made each analysis so it may be useful independently. The opening and closing chapters are intended as unifiers.

The bibliography repeats all titles cited in the footnotes and contains, in addition, titles of other studies that were particularly helpful.

An earlier, somewhat shorter, version of the chapter on *Suprema ley* appears in a volume (in press as I write this) honoring Luis Leal, edited by Donald W. Bleznick.

I am pleased to offer my thanks to a number of people who have helped in this study in one way or another, without suggesting that they are at all responsible for any of its deficiencies: to Pedro de Andrea, Demetrio Aguilera Malta, Ellen Brow, and Peggy Morrison for finding an edition or a piece of information at just the right time; to my colleagues at the University of Kansas, to Floyd Merrell and to Stella Clark for reading, questioning, and suggesting; to Raymond L. Williams and Jennifer Finch for fine research assistance; to Winifred Bryan Horner for opening up a new line of critical thought. The initial stage of the study was supported by the National Endowment for the Humanities; the remainder was supported, in part, by the General Research Fund of the University of Kansas. The concluding chapter was written and the final revisions were made at the Bellagio Study and Conference Center.

Genteel Barbarism

1

Major Movements and Spanish-American Variations

By virtually unanimous consent, a picaresque novel with a pun in its title, *El Periquillo Sarniento* (Mexico, 1816), enjoys the distinction of being the first real novel in Spanish America.[1] Periquillo's inventor, José Joaquín Fernández de Lizardi (1776–1827), was a journalist who found much to complain about—customs and institutions that seemed unreasonable to him—in the society of his time. When his journalistic objections nudged the Spanish colonial authorities too vigorously, they found ways of silencing him, and Fernández de Lizardi resorted to the novel. He chose a humorously derogatory name for his *pícaro,* placed him in the fault-ridden society, and later changed him into a serious man bent on advising his progeny how to comport themselves reasonably and morally.[2]

The narrator tells his story in the first person, as is generally the case in picaresque novels; however, there is a clear ambivalence in his tone. Although the narration is entirely retrospective, referring to what "I" did in the past, there are times when the "I" seems to be the rascal who was actually present, and other times when the "I" suggests the moralist, the *pícaro* reformed and now overwhelmed by didactic intent. The latter tone tends to prevail, especially because the author arranges to recount the death of the narrator and emphasize his message to following generations.

The literary activity of Fernández de Lizardi coincides chronologically with the struggle for independence from Spain, and his work is an expression of that movement. Certainly he was nothing like a freedom fighter, in the recent sense of the term, nor was he exactly an intellectual. Rather, he was what we now think of as an

1

informed citizen, one with a facile pen. Rousseau exercised the most apparent influence on his thinking, and in this respect his work is especially relevant to the independence movement. It may well be that, viewing the period from a distance of more than a century and a half, we place too much emphasis on the ideas that formed its intellectual base and too little on the militant attitude provoked by colonial authoritarianism. On the other hand, it does seem that the ideas of the Enlightenment were the basic cause of discontent. *El Periquillo Sarniento* is a statement of reason. It attacks meaningless custom, especially chicanery hidden by conventionality, and assumes that reasoning human beings will conduct themselves in a way acceptable to other reasoning human beings.

To a considerable extent, *El Periquillo Sarniento* corresponds to the further development of the Spanish-American novel in much the same way that the independence movement corresponds to the establishment of independent governments in the years immediately following. It is impossible to explain either the political movement or the novel without looking backward in time to the development of faith in rational man, to the new emphasis on individuality, and to the development of the sense of progress. If we look ahead from Fernández de Lizardi's novel, we find the romantic movement in fiction and a brave attempt (all too often frustrated) to establish functional republics in politics. On the face of it, *El Periquillo Sarniento* hardly suggests the coming romantic movement. Even its specific genre, the picaresque, is traditional rather than innovative. It is important, however, to recognize its emphasis on rational man as a transitional step in the history of ideas and attitudes. This view of the human individual seems clearly preliminary to the exaggerated emphasis on individual human values and reactions that characterizes the romantic movement. The mixture of rationality and romantic overstatement is apparent in many nineteenth-century novels, especially those based on historical themes. The anonymous *Jicoténcatl* (Mexico, 1826), before Spanish America is clearly within the romantic movement, offers an excruciatingly logical argument for the respect of man for man. Even the protagonist, an Aztec prince, participates in this illuminating discussion. The tradition continues; the rationalistic argument of *Jicoténcatl* is not basically different from the characterization of the ambivalent Jesuit in *La hija del judío* (Mexico, 1848–1850) by the elder Justo Sierra, or the examination of the Reformation in Vicente

Fidel López's *La novia del hereje* (Argentina, 1854), or Doctor Gutherzig's argument against all forms of religious dogma in Pascual Almazán's *Un hereje y un musulmán* (Mexico, 1870).

El periquillo Sarniento is certainly not a romantic novel, but it is a precursor, just as the struggle for independence, insofar as it was a rationally inspired movement, is the precursor of the political mixture of rational intent and practical anarchy that followed the achievement of independence. Even while looking backward, Fernández de Lizardi's novel sets the stage for romanticism, the movement that is basic in the history of the nineteenth-century novel.

ROMANTICISM

When the romantic movement reached Spanish America, its effect on the novel was to define the character of an incipient genre rather than to change the nature of one that already flourished. Fiction was not widely cultivated during the colonial period; after independence, novels appeared more frequently, but they were still relatively isolated. As for the number of titles published, it is probably safe to guess that more than 80 percent of nineteenth-century Spanish-American novels appeared during the second half of the century.

Some of the early novels are inadequately developed sketches that resemble plot synopses. They are by no means short stories, because the plot lines are very complicated and have the potential of detailed development; they are not sketches of customs, because the authors are obviously intent on telling a story. Other novels are extremely long and often loosely structured—the result, most likely, of serialized publication. Some novels were published many years after they were written; some that were published serially appeared as books years later; in other cases, the first part of a novel was published several years before the second. The first part of Cirilo Villaverde's famous *Cecilia Valdés* (Cuba), for example, appeared in 1839, the complete work in 1882.[3]

With reference to literature in general, it is possible to discuss intelligently the question of when romanticism reached Spanish America. Unlike the novel, poetry had a rich tradition, and the influence of the romantic movement can be seen, for example, when Esteban Echeverría returned to Buenos Aires, after a lengthy sojourn in France, and published a romantic narrative poem, *Elvira, o La novia del Plata,* in 1832. It was not uncommon to have the romantic movement brought to a given place, almost as if by special messenger. In Mexico, the particular reading experience of self-taught Ignacio Rodríguez Galván was a key factor; his self-directed reading turned him into a romantic. This orientation says as much about the generation as Echeverría's trip does. Among other things, it says that Spanish-American writers were reading some literature other than Spanish, because the romantic movement was imported into Spain at about the same time it was brought to the New World. In addition, the appearance of romanticism in the new national literatures indicates a certain readiness for that kind of expression.

Almost all the fiction in the years following the achievement of independence is romantic, and it would be difficult indeed to identify a starting point, but there is no doubt that the romantic novel in Spanish America is present and practiced in Villaverde's *Cecilia Valdés.* This story of an ill-fated love involves a problem of class distinction, leading to the slavery issue that is a major theme of the novel. Emphasis on this theme, along with the general conditions of life in Cuba during the early part of the last century, gives the novel a political shading—an especially important characteristic in view of the fact that Cuba did not gain independence as early as continental Spanish America.

Cecilia Valdés is also praised as a novel of customs, though many readers complain that it is heavy with detail. Its characters and its issues are categorically good or bad, a condition that usually offends readers of our time but is quite common in romantic fiction. Like many romantic novelists, Villaverde seems to have thought of his work as having sociological import. Even if the actions of the characters themselves do not constitute a denunciation, the implied author is clearly protesting the undesirable social consequences of a regime to which he objected.

Emphasis on the *costumbrista* (novel of customs) aspect of *Cecilia Valdés* suggests to some readers that it is "realistic"—a description that serves very well so long as it is not taken to mean Flaubertian realism but is understood more appropriately as mimetic. There is certainly no quarrel between realism in this sense and romanticism. The term *costumbrismo* may be best understood if it is associated with the writings of three Spanish authors who belong to the Romantic Period: Mariano José de Larra, Ramón Mesonero Romanos, and Serafín Estébanez Calderón. These writers view the customs of a particular place more carefully and critically than is normally the case. They wrote sketches, usually humorous and frequently satirical, in which mankind's foibles are exaggeratedly apparent. These short pieces make no pretense of systematic study as in *Madame Bovary,* but they do claim to be dealing with reality. By extension, many novels are called *costumbrista* even though they resemble the sketches of Larra et al. only in their emphasis on local color.[4]

Costumbrismo is not the name of a literary movement; it is a term that indicates special interest in portraying the customs of a particular time and a particular place, and it may be a characteristic of romantic novels, realist novels, or naturalist novels. The effect of *costumbrismo* in Spanish-American romantic novels was to produce a kind of fiction the authors thought of as social—that is, they believed they were painting a true picture of society and revealing its deficiencies. They did not think their works were unrealistic. They often explained that they were showing life as it really was, and the term *novela social* frequently appears as a descriptive subtitle. Present-day readers find these novels declamatory in tone, improbable in plot, and exaggerated in sensitivity. They are social novels—at their best—in the same sense that Victor Hugo's *Les misérables* is a social novel; moving down the scale of artistic achievement, we find a much larger number resembling Eugène Sue's *Les mystères de Paris.* The latter's influence was phenomenal, and is even manifest in some titles—for example, the first Bolivian novel, *Los misterios de Sucre* (1861) by Sebastián Dalence, and *Los misterios de San Cosme* (Mexico, 1851) by José Rivera y Río.

This kind of social novel is obviously very important in Spanish-American romanticism, but the historical novel is also highly visible, as is the political novel (sometimes hard to distinguish from the social novel). Historical novels were often inspired by Sir Walter Scott, but in this kind of fiction, as in the social novel, lesser writers frequently became models. The Spanish-American novelists' search into the national past took them, not to an age of chivalry, but to the colonial period or the pre-Hispanic civilizations. The role of the Inquisition, in the first case, and the injustice of the Spanish conquest, in the second, established a link between the historical and social themes. Gertrudis Gómez de Avellaneda's *Guatimozín* (1846) is a good example of this relationship, which is apparent in many other novels.

Avellaneda's novels, taken together, make an interesting showcase of the different facets of romanticism. Her earliest, *Sab* (Cuba, 1841), has some characteristics of the historical novel, but is recognized chiefly as a novel about slavery, a theme that gives it a social slant (we will not discuss here the question of how the author really felt about the problem). *Guatimozín* is basically historical, but it is very political in its attention to the science of governing. It deals with the time of the Spanish conquest of Mexico. Another historical novel, *El cacique de Turmequé* (Cuba, 1854), is set later in the colonial period. Two other novels, *Dos mujeres* (Cuba, 1842) and *Dolores* (Cuba, 1851), are feminist and clearly *costumbrista*-social. Their relationship with political novels is based on the assumption that social problems have their origin in a political organization that does not function properly.

José Mármol's *Amalia* (Argentina, 1855) was the most clearly political novel up to the time it was published, and quite possibly of the century, since all the action and all the ideological implications are produced by the existence of the Rosas dictatorship in Argentina. The distinction between social and political is much less clear in most novels. Manuel Payno's *El fistol del diablo* (Mexico, 1845–46), for example, shows grave concern about the anarchic conditions existing in Mexico—conditions obviously caused by an inadequate political system. However, the experience of the novel creates awareness not so much of political systems as of individualism turned to personalistic opportunism. The message of the novel is a plea for common sense of the kind that makes individuals take account of society's needs.

Payno and Mármol share with many other novelists of their time the problems created by writing for serial publication. Mármol was far more successful in maintaining a cohesive plot line, and that is probably the main reason his novel has been more read throughout its history. *El fistol del diablo* is so fragmentary that we tend to think of it as a series of *costumbrista* sketches; as a result, the effect of its political message is diminished. Since the study of Spanish-American literature has not traditionally paid much attention to narrative technique in the romantic novel, it is interesting to note here that the structure is influential in our definition and experience of the work.

It is only fair to regard the early romantics as apprentices in the art of fiction. They were without a tradition, without teachers. Particular experiences, like Avellaneda's residence in Spain, could make an enormous difference in the capacity of a given writer, and, in view of the relatively sparse production during the first half of the century, the results of such a personal experience may loom large in our idea of what the genre was like. She understood the historical novel, for example, better than most of her Spanish-American contemporaries. In general, the early romantics were more concerned with theme than with technique. It is practically impossible to make significant statements about their novels without referring to political, social, or *costumbrista* aspects. On the other hand, the emphasis they placed on plot involvement frequently suggests that the act of narrating, in itself, is what mattered—that is, storytelling for its own sake. An interesting, if puzzling, case is Bartolomé Mitre's *Soledad* (Argentina, 1847). The novel is a love story set in La Paz (Mitre was living in La Paz when he wrote the novel) in the eighteen-twenties. We may avoid detailed analysis by saying that it has the general characteristics of a romantic novel without any particular distinction. Mitre's preface, however, is quite a different matter. He deplores the scarcity of good novels in South America and defines a kind of mission for the genre: to teach readers the history of America, their heritage, and to describe the customs of different peoples of the continent—a program similar to the proposal of Ignacio Manuel Altamirano about twenty years later. The puzzling fact is that Mitre's novel does not even come close to accomplishing what he proposes, even though one might argue that it is somewhat *costumbrista* and is of a certain historical interest because it is set in an important period in history. A possible clue to understanding this divergence between the preface and the work may be found in the characteristics of the narrative voice. The story is told in the third person by a narrator who reveals his sympathy for the good characters and wishes to bring about a happy ending for morally approved people. This sense of moral anxiety is rather common among the romantics. When the influence of this anxiety upon the narrative situation is lessened, a novel seems to benefit artistically from the freedom. Of course, there is no radically different narrative situation among the romantics, but the degree of control—and of intrusion to instruct the reader—is variable. The degree of coordination of the love story with other themes also varies.

In the case of *Amalia,* David Viñas says that it reveals a fundamental contrast expressed in the characterizations of Amalia and Rosas.[5] Stated in other terms, this same contrast may be described as urbane-versus-rustic, refinement-versus-grossness, or European-versus-American. Viñas says that the dream of the Argentine romantics was to bring about a synthesis of these opposites, but the Rosas regime polarized them instead. There is some merit in borrowing this notion for application to the analysis of the nineteenth-century novel in Spanish America without, of course, claiming that the polarizing effect of the Rosas regime affected more than Argentina.

If we recognize the kind of contrast suggested by Viñas, we may find in it a binary opposition that cannot be resolved, even though a resolution may seem possible at some point in history. The nineteenth-century novel appears to be based on such a contrast, expressed in a number of different ways. The political aspect of the novel, even among the early romantics, seems to contrast the personalism and anarchy of the American side with the ordered, progressive political organization of Europe. The contrast of customs is amply apparent: the barbarous (at worst) or the folkloric (at best) are set against refinement. In the case of the Indian, ethnic reality contrasts with the noble savage. When slavery becomes a theme, the contrast is between that condition and the idea of individual freedom. References to nature are surprisingly rare among the early Romantics. The novels deal mainly with the city. The contrasts observed here, or the metaphors in which the basic contrast is expressed, are not related to any differing sets of narrative techniques. Although techniques may vary somewhat among different novels, they are not related to the contrasts mentioned.

REALISM

There is no way to indicate a beginning point for realism in Spanish-American fiction, though it is possible, of course, to point to novels that are realist. One of the problems is a matter of definition. If *costumbrismo* is realism—and it may be reasonably understood that way, if we think of realism as mimesis—then it has been present in Spanish-American fiction throughout the century, beginning with the novel generally considered to be the first in the New World. If, on the other hand, we require an explicit narrative procedure set forth—if not always followed—by Gustave Flaubert, we must wait until the last two decades of the century. According to this definition, the probable best candidate for designation as the first realist novel is *La gran aldea* (Argentina, 1884) by Lucio V. López. However, it is important to note that this kind of realism does not precede naturalism in Spanish-American fiction. The Argentine Eugenio Cambaceres had already published a naturalist novel, *Pot-pourri*, in 1881. His second naturalist novel, *Música sentimental*, appeared in 1884. Cambaceres had lived in France, and he imported naturalism to Argentina just as Echeverría had imported romanticism.

A third definition—one that approaches rather closely the equating of *costumbrismo* and realism—refers to the novels of Honoré de Balzac, who is certainly a realist according to the first definition, and a novelist of transition according to the second. If we try to pinpoint the earliest specific Balzacian influence, *Martín Rivas* (Chile, 1862) may be the most satisfactory choice. Romanticism is still present; however, it may be described as relatively subdued.[6]

The case for *Martín Rivas* is strengthened by the author's expressed admiration for Balzac, a fact noted in practically every discussion of the man and his work. Alberto Blest Gana was a student in France from 1847 and 1851. His studies were not literary, but his inclinations were, and he was so strongly impressed by Balzac's work that he decided to become a novelist. He wrote seven novels before producing one, *La aritmética en el amor* (Chile, 1860), of enough merit to win praise as a mature work, in his day and even later. His critics are not very clear regarding the nature of their objections to his earlier works. It seems probable that they were not sufficiently *costumbrista;* if that is the case, critical preference appears, once again, to favor regionalism as a required characteristic of the Spanish-American novel. There is no question at all about the literary portraiture in *La aritmética en el amor.* Its major theme is quite universal, but the novel also provides a picture of Santiago society that is generally accepted as authentic.

Although the romanticism of Blest Gana's novels is subdued, it should be clear that they are still basically romantic, not realist; it should be equally clear that they do not initiate a period of realism. The publication of *Los misterios de Sucre* (Bolivia, 1861), between *La aritmética en el amor* and *Martín Rivas,* suggests that the change observed in Blest Gana's work is personal, or at most Chilean. The appearance of Isaacs's *María* (Colombia, 1867), of Juan León Mera's *Cumandá* (Ecuador, 1879), and of the first complete *Cecilia Valdés* in 1882, to name only some of the best-known novels, indicates that the canons of taste had by no means cast romanticism aside.

It may be helpful to think of a second wave of romantics ("generation" may be too precise a term), many of whom had read more extensively than their immediate predecessors, or who belonged to one of the many literary societies that were founded as Spanish America achieved a sharper awareness of its own identity, or who had discovered an object for study in the middle class. Any of these circumstances might well add a certain element of restraint to the continuation of romantic qualities in fiction. Such reference to restraint may sound odd to readers who know the declamatory scenes in *Cumandá,* the exaggerated sighs in *María,* or Martín Rivas's pouting sensitivity; nevertheless, they are different from the accumulation of disasters and the persistent melodrama of many earlier novels.

To speak of realism in *María* is to miss the point of the novel. In the first place, there is no evident awareness of Balzac or Flaubert; rather, we find strong suggestions of Bernardin de Saint-Pierre and, to a far less extent, of Chauteaubriand. The novel does have a *costumbrista* facet, not just related to the humble people (as is most frequently noted) but also to the protagonist's family and their way of life. A more interesting modification of romantic characteristics in *María* is the combination of a simple story with a very complicated narrative situation (the characterization of the narrator, and his relationship to the events).

In *Cumandá,* the course of events is complicated enough to satisfy the wildest romantic imagination, but it is tempered by a certain displacement of focus in favor of the natural setting, specifically the forest. Although the rain forests, the rivers, and the mountains later became extremely important in Spanish-American fiction, there is surprisingly little about them before the last third of the century. Luis G. Inclán's *Astucia* (Mexico, 1865) uses the provincial ambience with an effect similar to the role of nature in *Cumandá.* Both novels are intensely romantic: *Cumandá* offers a combination of familiar motifs including the noble savage, impossible love, hidden identity, and hairbreadth escape; *Astucia* is obviously influenced by *The Three Musketeers* and by a long tradition of mindboggling complications that stimulate heartrending reactions. In somewhat different ways, the two novels modify their romantic characteristics by making the non-urban settings function as techniques of narration. In *Cumandá,* the forest is essential to the characterization; in *Astucia,* the rural setting permits the introduction of social values different from those found in Sue-type social novels of the city, and the narrator enhances the reader's sense of mimesis by reproducing rural speech in the dialogue of his characters (the summary passages are written in a presumably high style that is dull when it is not unintentionally amusing).

Ignacio Manuel Altamirano's *Clemencia* (Mexico, 1869) differs from the romantic norm in several different ways. The author invents a framing situation in which the story is told to him, but he is still the implied author; therefore, a present-day reader is aware of three contexts (contextual perspectives) instead of two: the context applicable to the message of the invented narrator directed toward the author, the context of the implicit author's message directed to an outside receiver in the same general time and place, and the context that corresponds to the involvement of a reader in a distanced position (see the chapter on *María*). Careful narrative structure is another quality. Altamirano was not a writer of great imagination, but he was able to achieve an unusual structural harmony simply by sensing how long a chapter should be and how its content should be organized. A third important difference from the romantic norm is a switch in the moral quality of the dual protagonists. The good-bad dichotomy is as apparent in *Clemencia* as in any romantic novel; the difference is that the novelist, through gradually developing characterization, shows that the apparently ideal hero is basically a scoundrel and that his unpromising counterpart is a man of noble spirit. These aspects of the novel do not make it realist, but it is certainty an uncommonly deliberate fictional study for its time in regard to characterization, narrative structure, and historical setting (the time of the French Intervention).

Some historical novels of this second wave of romanticism seem to indicate a kind of spirit of realism by insisting on the accuracy of the story and even by using documentation. One of the more interesting is

Manuel de Jesús Galván's *Enriquillo* (Cuba, 1882), which was published in an incomplete version in 1879. It is the story of an eighteenth-century Indian uprising in Cuba. The chieftain Enriquillo acquires heroic dimensions, and Fray Bartolomé de Las Casas functions, within the novel, as the protector of the weak. The author refers to his material as a "leyenda" (legend), but he is quite particular about explaining the historical accuracy of his account. The use of extra-narrative references—even footnotes—was not new in Spanish America's historical novels; they are present in *Guatimozín,* for example. However, Galván is much more insistent, and his work resembles a number of other novels based on legends and also some in which documentation and data become oppressively important—for example, the *Episodios nacionales mexicanos* published by Enrique de Olavarría y Ferrari from 1880 to 1887. In a slightly different sense, *Enriquillo* may be related to Lucio V. Mansilla's *Una excursión a los indios Ranqueles* (Argentina, 1870). *Enriquillo,* in addition to being a historical novel, is important because of its picture of the Indian; the idea of the noble savage is present, but the novel also approaches later works that denounce injustice toward the indigenous peoples. Mansilla's work is an account of his acts and impressions on a mission to clarify the relationships between his government and a tribe descended from the Araucanians. The account is written in the form of letters from Mansilla to a friend, and it contains much information about the customs of the Ranqueles, whose culture he finds admirable. Mansilla relates this information to his own background, and so complicates the political overtones of the work. Critics point out quite rightly that *Una excursión a los indios Ranqueles* is not a novel; however, it is unquestionably a narrative.

Not surprisingly, all the novels produced by this second wave of romantics are intensely *costumbrista.* Indian customs from the sixteenth century or the nineteenth, pictures of salon society during Christmas in Guadalajara at the time of the French Intervention, Santiago's elite on Independence Day at mid-century, and much more: there is no question about the importance of *costumbrismo* in the nineteenth-century novel. However, the works of José Tomás de Cuéllar cast a slightly different light on the meaning of this term, which is sometimes carelessly used. His novels, mostly short, bear the collective title *La linterna mágica* and were published in two series over more than a decade, beginning in 1871. Many of them are named for the social type caricatured in each work. Cuéllar was a photographer, and at least one critic thinks the visual emphasis characteristic of this occupation explains the lack of development of his novels—that is, they consist of literary snapshots with minimal characterization.[7] His subjects are members of Mexico City's lower middle class. He writes satirically but with a basic affection for the characters he creates. A very considerable portion of overwrought emotional reaction (sometimes it seems more a convention than a meaningful aspect of his fiction) makes a strange combination with the satire. Of all the Spanish-American *costumbristas,* Cuéllar is probably the closest to the Spanish writers who cultivated the *artículo de costumbres.* His work raises a question about the appropriateness of the term *costumbrismo* as it is applied to such a wide range of novels of the last century. It is possible that satirical sketches like Cuéllar's might be most properly called *costumbrista* and that novels like *Martín Rivas* or *Cecilia Valdés* might be thought of as novels of manners.

Cuéllar's treatment of the lower middle class is something of a rarity for its time. Novels by other authors often portray its members in the subservient role of the underprivileged. Not so in the case of Cuéllar's people, who are similar to the Molina family of *Martín Rivas.* There is a difference between the vulgarity of these people and the sentimentally described middle class that functions as a substitute for the proletariat in some novels. Here we find another metaphor for the European-American dichotomy proposed by David Viñas. The suffering middle class is the literary issue of Eugène Sue's novels; Cuéllar's middle class and Blest Gana's *gente de medio pelo* have both virtues and vices but are, generally speaking, more earthy, more believable human beings.

The forest also becomes a factor with this second wave of romantics, specifically in *María* and *Cumandá* among the novels mentioned here. These novels are still at some distance from the devouring *selva* (forest) that becomes a major theme later on. Still, a tendency in that direction is quite apparent in *Cumandá.* In *María,* the forest is related to Efraín's sense of belonging—an interesting phenomenon because the *criollista* novels of later years find their basis in the authors' sense of belonging to the New World. (Although discussion of the meaning of *criollismo* is interminable, it is safe to say that it differs from *costumbrismo* mainly in that works in the latter mode could conceivably be written by an uncommitted observer but that *criollista* works could only be written by someone who belonged, who was a part of what he wrote about.) There is an ambivalent appreciation of the forest, in these two novels, that is similar to the contrast between portrayal of the Indian as noble savage on the one hand and as ethnological reality on the other. The forest, like the Indian, tends to be idealized, and thus conforms to the European-refinement component of the Viñas contrast; at the same time, the forest tends also to be a real fact of life in the continued conquest of the New World—a brutal, primitive force.

By 1880, the novel had acquired a considerable degree of literary sophistication. Awareness of narrative structure is especially apparent in the novels of Blest Gana and of Altamirano; interesting narrative situations appear in many novels—for example, the narrator's communication of his own sensitivity in *María*, the self-conscious creation of literary portraits in *La linterna mágica*, the narrator's insistence on documentation in *Enriquillo*. Every one of these novelists would insist that his work depicts reality exactly as it is; however, every one of their novels is replete with the trappings of romanticism: exaggerated emotions, unlikely coincidences, categorical division of good and evil. The difference, as compared with the early romantics, is one of degree rather than of kind; that is, the persistent characteristics of romanticism may well be regarded, among the later romantics, as tendencies in the direction of such characteristics rather than as fundamental commitments. An interesting comment on the literary tastes of the period is contained in the publication during the same year, 1882, of the first complete edition of *Cecilia Valdés* (begun in 1839) and of Eugenio Cambaceres's *Pot-pourri,* which might reasonably be called the first naturalist novel in Spanish America. At the same time in history, there is still no Spanish-American novel that can unreservedly be called realist.

NATURALISM

Lucio V. López published *La gran aldea,* a novel clearly in the tradition of *Madame Bovary,* in 1884; in the same year, Eugenio Cambeceres published his second novel, *Música sentimental,* a considerably more mature work than *Pot-pourri* and equally indebted to Emile Zola. Although it is possible to find suggestions of naturalism in some earlier novels and in a very large number of later ones, the year of *La gran aldea* and *Música sentimental* makes an attractive focal point because there can be no doubt about the naturalism of Cambaceres's novel, and the two works together exemplify the concurrence of realism and naturalism in Spanish America.

The character of Emma Bovary emerges in the experience of *La gran aldea* like the memory of a friend recalled by the face of a passing stranger. It is a tragic story of a woman whose materialistic (and social) ambition turns her into an agent of destruction. The setting is Buenos Aires during a period of great change; the narrator refers back to the Buenos Aires of a generation earlier in order to criticize the city's development toward modern metropolitan status, materialistic and impersonal. As is so often the fate of Spanish American novels, critics tend to dismiss the story as slight or inconsequential and to concentrate on the charming accuracy of the local color. This aspect of the novel is unquestionably interesting, and its documentary character certainly enhances the realist quality of the book as a whole; at the same time, critical insistence on the setting rather than on the story suggests once again that Spanish-American novels have generally been valued for their *costumbrista* interest rather than for their general effect as literary experience. On the other hand, the overwhelming ugliness of Cambaceres's *Música sentimental* concentrates attention on its passion-driven characters, who move from flirtation to tragedy. Fernando Alegría says the novel surpasses Zolaesque naturalism and substitutes the morbidness of Baudelaire.[8] Commentary generally notes that the scene is Paris rather than Buenos Aires, but concludes that *Música sentimental* emphasizes narrative rather than setting.[9] However, all the critics seem happier—or at least more comfortable— when they speak of his third novel, *Sin rumbo* (Argentina, 1885), which is set in Buenos Aires.

Buenos Aires during the last two decades of the nineteenth century was going through a period of social change that made realism and naturalism especially appropriate modes of expression. The process of becoming a great city threatened traditional values and particularly emphasized the kind of materialism associated with financial speculation. The boom-and-bust frenzy that created a few great fortunes and destroyed others reached an inflationary peak in

1890 and led to the fall of Miguel Juárez Celman's government. The period following was one of struggle between the traditionally dominant oligarchy and the new public created by massive immigration from Europe. In 1890, Buenos Aires was a city of about 300,000, approximately nine-tenths of whom were foreign born.[10] Naturalist determinism often seems to be especially applicable to the urban middle class in the economic setting of late nineteenth-century materialism—a condition that suggests a considerable, if unspecified, degree of dehumanization.[11]

There is no reason why naturalist doctrine should apply to any particular class, and it is fortunate that Cambaceres—possibly the outstanding exponent of naturalism in Spanish America—covers a fairly wide range of Argentine social life in his four novels. His third, *Sin rumbo,* actually introduces the countryside, even though it is not of great organic importance in the narration. More important are the adherence to naturalist principles and the careful structuring of narrative. There is no question that, in this novel, narrative dominates setting; the prose style itself is also important because it adds to the tension of the narration.[12] There are very few Spanish-American novels prior to this time that count on anything but events themselves to capture the reader's breathless attention.

Cambaceres's fourth and last novel, *En la sangre* (1887), is a textbook example of naturalism. In fact, the narrator concentrates so pointedly on the protagonist's case that the other characters tend to lose individual identity (the use of names is minimal). Genaro Piazza, the son of immigrants, has a single purpose—to rise from poverty to wealth. The nature of the man combines with the economic situation (the boom-and-bust cycle in Buenos Aires) to produce a sordid portrait of frustrated ambition. There is also a suggestion of continuity in the birth of his son. The clearly naturalist characteristics of *En la sangre,* however, are really not indicative of Spanish-American literary taste of that time. Several other novels published the same year indicate quite different inclinations.

The publication of *Eleodora* (Peru, 1887) by Mercedes Cabello de Carbonera is interesting in a consideration of literary movements and variations of taste. Schwartz states that this work was a final romantic novel before her turn to naturalism.[13] Her interest in naturalism did not quite end the romantic proclivity mentioned by

Schwartz; like a number of other Spanish-American writers, she produced an awkward hybrid that might be described as romantic naturalism. Her attraction to naturalism very likely was encouraged by a desire to denounce behavior that seemed immoral to her. *Blanca Sol* (Peru, 1889), pointed out by Schwartz as her first naturalist novel, is an attack on a morally corrupt Peruvian aristocracy; *El conspirador* (Peru, 1892) exposes corruption in politics. The latter novel confuses the forces of heritage and environment with an insistent vision of the ideal, expressed in the form of intrusive moralizing passages and a perfect heroine. The narrative voice belongs to the protagonist, who recounts from his prison cell the story of his rise and fall. The narrative device, unfortunately, does not ring true, because the moralizations betray the author's presence. The naturalist portrayal of political corruption is also weakened by the fact that the most dramatic moment is not related to a political development but to the death of an idealized beloved. The use of naturalism as in Mercedes Cabello's work is more common in Spanish-American fiction than is a truly Zolaesque novel like *En la sangre*. A similar criticism might be made, for example, of a later and much more widely known novel, Carlos Reyles's *Beba* (Uruguay, 1894). In other words, there was much naturalism in Spanish-American novels, but few of them were naturalist novels; it is also apparent that the influence of naturalism was modified not only by realism but even more by continued commitment to romanticism.

A second interesting phenomenon of the year 1887, also contemporary with *En la sangre,* is the publication of three novels of picaresque *costumbrismo,* two by Emilio Rabasa and one by Ramón Meza. The function of the picaresque code, in Meza's *Mi tío el empleado* (Cuba, 1887), is discussed in another chapter of this study. Basically, it portrays customs with a satirical slant created by means of a protagonist whose characteristics are associated with the picaresque—for example, the protagonist's innocence in facing the world, his upward movement in society, his egocentricity. Rabasa's *La bola* (Mexico, 1887) and *La gran ciencia* (Mexico, 1887) are similar to Meza's work. They share the picaresque *costumbrista* character; all three novels are directed toward specific politically-oriented objects of criticism; all three use narrative techniques that alternately place the narrator close to the characters and away from them. Readers are

likely to associate these novels not only with a centuries-old
picaresque tradition but with *El Periquillo Sarniento* and *La linterna
mágica* as well. They seem a good deal less pretentious, more natural,
than the partially naturalist novels. They make no effort at objectivity
or documentation, though their tone suggests that the narrator at least
believes he knows what he is talking about; a kind of ingenuous
determinism is apparent, but there is no suggestion of scientific study;
there is hardly any shading in characterization, good is good and bad
is bad; the author all but enters to state his intent. These novels are
also mixtures—not of romanticism with naturalism or even with
Flaubertian realism, but of romanticism with a particularly Hispanic,
down-to-earth view of reality that states its case without leaving much
time for questions.

The crossing currents of movements and influence created still a
third mixture in 1887—the Colombian José María Vargas Vila's *Aura
o las violetas,* a scandal in its time and largely forgotten today,
but interesting because it essays a poetic naturalism that suggests
the influence of *modernismo,* a particularly Spanish-American development.[14] The love story dominates; *costumbrismo* is of no consequence. Circumstances prohibit a happy ending, and the first-
person narrator pours out the details in exclamatory language that
does not become truly poetic but seems to be so intended. It is possible
that early readers of this novel may have objected to its erotic theme,
but it is even more likely that traditionalists may have been shaken by
the unorthodox attitudes toward religion. *Aura o las violetas* is
romanticism in a state of deterioration, and it certainly leans toward
decadentism.

Modernismo, which means above all a Spanish-American
renaissance in poetry, includes and absorbs the influence of French
Parnassianism and symbolism. These interests also affected prose
fiction, in two principal ways: first, a greater concern, on the part of
novelists, for sound artistic accomplishment; second, the extensive use
of imagery as an aspect of prose style. The influence of *modernismo*
on the novel may reasonably be seen as early as José Martí's *Amistad
funesta* (Cuba, 1885), in which the lyric quality is amply apparent.
Some later novels combine this quality with naturalism and border on
decadentism. The combination produced no great novels, but it
modified naturalism in still another way. Other novels—Federico

Gamboa's, for example—reflect *modernista* influence in their use of imagery while remaining intrinsically naturalist.

Clorinda Matto de Turner's *Aves sin nido* (Peru, 1889) reveals the fundamentally romantic proclivity of the author and, at the same time, suggests her awareness (less than complete) of naturalism. This novel is distinguished from other mixtures of romanticism and naturalism by its emphasis on the Indian problem, that is, on the social injustice suffered by the Indians of rural Peru. We may sense that she finds in naturalism the possibility of making a strong protest, and indeed the novel does indicate that the Indian will continue to be treated unjustly; on the other hand, the author cannot resist inserting a contradictory ray of hope. The romantic-naturalist combination is also evident in the plot design. Obviously, the author considers a love story essential to the novel; however, her control of naturalism (or perhaps naturalism's control of her) is not strong enough to produce this love story within the naturalist mode. The story of young love is integrated into the plot, but the tone of the narration becomes romantic in connection with it.

In spite of some halting steps, remarkable increases in both quality and quantity of fiction are apparent in the last twenty years of the century, and especially during the closing decade. Among the novelists best identified as realist, Carlos María Ocantos stands out for his series of novels that amount to a *Comédie Humaine* for Argentina. He was well recognized during his lifetime, but since then has been largely discounted, probably because his language makes his novels sound as if they were written by a Spaniard rather than by an Argentine (he actually spent many years in Spain as a diplomat). If he can be forgiven this idiosyncrasy, his works rank high in literary merit, especially because they are very carefully constructed narratives. Their subject matter includes many social situations that were quite real in the Argentina of that period—for instance, the stock market as a gamble, the adjustment of immigrants. Ocantos's studies, however, do not emphasize local problems, but rather the human relationships that exist within the problems. Choosing a title or two from the work of such a prolific novelist is far from easy. His first novel, *León Zaldívar* (Argentina, 1888) is probably the most frequently cited, though *Quilito* (Argentina, 1891) may well be the most praised; a good case could be made for *Promisión* (Argentina,

1897) because it is a very well structured novel that includes a large cast of characters with different backgrounds, problems, and expectations.

A similar quality of craftsmanship is apparent in Federico Gamboa's *Suprema ley* (Mexico, 1896). Whatever we may say about his faithfulness to naturalist procedures or the lingering romanticism in his works, the narratives are carefully made, and well proportioned with respect to the use of conflict, tension, and different methods of characterization. *Suprema ley,* and his other novels as well, have the flavor of a time past that sometimes attracts an inordinately large portion of the reader's attention—negatively or affirmatively, depending on the reader. These reactions, however, do not alter the fact of good literary craftsmanship.

We can only speculate on the extent to which the artistic awareness of the *modernista* poets influenced the care with which novelists made their fictions. We have observed that the romantics—especially the earlier ones—were more concerned with theme than with technique. Speaking of writers like Ocantos and Gamboa, it would be absurd to say that they are not concerned about theme; on the other hand, they certainly are more concerned with technique than were most of their predecessors. These two writers lived abroad (Gamboa in France) for considerable periods, and it is possible that foreign literary associations may have strengthened their discipline. Nevertheless, *modernismo* was a highly self-conscious tendency, and it was also the first literary trend that stimulated communication among writers throughout Spanish America. The goal of *modernismo* was artistic creativity. In prose style, the imagery of Gamboa and some other writers reflects the *modernista* influence; regarding the general question of artistic discipline, we can suspect but cannot be sure.

A *modernista* poet, Amado Nervo, published a short novel, *Pascual Aguilera* (Mexico, 1896), that coincided in time with *Suprema ley.* It combines a Mexican social theme with scientific analysis of character; the author's poetic presence is manifest in highly suggestive imagery and in an almost sonnet-like concentration on a single idea. The story contains an element of protest, since it deals with the abuse of class privilege—specifically, a master's right to sleep with his servant's betrothed. Nervo's version of this basic story has an unexpected outcome, which the narrator explains in terms of psychology, the intriguing new science of that age.

Pascual Aguilera may be thought of as taking a step toward *modernismo* in the combination naturalism-*modernismo* that it shares with *Suprema ley*. Another novel published in the same year, José Asunción Silva's *De sobremesa* (Colombia, 1896), is of considerable importance to the understanding of prose fiction at this time because its protagonist represents the aestheticism that can best be described as decadentist and is a fundamental characteristic of Spanish-American culture in the late nineteenth century.[15] Two interesting corollary expressions are *Bohemia sentimental* (Guatemala, 1899) by Enrique Gómez Carrillo and *La tristeza voluptuosa* (Venezuela, 1899) by Pedro César Domínici. Both novels deal with attitudes toward the importance of art. Gómez Carrillo's turns on the conflict between art and materialism, and discusses the question of artistic integrity. It also contains a rather weakly exploited factor of creativity commenting on itself. Domínici's novel is more pretentiously philosophical; the protagonist experiences a diminishing sense of attachment to reality. He gives up study to devote himself to art, but mainly he indulges in erotic episodes with intercalated periods of reading philosophy. Eventually he gives up everything as meaningless. Life is simply a matter of waiting for death; suicide is the only way to beat the game.

The question concerning the extent of *modernismo's* influence on naturalism may now be turned in the opposite direction to ask how much naturalism there is in this neurotic aestheticism. Paradoxically, neither *Bohemia sentimental* nor *La tristeza voluptuosa* is well written. Gómez Carrillo reveals all too clearly his eagerness to explain just what bohemianism is, with the result that his characters seem to be handled by him for that purpose. Domínici misses some outstanding opportunities to turn *La tristeza voluptuosa* into a satisfying literary experience. He persists in third-person narration, for example, in places where shifting to an interior voice would be greatly to his advantage. Indeed, it seems that his ideas about how a novel should be made, from a technical standpoint, must have come from a rather pedestrian reading of realist fiction; the result combines poorly with the decadentist notions of his protagonist.

Whatever the faults or merits of particular novels, it appears that naturalism (or naturalism-realism) and ·*modernismo* are mutually influential. In *El sargento Felipe* (Venezuela, 1899) by Gonzalo Picón-Febres, the naturalist-realist tendency becomes quite *criollista*, with the narrator showing what "our" situation is. At the same time, the *modernista* tendency enables him to define the *criollista* circumstance in contrast to a larger cultural context, but with a protagonist who functions in both. Picón-Febre's novel, therefore, creates the illusion of reconciling, within a single narrative, the two components of the binary opposition suggested by David Viñas's commentary on *Amalia*. In the story of the Spanish-American novel, subsequent developments show that this reconciliation was illusory; it marks a point in literary history when *criollismo* was about to give the Spanish-American novel a special identity that soon would be in partial conflict with vanguardist inventiveness.

2

Narrative Transformation and Amplification

Gertrudis Gómez de Avellaneda's Guatimozín

Studies of Gertrudis Gómez de Avellaneda (1814–73) and her work probably contain a higher percentage of biography than would be found in the case of any other Hispanic writer. She was a highly successful poet, dramatist, and novelist—in that order. But literary talent was not her only attraction. Her fame as a writer combined with an independent spirit to suggest a certain resemblance to George Sand, and this suggestion produced many pages of anecdote and speculation that are sometimes relevant to her literary production and sometimes quite extraneous to it. The essential facts, for a study of *Guatimozín* (1846), are relatively few. She was born in Cuba. Her mother was Cuban; her father, Manuel Gómez de Avellaneda, was a Spanish naval officer whose distinguished family heritage was a source of some pride on the author's part. She spent many years in Spain—a situation that was favorable to her work as a dramatist and also advantageous with respect to general contacts with the literary world. In mid-career, she returned to Cuba for a period of about five years and was active and influential in literary circles there. Her two best known novels, *Sab* (1841) and *Guatimozín,* are both thematically tied to the New World.

The standard life and works study of the author is *La Avellaneda y sus obras,* by Emilio Cotarelo y Mori.[1] It is notable for its painstaking scholarship and great detail. The critic tends to use Avellaneda's works as a means of explaining or commenting on her biography. Interest in her prose fiction has focused mainly on *Sab,* a novel whose protagonist is a black slave in Cuba.[2] *Guatimozín* is mentioned almost exclusively in connection with Indianist novels; the most valuable reference in this connection is by Concha Meléndez in *La novela indianista en Hispanoamérica*.[3] Studies of *Sab* are of some interest in the analysis of *Guatimozín* because (1) they deal with Avellaneda's literary filiation, (2) the protagonists of both novels are idealized in the romantic fashion, and (3) narrative techniques are similar in both works. The recent edition of *Sab,* by Mary Cruz, contains a detailed analysis of that novel. Unfortunately, there is no modern edition of *Guatimozín,* even though it was important enough to be given four editions and an English translation in the nineteenth century.[4]

Concha Meléndez takes the position that *Guatimozín* deserves better than the relative oblivion into which it has fallen, because it is typical of the period in which it was written and because Avellaneda tells the story of the conquest of Mexico in a poetic manner.[5] Both reasons are important in a study of the novel and are worth further consideration.

One of the characteristics of the romantic period was interest in the national past. In Europe, this emphasis produced many novels set in a medieval historical frame, partly because the setting added glamor to the national identity. The romantic inclination was to establish some vaguely familiar but quasi-exotic object-place as the goal or haven that incorporated a sought-for ideal. Most historical novels of the time served this purpose, and some promoted the nineteenth-century idea of history as a record of man's progress. In America there was no medieval past, but there was a colonial period and a pre-conquest civilization that provided adequate substitutes. At the same time, the "noble savage" theme, picked up from European writers, coincided with the admiration of indigenous heroes—an anti-Spanish phenomenon produced by the independence movement. No one should be encouraged to think that poetic references to Cuauhtémoc or the naming of Chilean warships for Araucanian chieftains signaled the emancipation of the Indian in Spanish America. Far from that, these acts referred to ideals, to abstractions, rather than to social change. Avellaneda had read the novels of Sir Walter Scott and also knew the work of Chateaubriand. She finds in her subject matter a combination of adventure and nobility of spirit. This ideal combination, expressed in certain attitudes and acts of the characters in the novel, advises a present-day reader to expect a familiar complex of relationships and events.

Meléndez's second reason for defending *Guatimozín* (that the author tells the story of the conquest poetically) has to do with the way the novel is made. We cannot be certain whether Meléndez's statement refers only to the sensitivity with which the novel is written or may also be taken as a reference to invention. Either way, however, the reference is undoubtedly directed toward technique.

Cotarelo y Mori is less enthusiastic than Meléndez about *Guatimozín*.[6] He notes that Avellaneda prepared herself well with respect to the historical material and that she succeeded in creating a poetic and dramatic story of the conquest—a vivid, warm, eloquent narration. Then he states that the book contains too much history that is not really history, and very little novel. After making some complaints about the credibility of the characters, he concludes that the author did as well as she could with an impossible task. The historical event itself, according to the critic, transcends fiction and makes a novel impossible.

Obviously, a similar statement might be made concerning many other astonishing moments in history. At the same time, one must remember that the function of a historical novel is not to recount history but to create a particular experience through fiction. It would be possible to identify this function as the intent of Avellaneda, simply by analyzing the work. However, we know by her own statement that she worked carefully to make a historical novel that would be comparable to the good ones she had read.[7]

The experience of *Guatimozín*—as a novel rather than as a historical account—seems to depend mainly on two aspects of narrative technique: (1) the function of scene as distinguished from summary and (2) the interrelationship of scene with narrative point of view. The problem may be stated in the form of questions. First, what does the author accomplish by using scene in various situations? Second, what is the relationship, if any, between the use of scene and who is seeing the action? Both phenomena require some definition.

The difference between scene and summary is related to the Aristotelian differentiation between dramatic manner and narrative manner, and, in more recent terminology, to the distinction between showing and telling. Scene usually involves dialogue and makes the reader aware of an event in approximately the same amount of time that one would spend in becoming aware of the same event in real life. Summary, on the other hand, requires less time than the real happening would require. A warning is in order here because some writers and critics have taken the position that scene (showing) is more realistic than summary (telling). The notion of relative realism may have some merit with respect to the narrator's absenting himself, but a one-to-one correspondence of time's passage in art and in real life has produced some of the most soporific narrative, not to mention film, ever offered the public. The debate over such matters does not enter into the analysis of *Guatimozín*. We are concerned with the effect that scene produces and with the narrator's identity and characteristics. Wayne Booth shows this relationship through his analysis of the narrator.[8]

Two other refinements of the scene-summary contrast, expositions by Brooks and Warren and by Gérard Genette, are helpful in understanding how basic anecdotal material is transformed into the experience of a novel. Brooks and Warren refer to the problem as "pace."[9] They point out that "summary is faster in rendering an action than is narrative; narrative tends to be faster than full rendering in terms of scene; scene tends to be faster than analysis." They think of the importance of changing pace in terms of changing emphasis. Gérard Genette, in his *durée,* is more concerned with the comparative duration of a time segment in the *histoire* (the sequence of events, existing in the abstract, that are transformed into the fiction we read) and the *récit* (the fiction that we read).[10] In this formulation, scene takes the same amount of time in the *récit* and the *histoire.* Summary takes less time in the *récit* than in the *histoire.* Descriptive pause takes up immeasurably (incapable of being measured) more time in the *récit* than in the *histoire.* Ellipse takes up immeasurably less time in the *récit* than in the *histoire.* Genette's exposition points up the difference and the relationship between reality and the illusion of reality. The sense of realistic passage of time in fiction is communicated not by a one-to-one correspondence of *récit* and *histoire* but by imaginative use of the four situations described by Genette. All three of these major analyses of scene and summary (Booth, Brooks and Warren, Genette) are useful in the analysis of *Guatimozín* because they emphasize, respectively: (1) the relationship of the narrator's identity to the use of scene versus summary, (2) variations in pace used for the sake of changing emphasis, and (3) the reader's perception of time's duration.

Recalling Cotarelo y Mori's assertion regarding the impossibility of a novel about the conquest, we must reduce the problem to its simplest form. Successfully or not, Avellaneda made a novel about the conquest. What did she do? We may guess, on the basis of the title, that she focuses on Guatimozín (Cuauhtémoc) rather than on Moctezuma (Montezuma) or Cortés. Because of the period in which the novel was written, we may expect the narrator to show Guatimozín as courageous and also deeply sensitive; there is no reason to expect ethnological expertise on the part of the author.

It would be foolish to deny that the historical event itself is fascinating. In a period of two years and a few months, Cortés invaded Mexico with a few men and some horses, mastiffs, and cannon, faced a culture so complicated it was a source of wonder to the invaders, and gradually succeeded in wresting power from the Aztec rulers. The principal events, as history records and usually emphasizes them, are the following:

1. Cortés landed near what is now Veracruz. He acquired Doña Marina (La Malinche) as interpreter and mistress, moved into the interior, executed a brutal object lesson at Cholula, and formed what became a crucially important alliance with the Tlaxcalans.

2. He was met by Moctezuma's emissaries and led into Tenochtitlan (Mexico City), where he was granted an audience with the emperor. The latter associated him with Quetzalcóatl, the benevolent god who was supposed to return from the east.

3. On the basis of a report concerning treacherous acts by subjects of Moctezuma, Cortés "arrested" the emperor and confined him to a palace under guard. Moctezuma's quandary, based on his religious expectation, prohibited his ordering a counter action.

4. Some Aztec nobles were imprisoned when they were suspected of fomenting rebellion.

5. Cortés received news that a Spanish expedition from Cuba had landed in Veracruz to arrest him for undertaking his own expedition against orders. He marched to Veracruz with some of his men to confront this threat, leaving Pedro de Alvarado in charge of the forces in Tenochtitlan. Alvarado's cruelty incited the wrath of the populace.

6. Cortés settled the issue at Veracruz and returned with more Tlaxcalan allies, but he was unable to quell the unrest. He also brought smallpox, a disease new to the Mexicans.

7. Moctezuma's subjects became disrespectful of him because of his

indecisiveness. When Cortés caused him to appear publicly in order to quiet the people, Moctezuma was killed by a stone thrown from the crowd.

8. Cuitláhuac (Quetlahuaca in the novel) became emperor.
9. Cortés and his forces retreated to Tacuba, scene of the "Sad Night," and later to Tlaxcala.
10. Cortés ordered some ships built for use on the lake around Tenochtitlan, secured more Tlaxcalan forces, and attacked the city some nine months after his retreat. By this time, Cuitláhuac had died of smallpox and Cuauhtémoc (Guatimozín) had become emperor.
11. The attack was stymied, but the Spaniards effected a blockade and set about destroying the city. The siege lasted more than three months.
12. Cuauhtémoc appeared before Cortés and asked to be killed. Cortés ordered that he be tortured so that he would reveal the whereabouts of the gold he was supposed to have hidden.

Analysis of a historical novel must always take account of the difference between historical fact and *histoire*. Obviously, the author must know the facts, and it is generally conceded that Avellaneda prepared herself well. However, what we experience in our reading is not simply a transformation of the event as it is reported by historians, but a transformation of the event as conceived by the novelist before actually writing the novel. In the case of *Guatimozín,* the protagonist is present from the very beginning, even though historians do not mention him until he actually becomes emperor (phase 10 of the twelve phases listed above). The narrative techniques employed by the novelist are not designed to transform history by adding Guatimozín; they are intended to transform Guatimozín from a presumed role in the basic anecdotal material (*histoire*) into part of an experience in fiction.

The difference between historical fact and *histoire* constitutes a problem in any historical novel. Naturally, the problem is more intense if the protagonist performs a decisive role in history. In *Guatimozín,* there is never any doubt that the protagonist will be a historical personage rather than an invented one acting against a historical backdrop. One might argue that Cortés is the protagonist, rather than Guatimozín, especially since Avellaneda, at the beginning, casts him in a rather favorable light. If we accept Genette's proposition that any *récit* is the expansion of a verb, the basic act in *Guatimozín* might be stated as *Cortés destroys the power of the Aztec empire.*[11] Such is, in fact, the case, and it suggests that Guatimozín could hardly be the dominant personage in the novel. However, the young emperor's role, although it necessarily ends in military defeat, is not a passive one. Actually, the basic act is *Guatimozín struggles to save the Aztec empire.* The *récit* is an expansion of this statement.

Avellaneda points out in a footnote that historians do not account for Guatimozín prior to his becoming emperor, and then she states that this exclusion seems extraordinary to her because very special qualities must have characterized a young prince of twenty-two years who was chosen as emperor over older princes (footnote, pp. 57–58). Therefore, the author deals with an *histoire* that included Guatimozín in an important role from a much earlier date. The story of Guatimozín is similar to the trajectory of the archetypal hero. We see him initially as a member of Moctezuma's council. The scene recognizes his youthfulness and justifies his presence. Almost immediately thereafter, he proves his determination and dexterity in a knightly tournament arranged for the entertainment of the visiting Spaniards. Later, Moctezuma orders him into exile (during the fourth phase of the historical account), from which he returns to deal with the tragic situation he has inherited. Following this same pattern, Moctezuma may be thought of as the scapegoat (*pharmakos*) whose sacrifice is necessary to give others strength. This notion is especially interesting in view of the characterization of Guatimozín as a stronger version of Moctezuma.

The novel's title is an important signifier of what the author has in mind. The suffix "-zin" (in Náhuatl, "-tzin") is a mark of respect; the reference in the subtitle to the "last emperor of Mexico" suggests a tragic end.[12] However, the narrator does not follow through immediately on these suggestions. The first chapter is really a kind of prologue, sketching the historical situation, in the manner of Scott. Using summary only, the narrator explains the unauthorized status of Cortés's expedition, refers to his acts in Tlaxcala and Cholula, sketches briefly the role of Moctezuma before the arrival of Cortés, and emphasizes, in closing, that they met on a basis of absolute equality. In this connection, Cortés is described as the "fortunate adventurer" (p. 6). Chapter two turns specifically to Moctezuma and his counselors, including Guatimozín. It opens with a "descriptive pause" that sets the scene in the palace, the palace in the city, and three unidentified persons in the room where Moctezuma sits thinking as he awaits the arrival of Cortés. The narrator communicates a sense of regal splendor, urban bustling, and respectful subjects. References to aquatic birds and floating gardens provide an exotic effect, but the narrator's emphasis is less on exoticism than on portraying a scene characterized by civilization and stability. Toward the end of the descriptive pause, the narrator refers to the visible characteristics of the three counselors, withholding their identities in good romantic fashion. Then begins the first true scene of the novel, with Moctezuma summoning each of the three by name and identifying them further. Such a procedure of addressing people and informing them of their own positions seems unnatural in the everyday world; in the idealized *Guatimozín,* it enhances the emperor's regal dignity. He speaks to the three—Quetlahuaca, Cacumatzín, and Guatimozín—about the newly arrived strangers, wondering who they may be and how they should be treated. In this discourse, he speaks of Quetzalcóatl's promised return and of the apparently miraculous qualities of the strangers (mastery of horses, cannon associated with lightning). The point of view is clearly Moctezuma's, quite different from the admiring but detached point of view in the descriptive pause. In effect, the basic narrator wisely allows Moctezuma to speak of things that reasonably would be best known to the Mexicans. This passage is scene from the standpoint of narrator Avellaneda but summary from the standpoint of narrator Moctezuma. However, long before the end of the exposition, the basic narrator's control becomes apparent through descriptive pauses that indicate Moctezuma's attitude. This fact is of considerable importance because it defines the narrator's permissiveness with respect to the Indian point of view. More than once, the situation is seen as it might have been seen by one of the Mexican characters, but this view is always carefully controlled. That is why Cortés appears often to be at fault but still attractive. A similar degree of narrator control persists throughout the novel and culminates in the Epilogue, where historical assumption is refuted in favor of a fictional ending that is dramatically effective but certainly not in any way proven.

Each of the three counselors expresses an opinion that corresponds to his personality. One of the principal uses of scene is characterization. Moctezuma closes this particular scene with some final remarks, and then the narrator makes a summary transition to the living quarters of the palace. After a descriptive pause, we witness another scene, involving Guatimozín's young wife and son, that establishes the intimate sensitivity of the hero. The closing summary adds to the reader's awareness two other important facts: Tecuixpa, the younger sister of Gualcazinla (Guatimozín's wife), is eager to see the Spaniards, and the two women (both are daughters of Moctezuma) are caring for some of the emperor's younger children.

Within this second chapter, we have seen most of the narrative procedures established. Scene is used for exposition, as in the case of Moctezuma's monologue, and the handling of it is most revealing because it is obviously the creation of an implied author who wishes to speak well of the Mexicans without surrendering completely to their point of view. The basic narrative voice, therefore, retains control, even while appearing to surrender its prerogative to the emperor. Scene has also served to establish a personality difference between Guatimozín and Cacumatzín—one is deliberate, the other hotheaded. This contrast is useful not so much in the characterization of the men as it is in signaling actions to come. It is a device, very common in romantic historical novels, that evokes reader interest corresponding to two entirely different moods. As a device, it serves in much the same way as Tecuixpa's interest in the Spaniards, which evolves into her tragic love affair with Velásquez de León. The narrator uses both devices to incorporate non-historical material into the story and reveals the implied author's romantic inclination in the process. Finally, scene reveals personalities and is especially useful in establishing a relationship between Moctezuma and Guatimozín that causes some of the former's qualities to adhere to the younger man, so using a historically familiar figure to build a largely fictional one. It is not quite accurate to speak of "noble savage" with reference to the implied author's idealized view of these men, because they are not in any way primitive. They might be called "noble exotics." In any case, they are noble in status and in their attitudes, which cover the ground from statesmanship to conjugal love. Given these revelations in the second chapter, it is interesting to observe the function of scene throughout the novel, grouping its uses in three categories: for characterization, for incorporation of non-historical material, and for exposition. Quantitatively, exposition is not a very important use of scene. However, there are two parts of the novel where it is of fundamental interest. One is the occasion when Moctezuma consults his three counselors (pp. 7–9); the other occurs when Moctezuma's ministers explain to Cortés the organization of their government (pp. 24–26). In the summary preliminary to this scene, the implied author is again apparent in the statement that the emperor invited the Spaniards to witness an audience granted by Moctezuma to his subjects, thinking that a display of imperial wisdom and justice might make the foreigners forget the Aztecs' "backwardness in the art of war" (p. 24). This seeming apology is hardly complimentary to the Spaniards, and when it is associated with some other incidents, its latent irony becomes apparent. There is a scene, for example, in which Moctezuma invites Cortés to dine with him in order to see if "our cooks are as far behind yours as our sages are" (p. 14). In terms of how scene functions, of course, this comment adds to the characterization of the emperor, and that is the most important use of scene in Avellaneda's novel.

The relationship between Moctezuma and Cortés resembles a brainwashing operation as we observe the two men together. The emperor's doubts are increased by Cortés's careful and constant reference to Moctezuma's status. He speaks of the latter's "visit" rather than of imprisonment (p. 34). This scene emphasizes the vacillation of Moctezuma and defines him as a weak personality—or, better, as one whose determination has been weakened by a circumstance he does not understand. In the same context, Cortés appears courteous but insistent. As a factor in the characterization of the invader, this scene is consummately important because it is basically critical of Cortés. The narrator never openly condemns him, and in fact the intruder often seems praiseworthy; however, in this case, his deceitfulness is apparent. Finally, a brief summary states it specifically: "Cortés le trataba con mayores respetos y le revestía de más alucinadoras apariencias de autoridad, cuanto era más extenso el poder que iba adquiriendo en aquel ánimo abatido" (p. 49). ("Cortés treated him with ever increasing respect and invested him with ever more imaginary authority, in proportion to the increase of his own power over that dejected spirit.") Characterization of Moctezuma is also an important function of scenes that reveal his relationship with Guatimozín. Its foundation is laid in chapter two, where a combination of scene and summary reveals the emperor's special affection for the young prince and also his high regard for the counsel he may offer. This passage anticipates the replacement of Moctezuma by Cuauhtémoc. Later development transposes this correspondence to a more intimate level when Guatimozín intrudes upon the emperor's lonely worrying to invite him to a family gathering. There is a brief scene during which Moctezuma asks Guatimozín to look at the man rather than the emperor. However, the prince cannot bear the possibility of seeing his majesty weep, and therefore offers to take up arms against the cause of his sorrow (p. 16). With respect to the characterization of both men, this scene is definitive because, in addition to the fundamental bond between them, we now see a deteriorating Moctezuma and a strong Cuauhtémoc. The displacement of the historical figure by the fictionalized one is established, even if the process is not yet complete. It is important that this definition is made through reference to intimate relationship rather than to affairs of state. By revealing it in this fashion, the implied author emphasizes a preference for the romantic hero with a streak of tenderness, and also accomplishes an addition to historical fact without making fictions that would operate in the public realm. She characterizes her hero and suggests that he functioned in history earlier than he actually is known to have done so, without proposing any change in the historical record.

Guatimozín's tenderness is a major factor in his characterization, especially in the part of the story that precedes his becoming emperor. However, this aspect of his personality is tied to his sense of obligation to the nation. The foundation again appears in chapter two, and the major reaffirmation occurs in a long scene with Gualcazinla that enhances the characterization of Moctezuma as well as of the two people participating in the episode (pp. 46–46). Cotarelo y Mori considers such refinement a deficiency in the novel. He thinks the author grants the Indians ideas that are inappropriately subtle, sentiments that belong to a more refined civilization, and an elegance of expression that would befit the most genteel Spanish society.[13] Meléndez points out that refinement of this kind is characteristic of all romantic Indianist novels.[14] There can be no doubt that the implied author intends it that way and uses scene specifically to make the point.

Characterization may be accomplished in scenes based either on the invented portion of the *histoire* or on accepted history or legend. Two memorable incidents are the final words of Quetlahuaca and the torture of Guatimozín. The former is extensive and does not belong to the historical record (pp. 104–6). Quetlahuaca is dying of smallpox, and the scene consists of his commission to Guatimozín and the latter's oath of compliance. To a considerable extent, this episode serves to characterize Cortés, because it is Quetlahuaca's evaluation of the invasion and its leader. Obviously, it serves also to characterize the dying emperor—always judicious and perceptive—since the problem is seen from his point of view. However, the image of Cortés—a bold and capable fighter, a crafty and devious person—reinforces once again the nature of the implied narrator. The episode of Guatimozín's torture is an interpretation of historical record. It is the final scene in the novel proper (the Epilogue later employs scene to great advantage). The basic fact of the torture is expanded by his wife's fainting and by an embrace between Guatimozín and his brother, who is to be tortured along with him. When they are on the grill, the brother moans, and the young emperor chastises him, asking "¿Estoy yo por ventura en tálamo de flores?".[15] In this particular instance, the novelist falls into the trap of referring to the historical record during the process of transforming the *histoire*. These words of Guatimozín are preceded by the narrator's statement that the hero silenced his brother by uttering "these famous words" (p. 173). The words might well have provided a sufficiently dramatic ending, but Avellaneda's *récit* includes two subsequent high points in the same scene. First, Cortés puts an end to the torture because he believes that either there is no gold to be surrendered or the victims are brave enough to die without revealing its location. Second, Gualcazinla (Guatimozín's wife) goes mad. By the end of the scene, therefore, the author has returned to the *histoire* as the basis of transformation.

In this final episode, it is apparent that characterization through the use of scene plays a role in the revelation of extra-historical material. For that reason, it is not always possible to state categorically that one scene functions as a characterizing agent and that another serves to introduce or develop non-historical aspects of the *histoire*. On the other hand, it is frequently accurate to say that a scene is significant primarily for one reason or another. In the introduction of non-historical matters, the novel uses three conventional devices that are especially interesting. Each one is related to characterization but is primarily important because of its role in developing the plot: (1) the personality contrast between the thoughtful Guatimozín and the impetuous Cacumatzín, (2) the triangle of impossible love, and (3) the I-will-go-with-you theme of the episode preceding Guatimozín's exile.

The Guatimozín-Cacumatzín contrast is apparent from the occasion when Moctezuma first asks the advice of his three counselors. Subsequently, the tournament reveals that there is no ill feeling between the two, but a difference of personality. Both perform well in the tournament, with Guatimozín holding a slight edge of superiority. The conventionality of this relationship even permits use of the archery contest in which Cacumatzín's arrow hits the center of the bull's-eye and Guatimozín's then splits the first arrow. In a later scene, the personality difference is apparent as the two men set forth their opinions as to how Moctezuma should deal with the cowardly behavior of the Mexican populace (pp. 22–24). The contrast signals misfortune for Cacumatzín that will exceed even that of the hero. He loses his bethrothed in an impossible (and extremely romantic) triangle and is assassinated in a cowardly fashion.

The members of the love triangle are Cacumatzín, Tecuixpa, who is Guatimozín's sister-in-law, and Velásquez de León. From the beginning of the novel, Tecuixpa seems extraordinarily interested in seeing the foreigners. Readers learn this through a summary statement by the narrator. Retrospectively, her interest seems to indicate some sort of predestined relationship. It develops into the book's major love theme. The triangle is set forth in an episode that begins as summary and ends as scene. It is a display of honor, flirtation, and discretion that would be appropriate in any historical novel of the period. Ultimately, for reasons that need not be explained here, both of Tecuixpa's lovers lose. Although this story line is not a part of the historical record, the novelist relates invention and history in various ways. Velásquez de León, for example, enters Moctezuma's household as an emissary to his family when the emperor is held prisoner. Connections of this kind meld history and invention. The triangle is useful because a love story is an important ingredient in the novel; at the same time, amorous involvement is much more suitable to Cacumatzín's personality than it would be to Guatimozín's sobriety. The implied author is, therefore, faithful to the requirements of a good historical novel.

The triangle functions in another way, one that may seem coincidental at first. It is through Velásquez de León that the principles of Christian religion are introduced into the imperial household. Tecuixpa accepts them in a partial way, as does the young wife of Moctezuma. They are identified by reference to "the God of Velásquez," and it is worth noting that they do not find ready and general acceptance. The most extensive elaboration through scene of the infusion of Christianity occurs when Tecuixpa points out a miraculous cure and participates in further discussion of the question with other characters (p. 128). The passage is essential to the characterization of Tecuixpa; however, it is even more important as a recognition of Christianity on the extra-historical level, where its human qualities contrast with Cortés's dogmatism. There is an interesting summary in which Moctezuma's wife, having been instructed by Doña Marina, wishes her husband to embrace Christianity and suggests that if the Mexican gods are unfavorable to him he had better look elsewhere (p. 64). We experience the infiltration of Christian ideas in a way that is reasonable within the narrative context; Christianity, in Avellaneda's novel, is not an overwhelming redemptive force.

The scene in which Gualcazinla states that she will go into exile with Guatimozín reaffirms the implied author's intention of characterizing a complete romantic hero (p. 46). This evidence of the great love is as clearly a part of the idealization of Guatimozín as is his prowess in archery. Of course, it does function in the characterization of both characters, but its principal use—what makes it essential to the novel—is to explain the absence of the hero from the city at a time when, according to historical record, other nobles were being imprisoned, but without weakening the devoted-husband side of his characterization.

Occasionally, Avellaneda inserts a single spoken expression in the midst of a summary passage and so creates some of the effect of scene. In the episode concerning Alvarado's cruelty, a "frenetic multitude" comes to Quetlahuaca and shouts, "Let us rise up and kill the Spaniards!" (p. 72). The narration immediately reverts to summary to account for Quetlahuaca's witnessing the slaughter and becoming properly furious. The summary account is broken once again by Quetlahuaca's "Follow me!" (p. 72). Such utterances emphasize dramatic effect in episodes that are inherently interesting but may lack dynamism. They are not part of historical record, nor do they need to be. They are transformation of the *histoire*.

The dominance of *histoire* over historical record reaches its extreme precisely at the end of the Epilogue. This chapter deals with the hanging of Guatimozín, and then adds an attempt by Gualcazinla to murder Cortés. He is saved by Doña Marina, who kills Gualcazinla and covers up the crime. The scene in which the soldier and his mistress discuss their highly compromising situation is dominated by Doña Marina's determination and discretion. Cortés, interestingly enough, is capable of no more than "What shall we do now, Marina?" (p. 178). The scene then fades into what was said the next day about Cortés's injury, ending with a quotation from Bernal Díaz that the narrator describes as the story used to cover up the truth.

Pure scene is never extensive in *Guatimozín,* though many long passages convey a total impression of scene in spite of the fact that they contain bits of summary or of descriptive pause. Generally speaking, the story is *told* rather than *shown,* with scene used to enhance the experience of fiction over the experience of history. On a few occasions, history is dialogued, as in the case of Moctezuma's setting forth the religious cause of his quandary. In other cases, scene confirms what the narrator says about the characters in narrative summary and provides dramatic effect.

Avellaneda's *histoire* is differently proportioned from the historical record. The tenth item in the list of twelve main historical events corresponds to a point approximately halfway through the novel. This difference is indicative of the emphasis on Guatimozín, whose role in the novel is much more complete than it is in history. Even after he becomes emperor, the narrator sustains development of the intimate side of his characterization. Scene is extremely useful in this procedure because it combines the legend with a sensitive human being and joins invention to the historical record. The result is entirely romantic and the narration is sometimes awkward, but some of the effects are extremely clever—the reflection of Moctezuma in the characterization of Guatimozín, for example.

The narrative voice is clearly transforming *histoire* rather than history. On the other hand, the implied author is constantly aware of history, a fact made evident by footnotes. The implied author may also impose on the narrative voice and make a reference to history that should not be made in a transformation of *histoire*. Nevertheless, the latter's predominance is always reasserted.

Although analysis of the use of scene emphasizes especially the character and role of Guatimozín, the implied author seems to be seeking more than the glorification of a particular hero. Underlying the novel one finds the proposition that Mexican civilization was as admirable as Spanish. Avellaneda was not an ethnologist. She knew some of the peculiarities of Mexican culture, but the implied author of *Guatimozín* frequently seems inclined to make that culture not only as good as, but often the same as, European culture. She seems to be especially eager to suggest a relationship between the rulers and the people that probably reflects the ideals of her time rather than the situation under the Aztec rulers. With regard to Christianity, she deals with its introduction into Mexico, though not always gently. The most favorable view of it is the case of Tecuixpa. The opposite extreme is a highly critical description of how the Tlaxcalans practice Christian ritual as learned from their Spanish masters. Their adopted system of worship is imbued with the fanaticism (essentially un-Christian, according to the narrator) that characterized the religion during that period of Spanish history (p. 145).

Guatimozín is the embodiment of the admirable aspects of Mexican civilization. At times, we do see the situation from the Mexican point of view, but that position is the exception. The prevailing point of view is from outside, though it carries the sense of one who wishes to see the Mexicans in a favorable light. This narrative situation (who is speaking and who is seeing) controls scene and its use.

Given the emphasis on Guatimozín, the novel is really not the story of the conquest of the Aztec Empire. J. Lloyd Read observes, in his study of the historical novel in Mexico, that the novel is "the story of the fall of the Aztec empire rather than a story of Cortés's triumph."[16] Indeed, by the end of the novel, Cortés, who initially is not wholly despicable, has become quite mean. There has been no conquest in the heroic sense, but a kind of fifth-column activity that has displaced the Aztec power.

3

The Focus of Action

José Mármol's Amalia

José Mármol's *Amalia* (1855) undoubtedly possesses a strong documentary significance with respect to the dictatorship of Juan Manuel de Rosas. Over the years, critics of the novel have paid more attention to this political base than to the narrative techniques used to tell an attractive story. In spite of his proximity to the events, José Mármol (1817–71) gave his work certain characteristics of a historical novel, and his inclination to expose the evils of the regime persuaded him to include some documents of the period within the narrative text. However, the documentary aspect of the book does not overwhelm the development of plot. The experience of the novel is not a conflict of ideologies but a sense of terrifying repression by violence. This effect is achieved by narrative skill, not by documentary reference. Scholarship, rather than the book itself, makes inordinate use of the historical record.

The political situation dealt with in *Amalia* was in fact the outgrowth of an ideological difference between unitarians (centralists) and federalists. The arguments on both sides were generally the same as in all countries attempting to establish representative governments. In Argentina, the problem was exacerbated by two principal factors: (1) the position of Buenos Aires as the center of commerce, population, and culture, and (2) the customs of the plainsmen, the gauchos, who were highly individualistic, accustomed to the un-sophisticated life of the provinces, and disinclined to conform to the elitism of the Buenos Aires culture. In most respects, this conflict is similar to the frontier versus the eastern seaboard in the history of the United States. One major difference was the absolute concentration of one component of the polarity in Buenos Aires.[1] In *Amalia,* Mármol shows how the conflict turned into a tragedy of hatred and violence. This tragedy—not the political principles involved at the roots— is the novelistic material of the book. In some special passages, the author sets forth, in essay form, certain aspects of the causes of the problem. The terms *unitario* and *federal* appear hundreds of times in the text; nevertheless, a casual reader might finish the novel with no clear idea of the ideological definition of those terms. The protagonist, Daniel Bello, is the son of a good *federal* family, but sides with the *unitarios* because of the barbarous practices of the *federal* dictatorship. The novel does not indicate that Daniel has rejected the basic political tenets of his family; he is portrayed as being opposed to the brutality of the regime.

The major historical figure in *Amalia* is Juan Manuel de Rosas, the *federal* leader who was the dominant force in Argentine politics from 1829 to 1851. During this entire period the nation was in a state of sporadic civil war. Rosas was first given executive power by the legislature in a desperate move to restore order. It was at that time that he was first referred to as "Restaurador de las Leyes." He was replaced in 1832 and empowered again in 1835, for a period of five years. (In the interim, he led a military campaign against the Indians.) In 1840, he was reelected by the legislature. During this same year the *unitarios* stood their best chance of driving him out of power. *Unitario* General Juan Lavalle, whose army had been active in the interior, led his men to the outskirts of Buenos Aires. He kept his troops in that position for a painfully long time, and then withdrew in order to control a counteraction to the rear. During this period, Rosas's government was beset by international as well as domestic problems. Not surprisingly, his policies became more repressive with respect to his political enemies. The crisis caused by the Lavalle threat produced a wave of terrorism in a situation that approach anarchy.

The historical setting of *Amalia* is during this crucial period in 1840, specifically from May 4 to October 6. (It is important for readers in the northern hemisphere to remind themselves that this time of the year, in Argentina, includes winter, not summer. The difference is important to the atmosphere of the novel.) Shortly after the terminal date of the plot, José Mármol took refuge in the embassy of the United States and soon joined other Argentine emigrants in Montevideo. Later he traveled to Río de Janeiro, Santiago de Chile, and back to

Montevideo. There he founded a newspaper, *La Semana,* in 1851, and published installments of *Amalia* in it until he ceased publication of the paper after Rosas's defeat in 1852. Most probably he thought of his novel as a means of stimulating his exiled compatriots in their struggle against Rosas.[2] The intense partisanship of the novel is expressed, for the most part, in terms of an assault on human dignity. The first complete edition of *Amalia* appeared in 1855. This edition was corrected and revised by the author. Some subsequent editions have followed the edition of 1855, others have deviated from it (pp. xliii–xlvi, lx). Juan Carlos Ghiano returned to the 1855 edition in preparing the text used here (see note 2). His introduction is an indispensable contribution to the study of *Amalia* because it deals with all the essential aspects of the work as a literary phenomenon related to a specific time in history.

Essays on *Amalia* have tended to concentrate on its denunciation of the Rosas regime or on its general value as a picture of an era. David Viñas is the author of the most interesting work of sociological criticism—an essay entitled "Mármol: Los dos ojos del romanticismo."[3] Viñas's analysis does not explicate the text as a mirror reflection of reality, but makes deductions, on the basis of the text, that give deeper insights into the nature of the society portrayed. A more general commentary on the novel may be found in Fernando Alegría's *Historia de la novela hispanoamericana*—a rather extensive criticism for a book of this kind.[4] Alegría tends to dismiss Mármol's "romántico diseño de amores y aventuras" and says that the basic material of the book is the characterization of Rosas and of his way of governing. This view of the novel is interesting for two reasons. First, it indicates how important Juan Manuel de Rosas is in the experience of *Amalia.* It is not that he is so frequently seen. In fact, he actually appears in the novel only twice—once in his office at night and once at Santos Lugares with his troops. The first of these scenes is a masterpiece of bitter satire, and no reader is likely to forget it. On the other hand, Rosas dominates the novel—like several other dictators in Spanish-American literature—not by his physical presence but by the pervasive effect of his rule. The second interesting aspect of Alegría's comments is the joining of "amores y aventuras" as one factor that may be separated from the presumably more realistic portrayal of Rosas and company.

Although this division emphasizes satisfactorily the denunciatory aspect of the novel, it underemphasizes the narrative procedure that probably won many readers for Mármol and continues to make the book attractive. The plot may be thought of as having three components: (1) a love story concerning Eduardo and Amalia, quite properly sensitive and ill-starred, as required by the epoch; (2) a historical factor centered on the excesses of the Rosas regime; (3) a story of intrigue, centered on Daniel, that connects the love story with the historical factor.

With reference to the criticism and the general readership of *Amalia,* Ghiano says that scholars have usually preferred to write about the novel's historical frame and the picture of Buenos Aires in 1840, and that almost all of them have forgotten the plot, which has attracted readers over the years because of its "mecánica folletinesca" (p. xlii). This comment clearly invites an analysis of the narrative process, with attention to the tripartite description mentioned above. As a basis for this consideration, it is helpful to point out, insofar as they may be relevant to the study of *Amalia,* some characteristics of this kind of novel. Another name for the *novela folletinesca* is *novela por entregas,* a phrase indicating that the author turned in episodes of the novel one at a time and suggesting that he probably wrote them with a deadline urging him on. This kind of fiction was widely cultivated during the nineteenth century and is characterized generally by overstatement of emotion, violence, mystery, and rare coincidence, in various combinations. Protagonists and other important characters tend to fit into clear categories of good or bad; minor characters sometimes appear more "realistic" than protagonists, but usually turn out to be types or caricatures. A frequently used technique is the withholding of information in order to create suspense. Such a novel, taken as a whole, very likely will lack symmetry with respect to the themes or lines of action on which the author focuses. That is, the author may concentrate on one aspect of the story for several episodes, then turn to another and seemingly forget what he has been dealing with, only to return unexpectedly in a future episode.

In order to deal with the narrative procedure in *Amalia,* it seems desirable to approach it by some means that deals with the act of making a fiction, while relegating to a position of secondary importance the matter of historical context. For this purpose, the analyses by Cleanth Brooks and Robert Penn Warren, in *Understanding Fiction,* are particularly useful because they show the relationship between narrative techniques and the effects these techniques create.[5] The appendix to the book is entitled "Technical Problems and Principles in the Composition of Fiction—A Summary." This title amounts to a significant statement of procedure—that is, Brooks and Warren deal with the problems confronting the author and the principles that form a basis for their solution. The reader, if he follows this process, becomes keenly aware of the act of making fiction. At the same time—since he is the reader—he appreciates the effect achieved.

In *Understanding Fiction*, Brooks and Warren deal specifically with short stories, though much of what they say is also applicable to longer fiction. Their emphasis on short fiction is helpful in the case of *Amalia* because Mármol's novel has the episodic character of a serialized novel. This characteristic is a major factor in the asymmetry that makes analysis of *Amalia* deceptive. If one deals with the novel as a whole, its asymmetry (poorly balanced emphases on different elements of plot, capricious intercalation of history, imagination, and document) is likely to evoke a negative judgment that seems contrary to the novel's obvious readability. The narrative procedures that Mármol used to attract readers (and that have continued to attract readers) may be seen most clearly by applying Brooks and Warren's "problems and principles" to one of the installments of this serialized novel. The following analysis, therefore, will focus on the first chapter, which can be read as a complete unit of fiction. This emphasis will point out the main features of the narrative procedure. Secondarily, the analysis will relate the first chapter to the novel as a whole. The analysis will follow the order of Brooks and Warren's "problems and procedures."

The fundamental story line of *Amalia* concerns Daniel Bello's attempt to protect his friend, Eduardo Belgrano, from discovery and assassination by the *federales*. The expansion of this fundamental action produces the love relationship of Eduardo with Daniel's cousin, Amalia, involves a number of other people in Daniel's intrigues, places Daniel in contact with people close to Rosas, and enables the author to use Daniel as his mouthpiece for the exposition of ideas concerning the causes and character of the Argentine situation in 1840 (p. xxviii). The basic action of the novel's first chapter is Daniel's rescue of Eduardo from an attack by *federal* thugs. He takes him to the safety of Amalia's house. This haven amounts to a satisfactory resolution in the first chapter (installment), but is only temporary in the novel as a whole. The expansion of the first chapter's basic action involves development of the situation in which Daniel intervenes: Eduardo's attempt, along with several friends, to escape to Uruguay; the treacherous attack on them; Eduardo's spectacular sword fight against overwhelming odds. Daniel appears at the crucial moment and rescues the seriously wounded Eduardo. Still another crisis occurs on the way to Amalia's house; Daniel is able to use his craftiness to advantage, and he also expresses several ideas related to the problems of the time.

BEGINNING AND EXPOSITION

The author must choose a satisfactory beginning point because his characters and their circumstance presumably have backgrounds. "The writer wants to strike into his story at a point which will lead fairly quickly and logically to the crucial moment" (BW, p. 646). Nevertheless, some information must be provided about who the characters are.

The opening sentence of *Amalia* reads: "El 4 de mayo de 1840, a las diez y media de la noche, seis hombres atravesaban el patio de una pequeña casa de la calle de Belgrano, en la ciudad de Buenos Aires" (p. 3). ("On the 4th of May, at ten-thirty at night, six men were crossing the patio of a small house on Belgrano street, in the city of Buenos Aires.") Obviously, we are beginning in the middle of an action, though the nature of the action is not immediately apparent. The specificity of the date will be significant for a reader who knows Argentine history, but is not very helpful if the story is not understood, from the beginning, as belonging to a historical context. The date takes on meaning if it is considered in sequence with a preceding "Explicación" by the author (p. 1). This note refers to the use of the past tense in spite of the slight difference between the time of the events and the time of composition; it also reveals Mármol's awareness of the significance of the historical period dealt with. In other words, the author projects his novel into a future time when it will be a historical novel. The effect of the date, however—if it does not take into account the historical context—is changed by the "a las diez y media de la noche" that follows immediately. This introduction is more suggestive of a crime novel than of a historical novel, and is, therefore, a suitable beginning for the sustained intrigue that is the basis of the work as a whole.

Mármol "strikes into his story" by choosing the moment when Eduardo and his companions are beginning their attempted escape to Montevideo. The author can certainly move quickly to the crucial point. As for the exposition that justifies beginning at this point, Mármol is initially more interested in explaining the situation than in identifying the characters. He makes us aware immediately of necessary precautions, identifies Rosas as the danger from which the men are escaping, and introduces a consideration of whether it is better to escape from Buenos Aires and fight Rosas from outside or stay in Buenos Aires and fight him from within. Once these matters are made clear, Mármol moves to the identification of his characters. It is typical of the narrative procedure in *Amalia* that identification is withheld until the situation is made clear. The purpose is apparently to create a secondary suspense. Obviously, the references to individuals sometimes become awkward—for instance, "el compañero del joven que conocemos por la distinción de una espada a la cintura, dijo a éste" (p. 3) ("the companion of the young man whom we know by the distinction of a sword at his waist, said to the latter"). After all the fugitives have been identified in some similar manner, the author introduces each one by name, with additional biographical information. This procedure interrupts the flow of the plot as mystery story but enhances the satisfaction it provides as a historical account.

DESCRIPTION AND SETTING

It is not enough that description and setting be realistic; they must also make a substantial contribution to the story (BW, pp. 647–48). The setting of Mármol's first chapter is Buenos Aires, with the focus moving from a central part to an isolated area near the shore. The description names streets and mentions other locations, thereby creating a ring of authenticity. At the same time, reference to the night hour precedes the mention of a dark entryway; then a description of Buenos Aires as a city with spies in every hiding place adds to the gloomy ambience, which becomes even more intense in the river area described as "uninhabited and wild" (p. 4). In all, the description creates a sense of foreboding that is very appropriate to the cloak-and-dagger behavior of the characters and to the generally strident suggestion of danger that leads into the attack itself. It is worth noting that the description serves both the historical and the intrigue factors of the novel.

The action of the attack scene dominates the setting, but when Daniel helps Eduardo toward Amalia's house the setting again becomes lugubrious. The description of the house itself (very brief in the first chapter) is an entirely different matter. It suggests the author's idea of good taste and therefore provides a perfect frame for Mármol's highly idealized portrait of Amalia. It is also the perfect refuge for aristocratic Eduardo. He is saved from almost certain death and restored to his element. This setting takes on considerable importance in the novel as a whole because it develops in contrast to the crudeness of Rosas's surroundings.[6]

ATMOSPHERE

Brooks and Warren point out that "atmosphere" refers to the general feel of a story (BW, pp. 649–50). They note that some stories are famous for their atmosphere because they are especially poetic or mysterious, but that all stories have an atmosphere that is created by a combination of other factors in the composition of the piece. The action in the first chapter of *Amalia* produces an atmosphere of ever-present danger; the comments made in dialogue associate this danger with Rosas and therefore with political repression. The narrator speaks directly to his audience, in a manner frequently used in romantic fiction, to confirm that the narrative has already established: "En la época a que nos referimos, además, la salud del ánimo empezaba a ser quebrantada por el terror: por esa enfermedad terrible del espíritu, conocida y estudiada por la Inglaterra y por la Francia, mucho tiempo antes que la conociéramos en la América" (p. 5). ("In addition, in the period to which we refer, the spiritual well-being was beginning to be shattered by terror, by that dreadful disease of the spirit, known and studied by England and France long before we knew of it in America.") This statement by the narrator does not create an atmosphere of terror; it amounts to information, not experience. The brutality apparent during the attack on Daniel and his friends does contribute to a feeling of terror initiated by the need to escape. Even so, this effect might be more sensationalist than deeply convincing if the fiction text were limited to the first chapter. In the novel as a whole, the atmosphere becomes overwhelming. It is impossible, of course, to measure the influence of context in this connection. Mármol himself enters repeatedly to comment on the circumstances of the time he writes about; the modern reader has knowledge, in addition, of terror in more recent history, not only in Argentina but in other parts of the world.

SELECTION AND SUGGESTION

This principle is similar to "Beginning and Exposition" because it involves choice of detail. If it is obvious that the author cannot provide all the background information concerning the situation and characters of a story, it is equally apparent that he cannot supply every detail of the fictional present. He must choose the actions that lead most directly to the point of the story, and emphasize the personal characteristics that suggest as well as show what the people are like. Economical use of space corresponds directly to the efficacy of selection and suggestion.

Application of this principle in the case of *Amalia* emphasizes the clear division of people into categories of good and bad. Considering either the first chapter as an independent entity or the novel as a whole, the details chosen by Mármol serve to contrast the brutality of one side with the nobility of the other. The episode of the sword fight is the most minutely described. Eduardo's actions show his courage and his cleverness; his opponents' actions reveal their bloodthirsty cruelty. A subsequent episode demonstrates their venality.

Two "suggestions" are of considerable importance in the first chapter. One of them is painfully obvious, but typical of the serialized novel. When Daniel comes to the aid of Eduardo, he makes use of a weapon "que Daniel tenía en sus manos, muy pequeño y que no conocemos todavía" (p. 12) ("that Daniel had in his hands, very small, that we don't yet know about"). Further information about the weapon is withheld until pp. 315–16, although it is mentioned more than once. Its presence has some effect as an interest-holding device, and Mármol deserves a word of praise for remembering it: authors of serialized novels were not noted for their long memories. However, the chief suggestive value of this secret weapon is that it confers a special importance on Daniel, indicating that he has his own methods of dealing with the situation and is capable of achieving success where others may fail. He becomes the take-charge man. In this way, he is differentiated from Eduardo in the first chapter, and the difference is sustained throughout the novel. The second important suggestion involves the appearance and character of Amalia. She is a young woman dressed in black when she admits Daniel and the wounded Eduardo into her house. A few moments later, she unhesitatingly supports Eduardo by holding his arm. In the first chapter alone, these details suggest a pleasant and safe retreat for Eduardo. In the whole novel, they lay the foundation for the characterization of Amalia—a young widow of exquisite taste, with great inner strength and with equally great doubt about the future.

KEY MOMENT AND CLIMAX

Brooks and Warren differentiate between these two phenomena by pointing out that the key moment is the "moment of illumination for the whole story" (BW, p. 651), and it may or may not be the same as the decisive episode in a physical sense (the climax). In the first chapter of *Amalia,* the instant of the treacherous attack on the refugees may be considered the key moment because it shows how the regime functions and therefore synthesizes, to a large extent, the experience of the chapter and of the novel as a whole. The climax, on the other hand, is Daniel's unexpected appearance when Eduardo is about to be done in by his adversaries.

However, the key moment is further taken to be the germ of the story—it "contains in itself, by implication at least, the total meaning of the story" (BW, p. 651). The moment of attack will not qualify according to this definition because it does not suggest the possibility of a better situation. In the first chapter, this change is added to the sense of the story when Eduardo takes refuge in Amalia's house; in the novel as a whole, a similar effect is achieved, in a limited way, by the escape to Uruguay and, on a larger scale, by the hoped-for victory of the liberating army.

Brooks and Warren point out that, if the author has not decided what the key moment is, or if the moment is not truly illuminating, the story's structure will be loose and vague (BW, p. 651). That is clearly the case in the first chapter of *Amalia* and is even more clearly so in the novel as a whole. The significance of the book is not vague in the sense of the reader's not knowing what is going on; the vagueness is related to the novel's lack of symmetry. There are a number of climactic moments in *Amalia*—a situation almost mandatory in a serialized novel. The most important one, in the context of the whole work, is the moment when Rosas's scheming sister-in-law discovers that Eduardo is the man who escaped the attack by her agents. This incident is an important element of the novel's intrigue factor. Another climactic moment is the withdrawal of Lavalle's liberation army. This incident belongs more to the historical component and is less intimately experienced by the reader. Neither of these incidents, nor any other moment in *Amalia,* could properly be singled out as a true moment of revelation. However, since the total meaning of the story depends on contrast, two moments may serve together—the description of Amalia's house and the description of Rosas in his office and at dinner. These passages come rather early in the novel and seem more like the basis of contrast than like a moment of revelation; nevertheless, they do incorporate a great deal of what the book is about.

David Viñas sees this contrast as indicative of an important social phenomenon. Rosas is associated with rusticity, Amalia with urbanity. These correspondences are, in turn, associated with Americanism and Europeanism. Their synthesis, which has been a goal of the Argentine romantics, changes to polarity under the Rosas regime. In *Amalia,* according to Viñas, the Rosas-rustic-American line becomes hateful, and the Amalia-urbane-European line becomes a frustrated ideal.[7]

CONFLICT

Viñas's exposition of the Amalia-Rosas polarity states very well the conflict that is central in the experience of the novel. It is suggested in the first chapter when we first see Amalia in the role of providing a refuge for Eduardo. This conflict emphasizes the importance of the intrigue factor in *Amalia* as the basis of the narrative process. There are other conflicts less directly related to the story itself. We know there is an ideological conflict between *unitarios* and *federales*, but the ideology itself is almost entirely external to the action of the novel. Another related conflict is the question of whether it is better to fight Rosas from within or take refuge in another country. This matter is presented early in the first chapter, as part of what Eduardo says to one of his refugee companions. The decision has a moral component as well as a tactical one, but the vitality of this conflict is generally overshadowed by the need to escape terrorism.

Brooks and Warren point out that development of the conflict leads to the moment of illumination, the "key moment" (BW, p. 652). In general, that is what happens in the first chapter of *Amalia,* with reservations made because of Mármol's uncertainty concerning the moment of revelation. In the book as a whole, the moment of revelation (the descriptions of Amalia's house and of Rosas's office, considered together) comes too early in the novel to be the culmination of conflict development. However, the conflict has, in fact, been presented. Therefore, we experience the novel's essential message very early in the first of its five parts. Subsequently, the same message is repeated on many occasions—or it might be better to say that the message is constantly present. A fundamental difference between the first chapter and the novel as a whole must be pointed out in this connection. If we take the act of finding refuge in Amalia's house to be the key moment of the chapter, then the chapter as an independent unit has a satisfactory resolution in favor of the Amalia side of the Rosas-Amalia polarity. The novel as a whole, however, ends in the frustration of the Amalia-urbane-European side.

COMPLICATION

The writer builds toward his moment of illumination "by establishing an ascending series of moments of *complication*" (BW, p. 653). On the other hand, "the increase in intensity may be simply the result of accumulation of complications, though the individual complications in themselves may be approximately equivalent" (BW, p. 654). The latter is obviously the case in *Amalia.* In the first chapter, the sword-fight episode contains its own ascending series of moments, but this process does not apply to the development of the chapter as story. In the novel as a whole, there are many episodes in which tension increases, but there is no regular progression. One major episode—the discovery of Eduardo by Rosas's sister-in-law—comes little more than halfway through the novel, and announces rather clearly that a happy ending is unlikely. Effective complication might have been developed beyond this point by a more imaginative use of historical materials; however, Mármol frequently chose to quote historical documents rather than transform them into a literary experience—probably because his righteous indignation persuaded him that a presentation of "the facts" would be more convincing than narrative itself. This procedure shifts the interest in the literary experience from concentration on incidents to concentration on Daniel. His frenzied activity and his gift for intrigue characterize an exceptional person who makes the novel vital.

PATTERN OR DESIGN

Effective narration is characterized by a phenomenon that is something like repetition. Incidents are not actually repeated, but each incident in a sequence refers to a central question and recalls the preceding ones. Mármol's narrative procedure adheres to this principle; the asymmetry in *Amalia*'s pattern is produced by extreme imbalance in the intensity of episodes or by departure from the principle line of development (the intrigue factor).

Brooks and Warren say that "the writer of a story has to fulfill conflicting demands in creating his pattern, the demand for variety on the one hand and the demand for repetition on the other" (BW, p. 655). Satisfaction of this principle can be seen most clearly if we think of the incidents as always related to Daniel's campaign to save Eduardo. It is true that multiple connotations expand this act into a very complicated affair, but the basis of the intrigue is this rescue attempt. In the first chapter, there are three principle incidents: Daniel's intervention in the sword fight, his success in outwitting two of the enemy and commandeering a horse, and his delivery of Eduardo into the care of Amalia. All three incidents are directly concerned with the rescue, but the circumstances offer great variety: sheer violence, humorous trickery, feminine gentleness. Repeatedly, in the novel as a whole, incidents can be reduced to the basic goal of saving Eduardo, and the variety is considerable. In the first chapter, the awesome intensity of the sword fight puts it out of balance with the other two incidents, and comments on the conditions of the time intervene rather than underline, in such a way that the pattern becomes messy. This characteristic is even more apparent in the novel as a whole, because the author's interventions do not constitute a pattern that corresponds to the narrative development, but appear, rather, to correspond to his impulse at a given time. On the other hand, there is always an awareness of the thread of intrigue (and interest in Daniel).

DENOUEMENT

Identification of the denouement as "the moment of success or failure" (BW, p. 655) is especially interesting in a comparison of the first chapter of *Amalia* with the novel as a whole. When Daniel introduces the wounded Eduardo into Amalia's house, he achieves success, so far as the first chapter is concerned. If we read the chapter without reference to its historical context, the only suspense factor remaining at the end of chapter one is the fact that Eduardo needs medical attention. Such a chapter ending provides a poor transition to the next installment of a serialized novel. Obviously, awareness of the context provides suspense that enhances interest in subsequent events.

The successful rescue effort in the first chapter turns into tragic failure in the novel. The denouement is very clearly the final result of Daniel's efforts to save Eduardo. Historical facts presage the denouement when Daniel learns that Lavalle's army has turned back. He knows that he must help Eduardo (and others) leave the country. The terrorism of the moment moves faster than he does; *federal* hoodlums sack Amalia's house (destruction of the Amalia side of the polarity explained by Viñas) and murder Eduardo. Amalia either dies or faints (the key word is "exánime," p. 427), and Daniel is seriously injured. Mármol elects to leave in obscurity the precise fate of these two characters.

It is important to note, in connection with the novel's denouement, that the Amalia-Eduardo love story is of little or no functional importance. The line of intrigue, focused on Daniel, is persistently dominant, and the historical factor is related to the love story by using Daniel as an agent. The Eduardo-Amalia idyll is more important to the setting than it is to the plot, because it serves mainly to enhance the refinement and sensibility that contrast with the vulgarity of the *federales*.

CHARACTER AND ACTION

Daniel Bello is the protagonist. Modifications of this statement must take into account factors other than the experience of reading the novel. Eduardo Belgrano is admired by the narrator, but he is a very passive character after the sword fight in the first chapter. Amalia herself is important as the embodiment of an ideal, and in this connection it is significant that her name is the title of the novel; however, she does not really act very much in the first chapter or in the novel as a whole. Rosas is a portrait—an exceptionally striking one—but less than a fully participating character in the story.

Trinidad Pérez, in an introduction to the Casa de las Américas edition of *Amalia*, recognizes Daniel as protagonist and sets forth the essential qualities of his character, but says that his "realistic" attitude (Pérez uses the term in quotation marks) keeps him from being a pure romantic hero.[8] This statement unfortunately suggests that a romantic hero must be a wilting bundle of exaggerated sensibility. Daniel is, in fact, a perfect example of the romantic hero, that is, the man of action as well as the sensitive lover.

Genius and energy are the romantic qualities pointed out by Jacques Barzun in his explanation of why Napoleon was so attractive to romantic writers.[9] These characteristics—genius and energy—constitute an appropriate description of Daniel Bello. He uses his imagination in dealing with the situation in Buenos Aires, risks his own safety time after time, has a nearly unlimited reservoir of energy. The reference to his realistic attitude is probably based on Daniel's ability to face a circumstance and do something about it—an entirely romantic quality. The idea that the romantics were not realistic, in this sense, is unfounded and can distort appreciation of the romantic novel.

Daniel's intense activity makes him the novel's most complete characterization. Brooks and Warren say "the most significant way of presenting character is through action" (BW, p. 656). This principle explains the difference between Daniel and Eduardo. In the first chapter, Eduardo's action in the escape attempt reveals his plan to leave Buenos Aires, and the sword fight reveals his valor. After that, he does little more than fall in love.

Brooks and Warren point out that the character should have the potential for different kinds of action but that these actions must be consistent with each other. In the case of Daniel, the goal of his actions is rescuing Eduardo. We see him in many different places, employing different means to achieve this goal. The goal itself expands to include other people and to refer directly to the Argentine political situation.

In the first chapter, Daniel's actions reveal three related aspects of his character: the swashbuckling rescuer, the ironic observer of an English diplomat, and the pragmatic problem-solver who leaves Eduardo in Amalia's house. The chapter also supplements this characterization of Daniel through what he says about the political situation, and even through what Eduardo says about him. These techniques continue throughout the novel and are augmented, of course, by the narrator's direct description.

Mármol tends to reveal other characterizations through action and to supplement them by commenting directly. The other characterizations are not complete, but reveal the qualities needed to supplement the revelation of Daniel or intensify the anti-Rosas bias of the novel.

FOCUS OF INTEREST

The problem involved here is how the author emphasizes answers to the various questions that the reader will have: Who are these people? What is the situation? When is it going on? Why is it happening? What does it mean? Since, the questions cannot be answered all at once, the experience of the reading is affected by the ordering of these expositions and the relative importance given to them.

Obviously, the author of *Amalia* considers the *when* to be essential information, because he opens the novel with a direct statement of the year and day. This date is of immediate importance only if the story is read with knowledge of the historical context. The time of night, following the date and year, is more related to *what* is going on (the escape attempt) than it is to historical chronology. Ending the first paragraph, Mármol identifies the *where* as a particular street in Buenos Aires. Shortly thereafter, the *what* (escape from the Rosas regime) and *why* become clear. The *who* information is withheld longest—not because it is least important, but as a means of creating suspense.

Throughout the novel, Mármol keeps the reader informed with respect to the passing of time. Undoubtedly, this information is useful to readers who know the historical context; it is also helpful as a narrative device because it compensates partially for Mármol's straying from his plot line. As the novel develops, *what* becomes much more important than any of the other questions, because the sense of terror escapes the limits of place and time.

FOCUS OF CHARACTER

"The problem of the *focus of character* may be stated thus: *whose story is it?*" (BW, p. 658). The events may be important to a single person or to a group of persons with one particular person singled out. Brooks and Warren state that the author faces this question and also a related one: *"whose fate is really at stake?"* (BW, p. 659).

The first chapter of *Amalia* is clearly Eduardo's story until Daniel intervenes to rescue him. From that point to the end of the chapter, Daniel is the dominant figure. Even so, it is still apparently Eduardo *whose fate is really at stake*. This fact is important because it reveals a great deal about the author's priorities in what was probably his original conception of the novel. Eduardo belongs to the idealized line of refinement, represented mainly by Amalia. The passivity caused by his injury is entirely in accord with his contribution to the message of the novel.[10]

In the novel as a whole, the story is Daniel's. Mármol's invention of Daniel keeps the novel from becoming a static contrast. Although such a contrast may well have been the basis of the author's original plan, he must have invented Daniel as a person on whom the story could focus. Interestingly enough, we could not readily say that it is Daniel *whose fate is really at stake,* since his activities are directed toward saving Eduardo and others. Indeed, it is not quite accurate to think of Daniel even as a single person within a special group on which the narration focuses. Eduardo is a more likely candidate for that distinction.

What, then, is the relationship of Daniel to the group with which he is allied? In what way does the author focus on him? Ghiano says Mármol uses Daniel as his mouthpiece (p. xxviii). This description, however, suggests a more mechanical characterization than is actually the case. Daniel does not really belong to the special group of persons, because that group represents one of the components of the contrast pointed out by Viñas in the analysis discussed under the headings "key moment and climax" and "conflict." He is on their side because he hates the terrorism of the regime. However, the character of Daniel, taken as a whole, approximates the synthesis mentioned by Viñas as the original intention of the generation that was polarized by Rosas. In this sense, he certainly is the character *whose fate is really at stake.*

FOCUS OF NARRATION: POINT OF VIEW

This problem, which can be extremely complex in some pieces of fiction, is of the utmost simplicity in *Amalia*—the point of view is that of an omniscient author. He knows everything that is going on, and all about the people who appear in the story. There is only one kind of situation when such omniscience is not assumed by the reader, and that is an excessively obvious artifice of narration: sometimes the author describes people or situations and remarks coyly that "we" do not yet know who or what they are. It is quite reasonable to think that Mármol's interest in making his point caused him to "manage" the novel, even to the extent of appearing to use the story as an illustration of his argument. This tendency is the least attractive feature of the book, which, fortunately, is rescued by the invented factor in the narration, chiefly the action of Daniel and his function in the intrigue as a unifying agent between the historical component and the love story—a role that is apparent throughout the novel, including the first chapter.

DISTANCE AND TONE

The problem of distance refers to how close the author seems to be to his characters. Mármol makes it perfectly clear, through judgmental statements and obvious attitudes, that he is in favor of certain characters and against others. However, he really is not "close" to any of them in that metaphorical sense that makes the reader aware of a narrative intimacy. Quite to the contrary, he seems far removed from his characters (except insofar as Daniel appears to represent the views of Mármol) and inclined to set them out in illustrative scenes. The greatest distance is felt when the narrator uses "we" in collusion with his readers. These effects are the same in the novel as a whole and in the first chapter as an independent entity. A single exception is the relative closeness that is effected when the narrative changes from past tense to present tense in the sword-fight episode of the first chapter.

The problem of tone refers to the shadings that a speaker may give to an expression when he says it. Although the author does not have the advantage of audio effects, various factors in the narrative procedure combine to create the tone. All the aspects of distance contribute; the sharp division of characters into good and bad is a major factor; the uninhibited elitism seen in Mármol's preferences indicates his distaste for the vulgarity of the Rosas people. This militant snobbery may be a result of the polarity pointed out by Viñas and possibly not a fundamental attitude of Mármol's, but it certainly is an aspect of the novel's tone. Fryda Schultz de Mantovani, in describing the author of *Amalia,* takes a line from his *Cantos del peregrino* and refers to him as "el más infortunado y ofendido."[11] This description seems particularly significant if it is understood to indicate not self-pity but righteous indignation, and especially if we bear in mind the idea of the romantic individual driven to the wall. Mármol indicates his frustration by writing that the novelist cannot possibly show how bad the situation really was (pp. 389, 425, for example).

SCALE AND PACE

The problem of scale raises the question of whether or not the work is the right size for its message. The author cannot tell everything, but he must tell enough. In the first chapter of Amalia, the scale seems about right if we think only in terms of rescuing Eduardo. However, the safety he finds in Amalia's house is part of a very complex statement of preference for European refinement. In the first chapter, this preference is suggested but not developed. If the chapter were chosen to stand by itself, some development of this attitude might be desirable at the cost of cutting down the length of some other part of the narrative text.

This question of proportion involves "pace," which should accomplish an agreeable balance of summary, narrative, and scene. These terms are used by Brooks and Warren with the explanation that summary "renders an action" faster than narrative, and narrative faster than scene. That is, the actions communicated by the narrator would take a certain amount of time in real life; however, the time spent in the narration does not always correspond to a real-life time. The pace of the first chapter of *Amalia* might have been changed advantageously, for example, by substituting summary for part of the narrative in the sword-fight episode. Its usefulness to the author is to demonstrate the wanton violence of the Rosas men and the courage of Eduardo, but this purpose might have been served better by shifting some emphasis to the significance of Amalia and her surroundings.

This particular change would make little or no difference in the novel as a whole, because the following chapter describes Eduardo's refuge in great detail. Throughout the novel, Mármol makes use of summary, narrative, and scene, but presumably with no particular awareness of their different functions. It is a fact that these three methods may be used to avoid boredom (the use of only one produces a very strange effect); however, Mármol's choice must not have followed any such awareness of principle, but rather an alternating sense of urgency, sometimes with respect to setting forth his ideas and sometimes in connection with a novelizing instinct. The principles of scale and pace are related to the asymmetry of *Amalia* pointed out early in this analysis.

Since lack of proportion is an obvious problem in *Amalia,* some observations on the ordering of material will provide a coherent notion of how Mármol constructed the novel. It is divided into five parts, not equal in length but with no startling variations. Following the first chapter of Part One—already fully discussed—the first important factor is a description of Amalia's house. The dominant characteristic of this passage is European refinement. It sets forth clearly the nature of Eduardo's refuge. Next comes a sketch of Daniel. As a supplement to description by the narrator, Daniel reveals the lines of his activity in a series of notes that he writes to several people. An exposition of the historical circumstance follows, and then comes the famous portrait of Rosas, which establishes the contrast with the world of Amalia. Coutiño, one of Rosas's hatchetmen, is the focal character in a reprise of the attack narrated in chapter one. Now we have two sides of the incident.

The rest of Part One is mainly a series of introductions of other characters, some taken from history and others invented. Several of them have important functions in the novel, even though they may not be especially interesting characterizations. Daniel's fiancée, Florencia, for example, is a lightly sketched stereotype of a young cosmopolitan lady; her function in the novel is to confirm Daniel's relationship to the Amalia-urbane-European ideal. Doña María Josefa, Rosas's sister-in-law, is taken from history and is fully as ruthless as the dictator. She functions as Daniel's antagonist in the development of the intrigue factor. In many ways, *Amalia* is reminiscent of a Spanish *comedia de capa y espada,* with Daniel as hero. Following this notion, we can say that Don Cándido, an old schoolteacher of Daniel's, serves as *gracioso.* Cándido is caricatured by his use of redundant adjectives and by his cowardice. Because of his personal qualities, he is a useful agent for Daniel, who makes the poor man an unwilling participant in his intrigues. A feminine counterpart, Doña Marcelina, is the mistress of a house of ill fame and is caricatured by her quotations from classical tragedy. These two, especially Don Cándido, provide the comic relief of the novel. It is typical of *Amalia's* asymmetry that both comic characters are presented in consecutive episodes rather than placed strategically apart.

The second part opens with a passage about Amalia's background and some suggestions about her nascent love relationship with Eduardo. This part of the novel deals with the Amalia-Eduardo story more than once; nevertheless, it is surprising in view of the impression created by general comments concerning the novel, that it occupies very little text space.

More people are introduced when Amalia attends a ball. Later we see Daniel at the ball, but the sequence is broken by Daniel's long statement concerning why Rosas's opponents should stay in Buenos Aires and fight him from within. Following the ball and banquet, Amalia's privacy is threatened by a Rosas partisan who has found her attractive. This incident highlights her relationship with Eduardo. Part Three is by far the most important section insofar as the development of intrigue is concerned. Daniel goes to Montevideo and is in contact there with exiled Argentines and with a representative of the French government. (As Mármol presents foreign relations, the French are good, the English are bad.) This action naturally approaches the documentary. More clearly within the novel's intrigue component, Doña María Josefa obtains circumstantial evidence that Eduardo is the escapee from the attack that takes place in chapter one. Daniel outbluffs Doña María Josefa's hoodlums when they come to get Eduardo. However, the police search Amalia's house—an invasion of the world of good taste. It is fairly apparent at the end of Part Three that there will be no happy ending for those on the Amalia-urbane-European side.

Part Four becomes heavily documentary. We discover that Amalia's house is being watched and that Rosas has left the city for Santos Lugares to ready his troops for the anticipated confrontation with Lavalle. At this point, Mármol inserts authenticated documents into the novel, so arresting the narrative procedure. A documentary episode comments on the political details of the moment. More documents follow. An episode involving Don Cándido makes the text somewhat more narrative. However, this episode is followed by Mármol's essay on the gaucho, his theory on the sociology of revolution, and the history of the Argentine struggle for independence. Part Four ends in a flurry of intrigue, with Daniel becoming suspect by the *federales* who have previously accepted him because of his family's traditional *federal* affiliation.

Part Five contains many more documents and much information about troop movements. The two agents of comic relief, Don Cándido and Doña Marcelina, both bring discouraging news regarding Lavalle. A considerable amount of cloak-and-dagger activity has to do with arrangements for Daniel's people to leave Buenos Aires. Daniel announces to his handful of followers Lavalle's decision to retreat. Extreme terrorism breaks out in the city. It is described in an editorial tone, as is a government decision to confiscate the property of *unitarios*. Before Eduardo can leave, terrorists sack Amalia's house in the final scene, intent upon destruction and murder. This intrusion amounts to a destruction of the enlightened side of the contrast. Only "Una especie de epílogo" (p. 428), following an ending that is not clear on all points, suggests the possibility of a future for the Amalia component of the polarity.

Clearly, the asymmetry of *Amalia* is a narrative defect. It may be granted that, if the episodes of a serialized novel are read separately, the well-constructed episode is more important than the well-constructed novel. On the other hand, it is important to remember that Mármol wrote with posterity in mind, even though *Amalia* served the immediate purpose of encouraging Argentine exiles in their struggle against Rosas (p. 1). It is interesting that the novel's most obvious technical fault is very closely related to one of its major triumphs: Mármol's uncertainty with respect to the "key moment" produced a loosely constructed novel, but it also placed early emphasis on the polarity represented by the Amalia-urbane-European component versus the Rosas-rustic-American side, the deepest expression of the novel's conflict.

According to Brooks and Warren, the development of the "conflict" should lead toward the "key moment," the moment of illumination. Presentation of the Amalia-Rosas polarity comes too early in the novel to be the culmination of a process; the first-chapter scene in Amalia's house is soon followed by the famous portrait of Rosas's bestiality. From this point, the conflict is apparent, though it may be expressed in different ways. The moment of illumination is experienced when the conflict becomes evident. Nevertheless, the narrative process of *Amalia* effects the desirable "complication" with great success by unfolding a series of incidents that create the experience of terror by oppression. Intensity of feeling is achieved by a cumulative effect rather than by a series of events in which each one is more terrifying than the one preceding. With respect to "pattern," the narrator functions admirably. In the sequence of events, he provides a variety of situations, but the ultimate goal is consistently to save Eduardo. Therefore, it may be seen that the asymmetry of *Amalia* is not caused by an irregular plot design but by the author's eagerness to make the case clear. Again, in this connection, a deficiency of one order produces an excellent effect of another—Mármol's eagerness to make the facts known led him to introduce actual documents into the narrative text, and this procedure lessens interest in the historical events that take place, while increasing attention to Daniel as the ideal hero.

The characterization of Daniel is unquestionably Mármol's greatest achievement as a narrator. This young man of action relates the intrigue factor to both the historical material and the love story. However, his role is much more than a unifying device—Daniel is the perfect romantic hero. The narrator underplays the importance of Daniel as lover and assigns that role to Eduardo. Daniel then is able to fulfill the role of ingenious schemer who can solve the problem, ubiquitous undercover man, tireless fighter, and noble human being who transcends partisan affiliation in order to be on the side of justice. In this role, Daniel is everybody's hero and the soul of the novel's intrigue. He stands out above all the others because, as Brooks and Warren point out, character is best presented through action. The basic conflict was real enough in Argentine culture, and certainly *Amalia* is important for that reason; however, it could have been a shallow business indeed if the narrative art of Mármol had not turned the basic conflict into intrigue with Daniel in the center, and concurrently developed a sense of terror that exists somewhere between hate and nausea.

4

Narrative Illusion of Paradox Resolved

Alberto Blest Gana's Martín Rivas

Martín Rivas (1862) is one of the best possible examples of *realismo romántico* as defined by Fernando Alegría.[1] This apparently contradictory term describes a substantial number of Spanish-American novels in which the authors combined a generally realistic presentation of the social setting with a highly conventionalized, almost stereotyped, romantic love story. Alberto Blest Gana (1830–1920), the author, was strongly influenced by Balzac's novelistic portrayal of French society and intended to make a similar contribution to Chilean literature.

Martín, the protagonist of the novel that bears his name, comes to Santiago from the provinces to study law. He has little money, but is invited to live in the home of Don Dámaso Encina, a wealthy *santiagueño* who owes Martín's family a favor. As a novel of customs, the narrative builds on the social, political, and financial relationships of the Encina family. As a love story, the plot focuses on Martín Rivas and Leonor Encina, proud daughter of Don Dámaso. Both aspects of the novel are complicated by involvement with the Molina family (*gente de medio pelo* who are socially inferior to the Encinas) and with the liberal uprising in 1851 against the government of Manuel Montt.[2]

In spite of the reference to a specific event in the past, *Martín Rivas* is not a historical novel either in the sense of having characters that are unquestionably products of a particular historical circumstance (Lukacs) or in the more general sense of recreating the atmosphere of a unique period.[3] The novel's action takes place approximately ten years before the date of publication. There is no reason to question the fundamental credibility of the social types portrayed, even though they are seen through the eyes of an external narrator who views them satirically. However, it is not probable that they are restricted to a single brief period of Chilean history. One of the pleasures of the novel, for Chileans (according to Algería, himself a Chilean), is the fact that these figures from the past take on a similarity to people of the present time.[4] As for the rebellion and other historical facts included in the novel, they suggest a degree of unrest in the country that underlines several contrasts, in the novel, between how things were in 1851 and how they had become by the time the book was written. These contrasts suggest, although hesitantly, a certain degree of progress, in the nineteenth-century understanding of the word.

There can be little doubt about the high regard in which Chileans hold *Martín Rivas*. Although it is less well known internationally than *Amalia* or *María,* it has been published in at least twenty-four editions, most of them Chilean.[5] At the same time, Chilean critics have been far from negligent of this favorite literary child. The most comprehensive study of Blest Gana's life and works is by Raúl Silva Castro, though it would be a mistake to overlook the valuable book-length study by Hernán Díaz Arrieta and a more recent volume in the Argentine *Genio y figura* series by Hernán Poblete Varas.[6] These studies, and others, contain interesting comments about *Martín Rivas,* but the most detailed analysis of the novel is by Cedomil Goic in his *La novela chilena.*[7] Goic cuts through the maze of a kind of legend of Martín Rivas and gets to the way the novel is constructed and what it means. His study is essential to any consideration of the work.

Goic points out that critical interpretations of *Martín Rivas* have been varied and contradictory. When it has been compared with European novels, especially with Stendhal's *Le Rouge et le noir,* Blest Gana's work is seen as very regionalistic, excessively vituperative in its social criticism, or inordinately picturesque as a novel of customs. Considered strictly within the framework of Chilean fiction, it seems quite authentic.[8] However, even in this context, the emphases of the critics' readings vary considerably. According to the annotations made by Goic on the studies he cites, one critic may consider mainly the picture of customs in a time past; another finds an underlying philosophical element that makes the novel a kind of handbook for young men who aspire to a good place in society; a third finds some of

the historical events rather lifeless; for still another, the nucleus of the
novel is Leonor's gradually coming to love Martín.[9] However one
understands the meaning of the novel, there is much to be said for this
last reaction, though it would be equally indicative to say that Martín
gradually wins the love of Leonor. In the process of doing so, he wins
a place for himself in society and, presumably, implants some of his
ideals in a social sphere where they have been sadly lacking. The full
meaning of this process may not be readily apparent. The protagonist's action, as stated here, smacks of superficiality; on the other
hand, in the experience of reading the novel, it is quite possible that
the Martín-Leonor relationship may seem, however vaguely, to imply
a deeper significance. In the interest of pursuing this significance and
how it is communicated, the following analysis will make use of a
theory and application set forth by Floyd Merrell in an essay called
"Toward a New Model of Narrative Structure."[10]

Two important caveats must be stated with respect to Merrell's
work and its use here. First, he proposes a model and shows, in a story
by Juan Rulfo, "La cuesta de las comadres," how his hypotheses function; he is quite aware of the tentative nature of his proposal. Second,
the following analysis of *Martín Rivas* may not be a flawless application of Merrell's design. However, primary references will be made to
Merrell's work rather than to the enormous body of theory that is
behind it.

Stated in the most general fashion, Merrell's purpose is to use
linguistic methods in such a way that the similarity of literary texts
may be seen without disregard for their dissimilarity. He points out,
with considerable care, the objections that have been raised against
the application of various theories (Saussure, Propp, Chomsky, and
others) to the analysis of modern narrative; then he sets forth the procedure that recognizes certain basic principles and, at the same time,
comes to grips with the dynamic factor in the narrative text. The
scheme of analysis includes three levels, which may be identified as (1)
axiological, (2) symbolico-semantic, and (3) praxemic.

The axiological is the "deepest" level. The structure here consists
of a fundamental opposition, such as life versus death, individual versus group, freedom versus necessity. These binary oppositions are absolutely opposed, without the possibility of one being partially the
other, and they are common to the thought of all peoples (Merrell, p.
154). The opposing elements seek resolution, though they may not

always be immediately apparent in the fiction text. This axiological tension represents the synchronic dimension of the narrative. It persists, through its representation may vary (Merrell, pp. 153–54).

In *Martín Rivas,* the axiological opposition is individual versus group. This contrast provides a better basis for experiencing the novel fully than do the more usual statements of conflict between province and capital city or between upper class and middle class. Obviously, these conflicts do exist; however, if we consider what Martín actually does in the novel, the fact that he is an individual seems more important than his provincial origin. There is an alienation factor involved in Martín's opposition to the group, but its special connotations can be appreciated best on the symbolico-semantic level.

This second level is the narrative clothing of the axiological contrast. The conflicts that appear on this level are symbolic of the underlying tension (Merrell, p. 155). The process of reading the fiction text produces recognition of these surface, symbolic conflicts; recognition of the underlying tension comes later. It seems possible that this deeper appreciation may not necessarily be on a conscious level. Certainly, if it does occur consciously, the experience of reading then reverses itself and appreciation of the narrative stems from the deepest level upward.

The following diagram will provide some idea of how the representation of the axiological opposition functions in Blest Gana's novel.

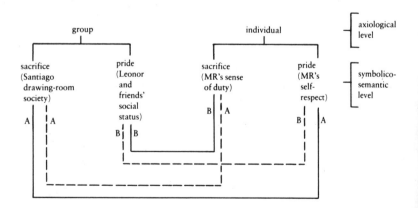

The use of the term "sacrifice," as applied to Santiago drawing-room society in the relationship indicated by broken line A, is ironic, and indicates the nature of Blest Gana's social satire. The members of this group are indeed willing to sacrifice many things—a daughter's happiness for financial advantage, ideological principle for political power, needed reform for social stability. This attitude contrasts with Martín's rectitude. Sacrifice, in his case, refers to his willingness to give up personal advantage for the sake of what he deems right. At the same time, "pride," as used in the first component of the contrast indicated by broken line B, also acquires some of the quality of irony when seen by the side of Martín's pride (self-respect). Disdainful pride is especially apparent in Leonor Encina and her circle of friends, because it becomes a major factor in the novel's dynamics; however, it is a characteristic of the whole drawing-room society.

The broken lines indicate the contrasting values of two terms that have quite different meanings depending on whether they are used with respect to the group or to the individual. The solid lines indicate how these qualities play upon each other. Solid line A refers to the contrast by which Martín's uncompromising principles show up the expediency of Santiago's elite. Solid line B highlights the contrast by which Martín's sense of duty basically ridicules Leonor's disdain, even as that very sense of duty requires him to lose an advantage he has gained with Leonor, whom he loves. It is possible to say, taking into consideration the meaning of the broken as well as the solid lines, that Martín's self-respect is to the expediency of Santiago drawing-room society as Martín's sense of duty is to the disdainful pride of Leonor.

This consideration pushes us toward the praxemic level. Before dealing with all the ramifications of that component, however, it is important to indicate that broken line B has a special significance. It is through the interplay of these contrasting elements, the pride of Leonor and the pride of Martín, that we see the diachronic axis of the novel.

The nucleus of Merrell's proposition is that, on the praxemic level, the synchronic axis and the diachronic axis of the narrative are temporarily joined and that the oppositions observed on the axiological and, subsequently, the symbolico-semantic level are subjected to possible reconciliation. This performance creates the illusion of resolving a paradox. A "mediating agent" is instrumental in this act (Merrell, p. 156). Merrell refers to this stage as "narrative performance," as a counterpart to Chomsky's "linguistic performance" (Merrell, p. 155).

The idea of "semantic praxis" (what happens on the praxemic level) comes from Roman Jakobson's linguistic differentiation between metaphor and metonymy (Merrell, pp. 155–56). Metaphor is association by selection. That is, one sign may be substituted for another, therefore selection—"selection allows for substitution between terms in the terms in the same context" (Merrell, p. 156). This is the paradigmatic, synchronic dimension. Metonymy is association by contiguity. That is, one sign is associated with another sign because one follows the other in a sequence. They cannot change places; they cannot be substituted for each other. This is the syntagmatic, diachronic dimension. Normally these dimensions are represented on a vertical axis and a horizontal axis. The vertical axis is metaphoric, paradigmatic, and synchronic; the horizontal axis is metonymic, syntagmatic, and diachronic. Now, in Merrell's words: "According to the model proposed in this study, at the praxemic level Jakobson's intransigent dualism between paradigm and syntagma is temporarily obliterated, the synchronic becomes 'diachronized,' and the basic antinomies of thought emanating from the axiological component via the symbolico-semantic component are at this point subjected to attempted reconciliation through *mediating agents*" (Merrell, p. 156).

In *Martín Rivas,* several variations on the opposition shown by solid line A appear early in the novel. They do not always refer specifically to Martín at the moment when they become apparent, but ultimately they are related to the interplay of Leonor's pride and Martín's pride (broken line B). Since they belong to the metaphoric-paradigmatic-synchronic dimension, reference to them in a vertical line will emphasize their nature:

1) conservatism versus progress (pp. 33–37)
2) materialism versus human emotional needs (p. 38)
3) financial reward versus sense of duty (p. 41)
4) external appearance versus inner worth (p. 47)

In each of the four oppositions, the first component refers to the attitude of Santiago's upper class, seen primarily in the drawing room of the Encina family; the second component reflects the attitude of Martín as an individual. (One or another of these worthy characteristics may be noted, from time to time, in another individual, but never as belonging to a group.) In other words, the group is ignoble; the individual is worthy.

The first of the four oppositions becomes clear in an early scene in the Encina house when the customary evening guests are present (pp. 33–37). Four distinct political positions become apparent. Dámaso Encina feels a certain sympathy toward the reformist cause of the *Sociedad de la Igualdad*. His enthusiasm is cooled by the fear that support of the cause might threaten his financial position. However, he vacillates throughout the novel because he is politically ambitious as well as ideologically uncertain. His brother-in-law, Fidel Elías, is the complete opportunist. He can interpret the political situation only in terms of his own advantage. His wife, Francisca, defends the reformist position, persisting gallantly for some time against unabashed shushing by her husband, who informs her that women know nothing of politics. Engracia, the wife of Dámaso Encina, plays the role of the submissive wife who stays in her place. Blest Gana makes her a caricature by emphasizing her attention to a lap dog as her only interest in life. This early scene is related to Martín's eventual participation in the rebellion of 1851 as a member of the *Sociedad de la Igualdad*.

The second opposition is revealed in a far less complex scene in which Fidel Elías points out to his wife the financial advantage of having their daughter, Matilde, marry her cousin, Agustín Encina (p. 38). The fact that Agustín is a witless dandy does nothing to deter Elías, even in the face of his wife's objections. This contrast between materialism and human emotional needs relates to the position of Martín when he becomes the advocate of Rafael San Luis, a former suitor of Matilde. The Rafael-Matilde love story is an important ingredient in the novel because it supplies the tragic note required by romantic taste. It would be impossible for Martín not to win Leonor, since the conquest of her kind of pride is the dynamic force in the novel (broken line B). It is also significant that, as the novel develops and complications increase, Rafael establishes a relationship between political reform and his love for Matilde (p. 319). After he has definitively lost her, he substitutes the reformist cause for his love, thereby suggesting an equivalence between the opposition "conservatism versus progress" and the opposition "conservatism versus love."

The third of the four listed oppostions ("financial reward versus sense of duty") directly involves Martín. Dámaso Encina, knowing that Martín's financial resources are very limited, offers him a part-time job as his secretary-bookkeeper (pp. 41–42). Martín accepts the job but refuses the salary offered. This determination to keep himself above reproach is the characteristic that makes Blest Gana's protagonist seem inordinately admirable.

The fourth opposition ("external appearance versus inner worth") is part of a statement by Rafael San Luis (p. 47). The latter is a fellow student of law. When he notices that Martín is being shunned because of his provincial dress and customs, he offers his friendship and explains that external appearance is the determining factor with regard to acceptance into Santiago society. It is interesting that Rafael, when he introduces Martín into the Molina household (the *gente de medio pelo*), indicates that they too make judgements on the basis of externals (p. 65). In the first instance, the statement is a simple declaration: "Aquí las gentes se pagan mucho de las exterioridades, cosa con la cual no convengo." ("Here, people base a lot on externals, something with which I disagree.") In the second, Rafael uses a popular locution: "Para las gentes de medio pelo, que no conocen nuestros salones, un *caballero* o, como ellas dicen, *un hijo de familia* es el tipo de la perfección, porque juzgan al monje por el hábito." ("For people of the lower middle class, who don't know our drawing-room society, a *gentleman* or, as they say, *a son of a family* is the perfect type, because they judge the monk by his habit.") The novelist chose to emphasize the expressions indicated in the quotation. In the present analysis, the words "juzgan el monje por el hábito" should be emphasized because the popular flavor of the expression accords with the social status of the Encina family. It is important to note that, although the inferior position of the Molina family is apparent in several different contexts during the course of the novel, the relationship between the Molinas and the Encinas does not symbolize an axiological opposition. In fact, there are some factors that suggest a metaphoric appreciation. It is hard to overlook Amador, for example, as a cheaper version of Agustín Encina. However, in terms of the axiological opposition, Edelmira Molina's role is the most important. She defends her honor, rejects convenience in favor of true love, sacrifices one aspect of her integrity to save another (by consenting to marry a man she does not love, in order to save the life of Martín, the object of her real, unrequited love). It may be said that Edelmira is to the *gente de medio pelo* as Martín is to drawing-room society.

Naturally, many sets of oppositions symbolize the axiological contrast throughout the novel. The preceding discussion of four indicates how one expression of the conflict may take the place of another. A slightly different kind of relationship may be noted in the possibility of exchanging one of the two components in each of two oppositions. For example, the second component of "conservatism versus reform" may be exchanged with the second component of "materialism versus human emotional needs," producing "conservatism versus human emotional needs" and "materialism versus reform," which are equally good symbolizations of the axiological opposition. This interchangeability emphasizes the metaphoric-paradigmatic-synchronic nature of the oppositions. The four that are discussed above are particularly significant because they come early in the novel, and also because there is very little plot development in the first half of *Martín Rivas*. In other words, very little happens on the novel's diachronic axis; therefore, the synchronic nature of the oppositions is all the more apparent. This peculiarity of *Martín Rivas* must be put aside for later consideration, because it is obvious that something must happen on the diachronic axis, and that it has to be taken into account.

It seems reasonable to think of the diachronic axis in two different ways: (1) as a series of signs in the form of actions of some particular kind, as in the "Martín-pride versus Leonor-pride" opposition (broken line B), or (2) as a series of signs in the form of narrative situations (scene, summary, descriptive pause, ellipse, or some other similar classification). Clearly a novel has a diachronic axis based on association by contiguity, even if it is no more than the sequence of pages. However, there is little point in considering the matter except as it applies to meaning. Roman Jakobson observes a line of contiguous (metonymic) relationships established by the realist novelist's movement from plot to ambience and character to setting.[11] This notion may do well enough—or almost well enough—if it is confined to realist novels, but serious problems arise when it is applied to many recent fiction texts. The contiguous relationship assumes nonreversibility—that is, if sign A is followed by sign B, the sequence cannot be rearranged so that sign B is followed by sign A, for the same reason that the words of a sentence may not be put in reverse order or otherwise placed according to choice. But such an anti-sequential arrangement is precisely what happens in many recent fiction texts. Indeed, not even the sequence of pages is inviolable (note Julio Cortázar's *Rayuela,* for example). What, then, is the diachronic axis of the novel? Even if we look at a series of events, the process of selection is apparent. They may appear to be related by contiguity, but this contiguity may sometimes be meaningful (and irreversible) only in connection with a preceding act of selection, especially if events in a series build tension by repeating essentially the same meaning through acts that are superficially different from each other but mean basically the same thing. This phenomenon is recognized by Brooks and Warren in the sections entitled "Complication" and "Pattern and Design," in "Technical Problems and Principles in the Composition of Fiction—a Summary."[12]

The contrast between Leonor Encina's pride (social status) and Martín Rivas's pride (self-respect), as indicated by broken line B, provides the best means of appreciating the diachronic axis of Blest Gana's novel. As the novel progresses, the temporary conjunction of the synchronic with the diachronic (metaphoric with metonymic, selective with contiguous, paradigmatic with syntagmatic) becomes increasingly apparent. The slow-moving first half of *Martín Rivas* makes the novel a convenient subject for analysis, because it emphasizes the synchronic axis first. However, this convenience cannot be assumed in the analyses of other novels.

The essence of the Martín-Leonor relationship, in the first half of the novel, is drawing-room coquetry contrasted with country-boy honesty. Martín knows, when he arrives in Santiago, the circumstances of his deceased father's relationship with Dámaso Encina. The latter's indebtedness is moral rather than legal. He discharges it willingly and well, a condition that is apparent from the earliest episodes. Martín, in turn, discharges his own indebtedness by refusing pay for his work as secretary-bookkeeper. His role with respect to Leonor, in the first part of the novel, consists of regarding her with moonstruck awe and serving as an agent to help her effect a reconciliation between Matilde and Rafael. Leonor senses the inner worth of Martín, or at least his difference from her accustomed bevy of suitors, but she is not about to show admiration for this awkward young man from the provinces. Martín, appropriately enough, supposes that the beautiful and sophisticated Leonor must despise him, but he has no inclination to bend to her whims or in any other way seek to ingratiate himself. If this description suggests that there is little movement, the description is accurate.[13] There are incidents, of course, but they are mainly interviews between Leonor and Martín, in the same situation—the drawing room—and with the same reactions. The novel, however, is more interesting than this series of encounters might indicate, because Blest Gana lays the groundwork of his social satire and begins to exploit it. Through the character types mentioned in the four synchronic oppositions described above, the narrator communicates his view of society. The synchronic signs illuminate Martín's position with respect to his personal integrity and also to his alienation from the group. From his point of view, Leonor embodies the group's characteristic exclusivism. The reader knows things that Martín does not know: Leonor's sense of the protagonist's inner worth and her doubts concerning some of her coterie. Speaking with Matilde at an evening gathering, she refers to one of her suitors as "este hombre con sus cadenas de reloj y brillantes que huelen a capitalista de mal gusto" (p. 31) ("that man with his watch chains and diamonds that smell of capitalists with poor taste").

Approximately halfway through the novel, a change in the Leonor-Martín relationship shows how the axiological opposition ("group versus individual") is subject to resolution on the praxemic level (Merrell, p. 159). The occasion is the celebration in the Campo de Marte of Chile's national holiday. It is well to remember, while examining this incident in some detail, that both man and woman have maintained a high degree of formality in their conversations. Although the reader knows that Leonor is disturbingly attracted to Martín and that the latter confesses to himself that he is in love with her, neither party has said or done anything that would openly indicate to the other any such state of sentiment. Martín has allowed himself some heavily veiled suggestions regarding his heart's dilemma, but they have been invariably sidetracked by Leonor's nimbleness in social repartee (or a less generous reading might consider her simply slow to catch on). On the day of the festive outing, Leonor goes on horseback, accompanied by her father, Matilde, Agustín, and Martín. It is of some importance that the mode of transportation is uncommon for these people, and though it is appropriate to the occasion, it is not the only way they could attend. The narrator describes the customs associated with the event, satirizing rather harshly the superficiality of the celebrants' interest—for example, the detailed comments on the quality and age of the ladies' attire, made by the ladies about each other. Then we are alerted by the narrator to an unusual circumstance. Referring to Leonor, he says:

El placer más vivo se retrataba francamente en su rostro. *No era en aquel instante la niña orgullosa de los salones,* la altiva belleza en cuya presencia perdía Rivas toda la energía de su pecho; *era una niña que se abandonaba sin afectación a la alegría de un paseo,* en el que latía de contento su corazón por la novedad de la situación, por la belleza del día y del paisaje. [P. 165, emphasis mine]

[The most vivid pleasure was reflected frankly on her face. *She was not at that instant the proud young woman of the salons,* the haughty beauty in whose presence Rivas shrank into himself; *she was a young girl abandoning herself without affectation to the enjoyment of an outing,* during which her heart beat with pleasure at the novelty of the situation, the beauty of the day and of the landscape.]

The change noted in Leonor is caused by the change of ambience. She is no less a member of the group than she has been all along, but in this particular situation she is more accessible to Martín.

A moment of ceremonial firing by a military unit frightens the horses and there is some milling around in the party. The following passage comes immediately after:

—*Aquí estamos mal*—dijo Leonor a Martín—. ¿Le gusta a usted galopar?
—Sí, señorita—contestó Rivas.
—*Sígame entonces*—repuso Leonor, volviendo su caballo hacia el sur. Hizo señas al mismo tiempo a Matilde, que emprendió el galope, mientras que don Dámaso . . . [here follow several lines of humorous reference to an awkward predicament of Dámaso, and his admonition to Agustín that he go ahead with the others].

Leonor azotaba a su caballo, que iba pasando del galope a la carrera, animado también por el movimiento del de Martín.

Este corría al lado de Leonor *sintiendo ensancharse su corazón por primera vez al influjo de una esperanza. . . .*

. . . Leonor se detuvo y contempló durante algunos momentos a los demás de la comitiva, que habiendo sólo galopado, venían aún muy distantes del punto en que ella se encontraba con Rivas.

—Nos *han dejado solos*—dijo, mirando a Martín, que en ese momento se creía feliz por primera vez desde que amaba. [Pp. 166–67, emphasis mine]

[*"We're in a poor place here,"* said Leonor to Martín. "Do you like to gallop?"

"Yes, señorita," answered Rivas.

"Follow me then," replied Leonor, turning her horse toward the south.

She signaled at the same time to Matilde, who started to gallop, while don Dámaso . . . *Leonor struck her horse with her riding crop* and he moved from a gallop to a run, urged on also by the movement of Martín's. The latter raced beside Leonor, *feeling his heart expand for the first time under the influence of a hope. . . .*

. . . Leonor stopped and contemplated for some moments the others of the retinue, who having only galloped, were still far away from the place where she found herself with Rivas.

"They have left us alone," she said, looking at Martín, who at that moment felt happy for the first time since he had fallen in love.]

For the first time in the novel, the first person plural appears with reference to Leonor and Martín, and this may be the single most important element in this crucial passage; however, it is only one of several indicators that should be noted. The movement that is narrated—that is, the activity of the fiesta and, even more notably, the Martín-Leonor chase—marks the point in the novel where the pace of the story quickens remarkably. The second part of the novel is much faster than the first; indeed, more happens. It is also fair to say that although the very act of narrating produces a provisional joining of the synchronic and the diachronic axes, in *Martín Rivas* the synchronic axis dominates in the first part and the diachronic dominates in the second. With this in mind, it is interesting to note Merrell's reference to the theories of Jacques Lacan, the French psychoanalyst: "Metaphor, repression of the object of desire, and metonymy, dynamic movement, are intimately related in the literary text" (Merrell, p. 161).

One could do worse than apply this statement to the personality change in Leonor, although such an application would be only a limited use of the hypothesis of Lacan as filtered through Merrell. Since the first part of the novel is predominantly synchronic (metaphoric), little imagination is required to see repression of the object of desire as characteristic of that part, whereas diachrony (metonymy) sets in motion the series of acts, in the second part, that refer to Martín's and Leonor's relationship, now modified by a change in the expression of Leonor's pride. Her new tone is variable; it may reveal flirtatiousness or pique, for example, depending on the circumstances, rather than the studied distance of the earlier drawing-room gamesmanship.

An erotic understanding of the central episode is strengthened by the symbolism of the horse, because the animal's significance goes deeper than the fact of Leonor's invitation to the chase ("Sígame entonces"). The horse, a very complicated symbol, appears related to cosmic origins as a generative force, and symbolizes overwhelming desires.[14] Although less insistent than the function of the horse, the "fiesta" is important as a reenactment of creation.[15] Of course, the Encina outing on the national holiday is not a fiesta in a truly participatory sense, and it would be difficult to substantiate such a symbolic function with respect to the whole party. However, the narrator does state and describe a change in Leonor that corresponds to the notion of regeneration. It is important that this regeneration happens only to Leonor (see preceding quotation from p. 165) and is reflected upon Martín. On the diachronic axis of the novel, the focus is sharply on the central pair and what they are doing. On the synchronic axis, the metaphoric opposition that persists is the fourth of those enumerated earlier in this analysis—"external appearances versus inner worth." The other metaphors have been repressed and are now symbolized by this one. With this situation in mind, the proposition that Merrell derives from Lacan becomes more generally significant.

Merrell understands the metonymic line of signifiers to constitute a dynamic factor that leads to the inexpressable (Merrell, pp. 161–62). He proposes, therefore, that this axis (metonymic-diachronic-syntagmatic) is not related to concrete reality "since literary fiction is only a mere semblance of reality" (Merrell, p. 162). The other line, however, leads directly to concrete reality. Merrell's formulation, insofar as it involves definition of fiction and reality, may be questioned. On the other hand, the general suggestion is extremely interesting with regard to *Martín Rivas* as a literary experience. There is no doubt that what seems real, at this point in the novel, is the opposition between external appearance and inner worth. The events of the story may be "made up," but there is nothing artificial about the opposition. Indeed, it seems all the more real because a change seems to be taking place, that is, inner worth and external appearance seem to be coming together rather than opposing each other, and in the paradigmatic line of substitutions this apparent reconciliation of opposites affects all the oppositions that it has come to signify. An event on the diachronic axis of the novel coincides with the presumed reconciliation mediated by the horse-fiesta-nature function. However, the axiological opposition "group versus individual" is not resolved, because the change in Leonor has affected her as an individual; the group has not changed. Her use of "we," with reference to Martín, opens a door to him, on the diachronic axis, to ally himself with one member of a specific set of persons who exemplify the "group" of the axiological opposition, but the fundamental contrast is not altered.

The next event on the diachronic axis (the first episode following the central event just discussed) brings Martín, still in the "we" relationship, into an intimate concern of the Encina family and reveals the unreconciled persistence of exterior appearance versus inner worth. Agustín Encina has very foolishly fallen into a difficult situation with respect to the Molina family. He arranged a secret meeting with Adelaida Molina, only to be discovered by Amador, her brother, who appeared opportunely by prearrangement with Adelaida. In this interesting variation on the badger game, Amador has a friend "marry" them on the spot. The ceremony is a farce, but Agustín is foolish enough to believe he is really married. Even when Martín proves that it has no legal basis, Doña Engracia fears the loss of good appearances.

—¡Qué dirán, por Dios, qué dirán!—volvió a exclamar doña Engracia, apretando con más fuerza a Diamela, que esta vez dió un gruñido de impaciencia, aumentando la desesperación de don Dámaso.

Este se volvió hacia Leonor, que permanecía impasible en medio de la confusión de sus padres.

—Dile, hija—repuso—, que el matrimonio es nulo y que hay cómo probarlo.

—Eso no basta, eso no basta—respondió doña Engracia—, ¡toda
la sociedad va a saber lo que ha sucedido y no se hablará de otra cosa!
[p. 201]

["What will they say, Dear God, what will they say!" Doña
Engracia exclaimed again, holding on tightly to Diamela, who this time
gave a growl of impatience, increasing the desperation of Don Dámoso.
He turned toward Leonor, who remained impassive in the midst of
her parents' confusion.
"Tell her, daughter," he replied, "that the marriage is null, and
that there's a way to prove it."
"That's not enough, that's not enough," answered Doña Engracia,
"everybody will know what has happened and they won't talk about
anything else!"]

The concern for external appearance is obvious; it is also apparent
that, whereas any individual might be satisfied with the knowledge of
the truth, the group demands a different solution. Leonor then points
out that Martín is the one who proved the marriage a farce and that he
can probably help keep it secret. Martín is called, and responds
promptly. Following his statement that he is certain the marriage is a
fake, Leonor speaks again:

—Lo que se necesita es asegurarse de todo eso, tener una prueba
irrecusable de la nulidad del matrimonio y comprar el silencio de esas
gentes—dijo Leonor a Martín, con tono tan perentorio y resuelto,
como si ella y el joven tuviesen solos el cargo de ventilar aquel asunto
de familia. [p. 202]

["What we need is to be sure of all that, to have irrefutable proof
that the marriage is null, and to buy the silence of those people," said
Leonor to Martín, in such a peremptory and decisive tone that it
seemed as though she and the young man alone carried the burden of
solving the family's problem.]

So it is that Martín, the paragon of inner worth, is committed to
maintaining the exterior appearance of respectability of the Encina
family, a model of Santiago drawing-room pretentiousness. The
conflict indicated by broken line A has turned into an alliance as the
novel moves along its diachronic axis—that is to say, Martín's sense of
duty moves him, at this point, to protect the interest of the family that
has befriended him. In so doing, he alters the relationship represented

by solid line A in such a way that the group appears to absorb the individual.

In order to justify Martín's act, the narrator portrays the Molina family in an unfavorable light. Amador is particularly unscrupulous. Adelaida can be influenced by her brother and, although she is not indecent, neither is her virtue unassailable. Their mother is strongwilled in some matters, but too addicted to the joys of drinking and gambling to keep her family in line. Edelmira, the second daughter, is admirable. In the process of settling Agustín's affair, Leonor becomes jealous of Martín's friendship (Leonor thinks it is love) for Edelmira. The basic contrast represented by broken line B—the dynamic line of the novel—seems to be restored to its original condition; however, it must be remembered that Leonor's pride is now affected by an element of jealousy.

In terms of the original diagram in this analysis, Martín's friendship with Edelmira serves to reaffirm his pride (self-respect) and his willingness to sacrifice his welfare in order to be dutiful (in this case, he risks the love of Leonor in order to help Edelmira). The narrator insists so strongly on reaffirming these qualities that Martín seems less than natural; instead, he is rather like a walking abstraction of noble manhood. The modified nature of broken line B (modified, that is, by the element of jealousy in Leonor's pride) still remains the dynamic factor throughout the second part of the novel. Edelmira eventually exhibits a sense of sacrifice similar to Martín's by agreeing to an undesired marriage in order to save his life. This act adds interest to the novel, but has little effect on appreciation of the axiological opposition.

Edelmira's unselfish act comes at the end of the reformist rebellion. It is with reference to that rebellion and to his loss of Matilde that Rafael substitutes reform for love. This substitution and other substitutions within the four oppositional signs identified earlier suggest the possibility of a new meaning—in place of the axiological opposition—that emanates from the coincidence of the synchronic and the diachronic. By the central episode of the novel, the metaphor "external appearance versus inner worth" has suppressed the others. It is true that, subsequently, suggestions of the others arise; however, the only one that is reactivated is "conservatism versus reform," in connection with the reformist rebellion. The following diagram illustrates the situation in the novel:

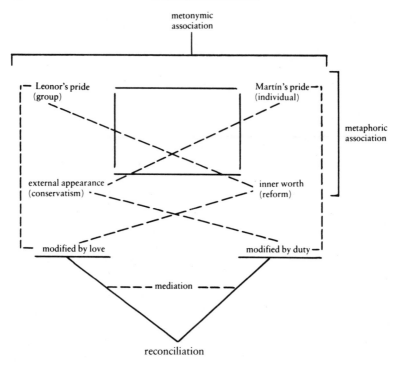

There is a metaphoric association between Leonor's pride and emphasis on external appearance, also between Martín's pride and emphasis on the individual's inner worth. At the same time, Leonor's pride and Martín's pride are in metonymic association, that is, they are associated by contiguity, and one is not replaceable by the other; the same may be said for "external appearance" and "inner worth." On the praxemic level, where the metaphoric (synchronic) and the metonymic (diachronic) provisionally join (Merrell, p. 156), Leonor's pride and Martín's pride are modified by an exchange of metaphoric associations—that is, Leonor's pride is modified by a sense of inner worth (modified by love for Martín), and Martín's pride is modified by external appearance (modified by his sense of duty toward the Encina family).

By the central episode of the novel, the "external appearance versus inner worth" sign has suppressed the others, and that situation prevails until it is challenged by the reemergence of "conservatism versus reform" in connection with the rebellion. Analogy, therefore, makes it possible to say that Martín's pride has been modified by conservatism and Leonor's pride by reform. With reference to the axiological opposition, there is an apparent reconciliation. The resurgence of the "conservatism versus reform" metaphor is once again suppressed by "external appearance versus inner worth"— Leonor's anxiety regarding Martín's welfare, Edelmira's abnegation, and Rafael's substitution of activism for love, all are acts in the novel that correspond to the supremacy of "external appearance versus inner worth." In the central episode of the novel, when it appears that a reconciliation of these two opposites may have been achieved, the mediating agent (Merrell, pp. 156, 163) is natural beauty, and Leonor's reaction to nature makes her a more genuine person. (This regenerative phenomenon is also expressed symbolically by the horse-fiesta combination.) However, on the diachronic axis, events occur that deny this possible reconciliation. After the rebellion, the opposition reappears, in its modified form, and the betrothal of Leonor and Martín mediates the apparent reconciliation. Modification of the opposition between her pride and his pride makes it appear that the axiological opposition ("group versus individual") has been resolved. In reality, the contrast remains inviolable; the supposed reconciliation takes place on the level where the synchronic and the diachronic are temporarily joined. Reconciliation has taken place between two individuals, not between individual and group.

As individuals, Martín has become a member of the Encina circle (he even takes over the family business) and Leonor has been liberated from her big-city pretentiousness (she even intends to visit Martín's provincial relatives). It is difficult to see, in *Martín Rivas,* anything like a victory of the province over the metropolis, or vice versa; it is even more difficult to see it as a struggle between the middle class and the upper class (if it is, the upper class is clearly the victor). Based on a fundamental, unresolvable opposition ("individual versus group"), the novel works out an apparent resolution that really consists of an accommodation between two individuals.

5

Codes of Character Definition
Jorge Isaacs's María

After more than a century, *María* continues to be a vivid presence in the history and criticism of Spanish-American fiction. Jorge Isaacs (1837–95) first published the novel in 1867. It is doubtful that anyone knows for sure how many editions have appeared since that time, because more than a few editors have taken liberties with this text, which has come to be regarded as a common property within Spanish-American culture. The most scholarly work dealing with *María* is the critical version published by Donald McGrady in 1970. Two other especially interesting editions are those with introductions by Enrique Anderson Imbert and Daniel Moreno.[1] The former is particularly useful because Anderson Imbert provides a clear exposition of the relationship of the author to his native region and to his protagonist. Moreno is uncommonly perceptive with respect to the complexities of the love relationship between María and Efraín.

In general, after realist fiction came to be accepted as a norm, readers tended to see a dichotomized *María:* (1) an idyllic love too charged with tearful sensitivity to be considered probable; (2) a regionalist novel with true-to-life pictures of the landscape and the people. To a very limited extent, these two aspects do describe Isaacs's novel; the danger is that, once such a dichotomy is suggested, it is likely to be taken as an absolutely accurate description, a phenomenon that leads readers to forget or ignore the fact that the characterization of María is inextricably combined with the region. In the aesthetic experience of the novel, it is impossible to separate one from the other. Two critics have been especially perceptive in recognizing the basic unity of the work. First, Anderson Imbert, in the introductory essay already mentioned, sees relationships between the Efraín-María idyll and some episodes that might appear extraneous to it, particularly an interpolated story of a black slave, based on the noble savage theme. More recently, Seymour Menton, in "La estructura dualística de *María*," points out several paired relationships that reveal a fundamental structure of the novel that is far more meaningful than the awareness of a dichotomy.[2] Continuing this kind of associative analysis and combining it with an analysis of the communication act that gives the novel meaning, we find that the parts of the novel usually thought of as *costumbrista* actually become extensions of the love theme, or constitute narrative techniques used to highlight that relationship.

The basic anecdote (the story before it is turned into plot) of Isaacs's novel is focussed on the idyllic love.[3] Efraín is the son of an hacienda owner in the Cauca Valley of Colombia. When he is eight years old, his father adopts María, the three-year-old daughter of a cousin who is also his closest friend. María becomes one of the family but maintains her identity as cousin rather than sibling. When Efraín is fourteen, he goes away to school in Bogotá. Six years later, he returns to the Cauca and finds his ideal in María. Their future happiness is threatened first by her illness and then by a marriage proposal from a friend of the family. Efraín's father insists that he go to London for a period of several years, to complete his medical education, after which he may return and marry María. During his absence, she suffers a recurrence of her illness, and, although he is called home, María dies before he can get there.

The transformation of this anecdote into the plot of the novel includes—indeed is dependent on—the *costumbrista* aspects of the work. The plot actually begins with Efraín, on his return from Bogotá, recalling the circumstances of his departure some six years earlier. Approximately five-sixths of the text has to do with a period of several months extending from the time of Efraín's return from Bogotá to the time of his departure for London. The narrator keeps us informed, with meticulous care, of the passage of time.[4] The use of regional factors—both people and places—combines with this emphasis on a short period of time to effect the transformation from *histoire* to *récit*.[5] The act of narrating this transformation makes effective use of references to time. They not only differentiate between basic anecdote and plot, they also emphasize the sense of immediate belonging and potential loss.

The sense of loss—or separation—is expressed by a narrative voice that is basically Efraín's, though there are important modifications to this fact. Efraín as narrator characterizes himself as a highly sensitive protagonist, and this characterization is the dynamic factor in the novel.

When a work acquires the age and status of *María*, it must inevitably be modifed by introductions, criticisms, and other comments that accompany editions. Of course, the narrative text is usually identifiable; however, if a reader learns, before beginning the text, that *María* is similar in some ways to *Paul et Virginie*, he is likely to combine this information with the knowledge that Isaacs's novel is partly autobiographical and, subsequently, spend as much time balancing and sorting this information as in experiencing the fiction. Obviously, the relationship between narrator and reader is changed substantially by this interposition of information.

In *María,* the narrator-reader relationship is extremely important and also very complicated. It is important because a satisfactory experience, in reading the novel, depends on maintaining an empathetic attitude, on the part of the reader, toward an intensely romantic protagonist-narrator. If this attitude is not maintained, Efraín seems absurd rather than tragic. The relationship is complicated because it may be affected by three kinds of addenda that appear in various editions of *María*, addenda that are different from the kind of introductory essay one ordinarily expects: comments by literary men who read the novel when it was relatively new; a piece entitled "Leyendo *María*," signed by Isaacs; and a dedicatory note to Efraín's siblings.

Undoubtedly, the experience of reading a novel is affected by the cultural context in which it is read. Therefore, a present-day reader, especially a non-Colombian, can hardly be expected to react to Efraín in quite the same way his contemporaries responded to him. On the other hand, the original communication act between Isaacs and his contemporary reader does have an effect on the context in which the novel is read today. In a recent study, Winifred Bryan Horner describes the differences between a speech act and a text act.[6] In the former, the speaker (sender) usually communicates face-to-face with the hearer (receiver). In a text act, naturally, somebody is saying something to somebody else, but a time lapse is practically immediate. Horner makes two points that are especially useful in the appreciation of how *María* functions as an aesthetic experience. First, she shows that, in spite of a time difference between the act of writing and the act of reading, the writer's intent is partially recoverable through analysis of the text. Second, she points out that the reader of the text act, when removed in time or space from the act of writing the text, does not have the benefit of the context in which the text was made. He has his own context and the text act itself.[7]

Of course, this "text act reader" may have some information about Isaacs and his circumstance that will provide an insight with respect to the original context. It appears, nevertheless, that a present-day reader of *María,* whatever his knowledge, can hardly be expected to put himself in the position of Isaacs's contemporary reader. A more accurate description of the present-day experience is to say that the text act, taken as a whole, becomes the sender in a secondary communication directed toward the text act reader in the latter's own context.[8]

Of the several addenda that influence a present-day reading of *María,* the dedication to Efraín's siblings is the most frequent and the most integral.[9] Its title is simple and direct: "A los hermanos de Efraín." The voice belongs to an invented editor of Efraín's memoirs. He assumes his primary readership will be the brothers and sisters of Efraín. Therefore, if this dedication is taken as a part of the narrative text (the fact that the editor is fictitious promotes this understanding), the narrative text contains both sender and receiver. However, within the act of narration, the siblings are of surprisingly little importance, except for Emma, the sister who is María's companion. The first-person narrator (Efraín) certainly does not address himself to a group of sibling-readers, because he makes many references that would be gratuitous if he were thinking only of members of his household. The fictitious editor reminds the *hermanos* that they must remember the night when Efraín handed him the memoirs and said the editor would know how to add what Efraín had omitted or erased with tears. The readers' tears will constitute proof that the fictitious editor will have complied with Efraín's request.

This definition of the anticipated reader helps define the nature of the text and the character of its protagonist. Other addenda, which appear in fewer editions, serve to support the expectation prompted by "A los hermanos de Efraín." The nineteenth-century reactions cited by Daniel Moreno indicate a very positive response to the narrator's sensitivity.[10] Isaacs's own statement, "Leyendo *María*," informs us that he weeps as he reads what he has written and that he has often felt almost unable to write the final pages.[11] In a very intimate tone, Isaacs indicates that he feels uprooted from his native region, cut off from what he has belonged to. It is known that Isaacs wrote *María* while working in another part of Colombia. His biographers also inform us that the love story is invented but that much of the other material has an autobiographical base. "Leyendo María," included as it is within the text (not the introduction) of the Porrúa edition, orients the reader toward a nostalgic narrator, but one whose nostalgia refers to loss of a place rather than of a person. Therefore, we are confronted again with the novel's apparent duality.

Gérard Genette proposes that *récit* may be considered the expansion of a verb that states essentially what happens in a story.[12] In the case of Isaacs's novel, it might be: *Efraín suffers the loss of María.* This statement identifies Efraín as the protagonist, quite properly, in spite of the novel's title. The verb itself coincides with the tone. A reasonable objection might be that, if one insists on a dichotomized *María,* the statement does not take into account the regionalistic aspect of the novel. Compounding the object amends this omission and defines Efraín's character more accurately: *Efraín suffers the loss of María and the region to which he belongs.* The expansion of this statement repeatedly associates María with the region as the protagonist's sense of separation develops.

We are dealing with a pyramiding text act (or narrative text act). First we have a presumed text written by Efraín and handed to his chosen editor. This fictitious editor—an invention of Jorge Isaacs, as is Efraín—is a presumed reader of Efraín's memoirs.[13] He in turn produces a text act and attempts an identification of his reader. The latter appears psychically analogous to the reader anticipated by Efraín, though the question of family relationship produces separate definitions. The common ground seems to be reaction to a great range of sensitivity—melancholia to desperation—without loss of a fundamental sense of reality. If a present-day reader rejects the weeping, it must be a rejection in degree rather than in kind, because weeping seems corollary to the tone of the novel, that is, a sense of loss and isolation.

Efraín's sensitivity—the basis of a characterization that is the novel's dynamic factor—is signaled in several ways that may be referred to as codes. Such a reference will most likely—and quite appropriately—suggest Roland Barthes's *S/Z*.[14] It should be understood, however, that the present analysis does not propose to emulate what Barthes does in his remarkable book. This essay on *María* will not deal with the way narrative operates, but rather with the means employed to develop a major characterization. The various codes used here might all be thought of as "connotative," in Barthes's terminology. Naturally, since this characterization is the novel's dynamic factor, it will be closely related to several aspects of the narrative act.

The selections ("lexias") are chosen with a certain purpose in mind: to illustrate several means used to make Efraín's sensitivity the most important factor in the novel's meaning. Following are descriptions of the five codes, with indications of the terms that will be used to refer to each one:

1. MARÍA-MILIEU. María is joined with the surrounding circumstance—both nature and people—whose loss Efraín suffers. In other words, María and her environment become one and the same through a process of associating her with various aspects of the world in which she lives. This code has the primary effect of characterizing María; however, the nature of the characterization reveals the combination that is the basis of Efraín's distress. This code might be referred to as "associative," because its function is to produce the oneness of María and milieu. Sometimes María is associated with the environment only in the mind of the narrator, who then communicates this appreciation to the reader. At other times, overt actions effect the association.

2. SEPARATION. Certain incidents and situations threaten the separation of the lovers or suggest the possibility of such a separation. This code might be referred to as "suggestive."

Sometimes the sense of threatened separation derives from a logically expected sequence of events; in other instances, the suggestion of separation is metaphoric. Therefore, the subtlety of the suggestions varies greatly.

3. OMEN. This code might be called "prophetic" or "augurial." Overt, symbolic threats are recognized as such by the narrator—the black bird so well known to readers of *María*. This overt symbol is different from the suggestions, in the SEPARATION code, that may be no more than a vague impression on Efraín's part.

4. TEST. Efraín's strength, courage, patience, and humaneness undergo a series of trials. This code might be described as "confirmative," because its function is to set forth the hero's manliness, so showing that he is fully endowed with this quality as well as with sensitivity.

5. INTENSIFICATION. The naming of this code is partly inconsistent with the naming of the first four. In those cases, it seems clearer to refer to the phenomenon (María-milieu, separation, omen, test) than to the nature of the function (associative, suggestive, prophetic, confirmative). If the procedure were followed exactly in the case of the fifth code, CRISIS might be the name of the phenomenon, and "intensifying" would be a satisfactory description of the code's function. However, the word "crisis," with reference to prose fiction, is likely to suggest a single, climactic event. In the present case, the fifth code consists of a series of actions and statements that intensify Efraín's growing sense of loss and heighten the emotion evoked by his narration.

In the following pages, a series of passages from *María* will be examined in terms of these five codes. It would be possible to examine the whole text profitably; however, the selections seem to reveal the important aspects of the meaning of Isaacs's novel. The codes could be treated as separate categories and dealt with one at a time. That is, it would be possible to write a section on the joining of María with her environment, a second section on the sense of separation, and so on. The difference that may be achieved by maintaining the order of the *récit* is a clearer awareness of the novel's structure or, to put it another way, an analysis of the experience of the novel, the process rather than the product. The first passage to be examined includes the last sentence of the novel's first chapter and the first two sentences of the second chapter. Observations on the passage will follow citation of the passage itself. The same order will be followed throughout the analysis—first the selection will be quoted, then the comments will follow.

Dábamos ya la vuelta a una de las colinas de la vereda en las que solían divisarse desde la casa viajeros deseados; volví la vista hacia ella buscando uno de tantos seres queridos; María estaba bajo las enredaderas que adornaban las ventanas del aposento di mi madre. Chapter one ends here and chapter two continues as follows: *Pasados los seis años, los últimos días de un lujoso agosto me recibieron al regresar al nativo valle. Mi corazón rebosaba de amor patrio.* (P. 50) (We were already rounding one of the hills of the path on which welcome travelers could be seen from the house. I looked back in that direction, hoping to see one of so many loved ones. María was standing beneath the vines that decorated the windows of my mother's room. . . . After six long years, the last days of a luxurious August received me upon my return to my native valley. My heart overflowed with love for my native land.) MARÍA-MILIEU; SEPARATION. The time of the principal action in *María* is established in the second chapter when Efraín returns after his years of study in Bogotá. The first chapter looks back to the time, six years earlier, when he left home. It serves to inform us of Efraín's sense of separation at that earlier time. However, it occurs as a flashback within a generally retrospective view. Efraín narrates from a point in time later than the time established in chapter two. He does not write in a diary present that would be contemporary with the main events of the novel. (The dedication "A los hermanos de Efraín" claims that an unidentified editor made the present text on the basis of Efraín's memoirs.)

As Efraín looks back to his original departure, it is María who stands out in his account—related to his mother and the vines. It is reasonable to assume that her importance in this flashback account is not a true representation of her importance to Efraín as a nine-year-old girl but instead a reflection of the importance she acquired for Efraín after his return from Bogotá. At the beginning of the second chapter, his identification is with the region first. (*Patrio* refers to the region, not to the nation.) His region *receives* him (the verb is important) even before María does; however, it is fundamental in the experience of the novel that María and the milieu share importance in the first two chapters and that both are related to the sense of loss and recovery.

Los esclavos, bien vestidos y contentos, hasta donde es posible estarlo en la servidumbre, eran sumisos y afectuosos para su amo. (P. 57) (The slaves, well dressed and content, insofar as it is possible to be so within a state of servitude, were submissive and affectionate towards their master.) María-milieu. Efraín, in this display of paternalism, takes the best view he can of an institution he deplores. It is important that the slaves be acceptable because they are part of the milieu, and María becomes more and more closely associated with all aspects of that milieu. In this regard, Efraín here anticipates an interpolated story—a kind of African *Atala,* the noble savage—that comes much later and functions as a surrogate idyll for Efraín and María. At the same time, Efraín must take the most favorable view possible of slavery as it is related to his family, and it sorely tries him. In many instances throughout the novel, he expresses his disapproval of the institution. Both McGrady and Menton deal with the element of social protest in *María.*[15] It is worth noting, in this connection, that social awareness does not make Isaacs's novel either less "romantic" or more "realistic." Social awareness is one of the characteristics of fiction during the romantic period, and we may be sure the novelists thought they were seeing reality.[16]

¡María! ¡María! ¡Cuánto te amé! ¡Cuánto te amara! (P. 62) (María! María! How I loved you! How I would have loved you!) Separation; intensification. Although this outburst of desperation seems retrospective, it actually occurs within plot time, at a point when Efraín thinks he has lost María. Of course, if we assume a retrospective act of narration, the intensity of the narrator (though not necessarily of the reader) may have been increased by knowledge of the ultimate loss.

Aquellas soledades, sus bosques silenciosos, sus flores, sus aves y sus aguas, ¿por qué me hablaban de ella? . . . Era que veía el Edén, pero faltaba ella. (p. 71) (Those solitary places, their silent forests, their flowers, their birds and their streams, why did they speak to me of her? . . . It was like seeing Eden, but she was not there.) MARÍA-MILIEU; SEPARATION. After a visit with humble but worthy friends in the country, Efraín returns home. He is pleased by his relationship with the people, and he is sensitive to the magnificence of the natural surroundings. The missing ingredient is María. She is suggested by nature; there is also an inevitable association between his need for her and his satisfactory relationship with people of different social categories: slaves, free tenants, landowners. Gradually, the story relates María to all these groups.

Mi hermana me refirió que María había sufrido un ataque nervioso; y al agregar que estaba aún sin sentido, procuró calmar cuanto le fue posible mi dolorosa ansiedad. (P. 79) (My sister informed me that María had suffered a nervous attack and upon adding that she was still unconscious, she tried, as far as possible, to calm my painful anxiety.) MARÍA-MILIEU; SEPARATION; INTENSIFICATION. Again Efraín returns from a period alone in the natural environment. Awareness of María's absence, as in the preceding selection, is intensified by her being in a state of unconsciousness. The illness carries a threat of permanent loss. Its psychosomatic nature becomes an important factor in the story, and this particular quality has its credibility supported when Efraín's father also suffers a psychosomatic illness as the result of a financial crisis (pp. 208–10).

No sé cuánto tiempo había pasado, cuando algo como el ala vibrante de un ave vino a rozar mi frente. Miré hacia los bosques inmediatos para seguirla: era una [sic] *ave negra.* (P. 81) (I don't know how much time had passed when something like the vibrating wing of a bird brushed against my forehead. I looked toward the nearby forest trying to follow it. It was a black bird.) OMEN. This incident occurs a few minutes after Efraín learns of María's illness. His recall does not inform him with respect to the amount of time spent in contemplation; this fact suggests that he was removed from reality, and so adds impact to the dolorous significance of the black bird. There is a different line of obvious symbolism, based on flowers, that signals changes in the relationships of Efraín and María. It is considerably less dramatiac in its effect and rather incidental to the development of Efraín's sensitivity.

One puzzling· aspect of the use of omen takes the form of an apparent contradiction. The black bird, a good romantic symbol, is accepted as an authentic, credible omen in several places in the novel. On the other hand, there is an occasion when Efraín's father takes the howling of a dog as a bad sign, and Efraín makes an apology to the reader, stating that his father, although a convert from Judaism to Christianity, had never freed himself from "cierta clase de pronósticos y agüeros, preocupaciones de su raza" (p. 133).

La imagen de María, tal como la había visto en el lecho aquella tarde, al decirme ese "hasta mañana" que tal vez no llegaría, iba conmigo, y avivando mi impaciencia me hacía medir incesantemente la distancia que me separaba del término del viaje, impaciencia que la velocidad del caballo no era bastante a moderar.

Las llanuras empezaban a desaparecer, huyendo en sentido contrario a mi carrera, semejantes a mantos inmensos arrollados por el huracán. Los bosques que más cercanos creía, parecían alejarse cuanto avanzaba hacia ellos. (P. 82) (The image of María, just as I had seen her in her bed that afternoon, saying that "until tomorrow" to me—a tomorrow that perhaps would never come—went with me and, increasing my impatience, made me measure incessantly the distance that separated me from the end of my journey, an impatience that even the horse's speed could not alleviate. The plains began to disappear, moving in the opposite direction to my flight, similar to huge blankets rolled up by a hurricane. The forests, which I thought to be closer, seemed to grow more distant as I advanced towards them.) TEST; SEPARATION; INTENSIFICATION. Efraín hurries, on horseback, to summon Dr. Mayn so he may attend María. Time is a factor of great consequence, and, in addition, Efraín has to overcome formidable and dangerous natural obstacles. The happy result of this test, even more than his triumph, is the fact that María learns of his willingness to face danger for her sake. The imagery is particularly effective in this passage. Faced with the possible loss of María, Efraín rides with her likeness before him; but the natural environment moves away from him, in one direction because of his haste, in the opposite direction because of his anxiety. The time factor, at this point, is strikingly different from the preceding selection. Here the narrator is hypersensitive to his surroundings, and uses them to stretch out time to accord with his uneasiness. The imperfect tense, of course, contributes to this lengthening effect, and the withdrawal of both plain and forest, in opposite directions, communicates Efraín's impatience and his isolation.

. . . puesto que esa noble resolución te anima, sí convendrás conmigo en que antes de cinco años no podrás ser esposo de María. (P. 89) (. . . since you are moved by such a noble resolution, you will certainly agree with me that you cannot be María's husband in less than five years.) SEPARATION. Efraín's father speaks. Assured of his son's devotion to María, he approves of their marrying eventually, but he insists that Efraín go to England first to complete his medical education. The absence means that Efraín will be separated from both María and his *patria*.

Como esos señores vienen mañana, las muchachas están afanadas porque queden muy bien hechos unos dulces; creo que han acabado ya y que vendrán ahora. (P. 111) (Since those gentlemen are coming tomorrow, the girls are anxious to have some specially made sweets. I think they've finished now, and they'll be here soon.) MARÍA-MILIEU. Here is a somewhat different manifestation of this code. Efraín has hoped to find María. His mother speaks, informing him that María has been busy at a household task. She is therefore identified in another way with the customs of the region. However, it should be noted that her work is not menial, but involves the preparation of sweets so they will be just right for expected guests.

Indecisa por un momento, en su sonrisa había tal dulzura y tan amorosa languidez en su mirada, que ya había ella desaparecido y aún la contemplaba yo extasiado. (P. 114) (Indecisive for a moment, in her smile there was such sweetness, and such an amorous languidness in her look, that even after she had disappeared I still looked at her ecstatically.) SEPARATION. Taken literally, this passage concludes a scene in which Efraín and María have been talking. She is called away by his baby brother, Juan, who is María's special charge. On the suggestive level, we find Efraín seeing María even after she has disappeared: "aún la contemplaba extasiado." This condition is the same as the one in which he narrates.

Entonces la fiera nos dio frente. Sólo mi escopeta estaba disponible: disparé; el tigre se sentó sobre la cola, tambaleó y cayó. (Pp. 122–23) (Then the beast confronted us. Mine was the only rifle available. I fired; the jaguar sat down on his tail, wavered, and fell.) TEST. A close call on a hunting trip reveals Efraín's sure marksmanship. This episode reaffirms his courage as demonstrated in the earlier trip to get the doctor. He is every inch a man no matter how sensitive or tender. Efraín narrates the story with dramatic effect, but with personal modesty.

—¿Conque todo, todo lo arrostras? me interrogó maravillado, apenas hube concluido mi relación. ¿Y esa enfermedad que probablemente es la de su madre? . . . ¿Y vas a pasar quizá la mitad de tu vida sentado sobre una tumba? (P. 170) ("So you'll face anything, anything?" he asked me, astounded, when I had barely finished my tale. "And this illness that is probably the same as her mother's? Are you going to spend perhaps half your life sitting on a grave?") SEPARATION. Efraín's close friend, Carlos, speaks. His direct, practical question characterizes him and places the situation in a new perspective, challenging the predominance of tenderness and loyalty.

Carlos's father had asked María's hand for his son, before the latter knew of Efraín's love. The passage quoted here comes after

Efraín has explained. The threat of separation implicit in the proposal made by Carlos's father is transformed here into a practical concern of Carlos for his friend. It is interesting that Carlos speaks of the illness as possibly inherited, thereby suggesting that there is nothing Efraín can do about it. Efraín's reaction is so strong that, in a narrative passage, he tells how he answered "sí," rather than include it in the course of the dialogue.

Después de nuestro diálogo, María no había vuelto a estar risueña. Inútilmente trataba yo de ocultarme la causa; bien la sabía por mi mal: ella pensaba al ver la felicidad de Tránsito y Braulio, en que pronto íbamos nosotros a separarnos, en que tal vez no volveríamos a vernos. (P. 180) (After our conversation, María had not become cheerful again. I tried unsuccessfully to hide the cause from myself, though to my sorrow I knew it well. She was thinking, upon seeing the happiness of Tránsito and Braulio, that we would separate, that perhaps we would never see one another again.) MARÍA-MILIEU; SEPARATION. This part of the story anticipates the rural wedding of two people whose family relationship suggests that of Efraín and María. It relates their love to the rustic idyll, linking Efraín's awareness of María to his sense of belonging to a region. This passage is a kind of summary statement used by the narrator to be sure his reader is entirely aware of the state of his and María's love relationship. It follows a rather extensive dialogue dealing with the customs related to the approaching wedding.

Tomó él la carta, y con los labios contraídos, mientras devoraba el contenido con los ojos, concluyó la lectura y arrojó el papel sobre la mesa diciendo:
"¡Ese hombre me ha muerto! lee esa carta; al cabo sucedió lo que tu madre temía." (Pp. 188–89) (He took the letter, and with pursed lips, while he devoured its contents with his eyes, he concluded his reading and threw the paper on the table, saying: "That man has killed me! Read that letter; at last what your mother feared has happened.")

INTENSIFICATION. Efraín's father learns that an employee has defrauded him of a large sum of money. This crisis diverts immediate attention from Efraín's growing sense of separation. It provokes his father's illness. The important connection with Efraín's problem, of course, is that it introduces the possibility that he may not have to go away. He soon learns, however, that there is still enough money left for his father to make a good investment in his son's career.

—*Abrimos la puerta, y vimos posada sobre una de las hojas de la ventana, que agitaba el viento, un ave negra y de tamaño como el de una paloma muy grande: dio un chillido que yo no había oído nunca: pareció encandilarse un momento con la luz que yo tenía en la mano, y la apagó pasando sobre nuestras cabezas a tiempo que íbamos a huir espantadas.* (P. 194) ("We opened the door, and saw perched on one of the shutters, which was blown by the wind, a black bird the size of a very large dove; it gave a cry that I had never heard before. For a moment it seemed dazzled by the light that I had in my hand, and put it out by flying over our heads just as we fled, horrified.") OMEN. María speaks, telling Efraín of an incident that occurred earlier when she was with Efraín's mother. He knows it happened at the exact moment when he and his father were reading the letter concerning the financial loss. He also knows it is the same black bird as before. Now Efraín can hardly doubt that the bird is an evil omen; however, he shares the relevant associations with the reader, not with María.

—*Me es más Fácil imaginarme la de Braulio. El va a ser desde hoy completamente dichoso; y yo voy a ausentarme, yo voy a dejarte por muchos años.* (P. 202) ("It is easier for me to imagine Braulio's. He will be completely happy from today on. And I am going away, I am going to leave you for many years.") MARÍA-MILIEU; SEPARATION. Efraín refers, in a dialogue with María, to the Tránsito-Braulio wedding, and specifically to Braulio's happiness ("la de Braulio"). María has earlier been related to this event. Now when Efraín thinks of leaving, the threat of separation includes both María and the rural situation.

Es tiempo de manifestar a usted, continuó después de una pausa, que si al venir el día no se hubiere presentado esa crisis, nada me resta por hacer. (P. 214) ("It is time for me to tell you," he continued after a pause, "that if this crisis does not occur before daybreak, there is nothing left for me to do.") INTENSIFICATION; SEPARATION. Dr. Mayn tells Efraín how gravely ill his father is. The time limit he sets provides an element of suspense. Now the sense of loss includes the possibility of his father's death, which may also determine whether or not Efraín will leave the Cauca. The narration reveals Efraín as being quite self-possessed.

—*Que me ames siempre así, respondió, y su mano se enlazó más estrechamente con la mía.* (P. 231) ("May you always love me like this," she answered, and she held my hand more tightly.) SEPARATION. The high point of the idyll. María's request for eternal love makes more poignant the threat of separation.

Pero he aquí su historia, que referida por Feliciana con rústico y patético lenguaje, entretuvo algunas veladas de mi infancia. (P. 232) (But here is her story, which, told by Feliciana in rustic and pathetic language, entertained me on many evenings during my childhood.) SEPARATION.

This passage is the introduction to the surrogate idyll, an African *Atala*. The protagonist, Feliciana (formerly Nay), was sold into slavery, so losing her beloved Sinar and also her native land. She was purchased by Efraín's father so she would not have to suffer inhumane treatment.

The story occupies about one-tenth the length of the novel and is not confined to a single chapter. Although Efraín describes Feliciana's language as "rústico y patético" in the version he remembers hearing as a child, he assumes the position of third-person narrator of the intercalated *récit,* and narrates it in his own way.

The noble-savage theme adds a dimension to the exposition of Efraín's and María's love. Significantly, it comes immediately after the scene in which María makes the request for eternal love. Immediately after the Feliciana story, there is a scene that places María in association with the natural setting (p. 261).[17]

Algo oscuro como la cabellera de María y veloz como el pensamiento cruzó por delante de nuestros ojos. María dio un grito ahogado, y cubriéndose el rostro con las manos, exclamó horrorizada: —¡El ave negra! (P. 271) (Something dark as María's hair and swift as thought crossed in front of our eyes. María gave a strangled cry and, covering her face with her hands, exclaimed in horror: "The black bird!") OMEN. Immediately after Efraín and María exchange rings in anticipation of his long absence, the black bird appears—this time to both of them. Efraín describes María's reaction of horror and also his own fear.

—Sí. Cuando tú y papá íbais a montar esta mañana, se me ocurrió por un momento que ya no volverías y que me engañaban. (P. 301) ("Yes. When you and Papa went riding this morning, it occurred to me for a moment that you would never return, that you were deceiving me.") SEPARATION. Here it is María who experiences the sense of impending loss—a variation that enhances the text act reader's awareness of their belonging to each other. This sharing follows their having seen the black bird when they were together. Again, Efraín speaks of María's anguish and also of his own, in the passage following her confession.

— . . . ¿Qué hiciste tú en la montaña?
—Sufrir mucho. Nunca creí que se afligirían tanto con mi despedida, ni que me causara tanto pesar decirles adiós. (P. 310) (". . . What did you do out on the mountain?"
"I suffered greatly. I never thought that they would be so afflicted by my going, nor that it would cause me so much grief to say goodbye.") TEST; SEPARATION.

In this fragment of dialogue between Efraín and María, he synthesizes the difficult experience of saying goodbye to the people and places he belongs to. These events take place in a broad spectrum of contexts that color Efraín's feeling of identity. The chapter precedes the one in which he actually takes leave of the family, including María.

Hacía dos semanas que estaba yo en Londres, y una noche recibí cartas de la familia. Rompí con mano trémula el paquete, cerrado con el sello de mi padre. Había una carta de María. Antes de desdoblarla, busqué en ella aquel perfume demasiado conocido para mí de la mano que la había escrito: aún lo conservaba; en sus pliegues iba un pedacito de cáliz de azucena. Mis ojos nublados quisieron inútilmente leer las primeras líneas. Abrí uno de los balcones de mi cuarto, porque parecía no serme suficiente el aire que había en él . . . ¡Rosales del huerto de mis amores! . . . ¡montañas americanas, montañas mías! . . . ¡noches azules! (P. 313) (I had been in London two weeks, and one night I received letters from my family. I broke open the package, closed with my father's seal, with trembling hands. There was a letter from María. Before unfolding it, I sought in it that perfume, all too well known to me, of the hand that had written it; it still conserved some; in its folds there was a tiny strip of lily's petal. My clouded eyes tried uselessly to read the first lines. I opened one of the balconies of my room, because the air inside seemed insufficient. Roses from the garden of my love! American mountains, my mountains! Azure nights!) MARÍA-MILIEU. This passage begins the first chapter following Efraín's departure. The reader is now approximately five-sixths of the way through the novel and, by this time, is quite aware that the *récit* concerns mainly what happened in the several months between Efraín's return from Bogotá and his leaving for London. Efraín says nothing about his arrival, and very little about being in London. The few things he says about it are directly related to his nostalgia for the Cauca. The most important aspect of this passage is the evocation by María's letter of the natural phenomena of his *patria*. This association comes about in a very logical progression from María's letter to the scent of her perfume to a flower petal included in the letter to the roses in the garden where his love for María has its roots to the mountains of his homeland to the melancholy suggestion of night.

The adjective "azul" may simply refer to the appearance of the night, or it may have a symbolist connotation. *María,* though indisputably a romantic novel, anticipates in more than one passage the symbolism and delicacy of *modernismo.* The reference to tears, in this passage, is an aspect of sensitivity probably related to this same delicacy. Tears are frequent in *María,* but I have intentionally avoided selections that would make them an important part of this commentary, because I believe that if the text act reader is aware of his context and understands his relationship to the text act (in which the text reader's tears are bidden), the frequency of weeping in *María* seems less "unreal" than has usually been the case.

—¡Al Cauca!, exclamé, olvidado por un momento de todo, menos de María y de mi país. (P. 316) ("To the Cauca!" I exclaimed, forgetful for a moment of everything except María and my homeland.) MARÍA-MILIEU. This is Efraín's reaction on learning from a family friend that he must go home. The obvious association of María with locale is a succinct confirmation of the progressive association noted in the preceding selection.

—Ella vivirá si usted llega a tiempo. (P. 316) ("She will live if you get there on time.") SEPARATION; TEST. The family friend informs Efraín of the seriousness of María's illness. The inheritance factor seems unimportant; the psychic aspect defines Efraín's next test—the trip to her side.

"*Yo quiero esperarte aquí: no quiero abandonar todo esto que amabas, porque se me figura que a mí me lo dejaste recomendado y que me amarías menos en otra parte.*" (Pp. 318–19) ("I want to wait for you here. I don't want to abandon all these things you loved, because it seems to me you left them in my care, and that you would love me less in some other place.") MARÍA-MILIEU; SEPARATION. This passage is part of a letter from María to Efraín, written at a time prior to its appearance in the *récit*. Efraín reads it during his trip back to the Cauca. María recognizes that, for Efraín, she is inextricably associated with the region. The sense of separation incorporates both woman and region.

El almuerzo de aquel día fue copia del anterior, salvo el aumento del tapado que Gregorio había prometido, potaje que preparó haciendo un hoyo en la playa, y una vez depositado en él, envuelto en hojas de biao, la carne, plátanos y demás que debían componer el cocido, lo cubrió con tierra y encima de todo encendió un fogón. (P. 336) (The lunch for that day was a copy of the one for the day before, except for the addition of the stew that Gregorio had promised, a dish that he prepared by making a pit on the beach, and after putting in the meat, the bananas, and other things to be cooked, all wrapped in *biao* leaves, he covered with earth, making a fire on top of it.) IN-TENSIFICATION. This passage is part of Efraín's account of the trip home, with emphasis on the voyage upriver to his native region. The text space occupied by the *récit* from the chapter in London to the end of the novel is about one-sixth of the book. The return trip itself occupies about one-half of this space.

If this prolonged account has any affirmative function in the story, it is to intensify anxiety about whether or not Efraín will arrive on time. Indeed, the repetitive quality of the trip is suggested by the first words of this passage. On the other hand, the narration of the trip upriver seems fundamentally different from the basic narration and, therefore, really does not contribute effectively to the increase of tension.

In the passage quoted here, the narrator describes in some detail how a regional dish is prepared. In other passages, we learn about the flora, the fauna, and the general appearance of the area. The important difference between these descriptions and the other references to nature in *María* is that here Efraín is learning, whereas in the rest of the novel he refers sensitively and lyrically to a known area to which he feels attached. Here he is a stranger. The objective detail in the passage quoted above signals his unfamiliarity, as does his reference elsewhere to what someone explained to him about the region.

The narrative voice, in this report of the trip up river, is technically Efraín's, but it is different from his voice in other parts of the novel. He is not characterizing himself in terms of his sensitive reaction to the circumstance he belongs to; rather he is describing something new. This trip is the most clearly *costumbrista* part of the novel. It is the least novelistic. Isaacs, the author, was employed, at one time, in the area described in the trip section. He felt foreign. Therefore, the account of the trip characterizes Isaacs rather than Efraín (even though we know that Efraín is partly an autobiographical creation). Although some may find the "realistic" quality of this account attractive, it seriously diminishes the vitality of the narration, which is recovered in the last stage of the trip home, when Efraín is again on horseback.

Quien aquello crió, me decía yo, no puede destruir aún la más bellas [sic, in this edition] *de sus criaturas y lo que él ha querido que yo más ame.* (P. 346) (The one who created that, I told myself, cannot destroy the most beautiful of his creatures and what he has willed that I love most.) MARÍA-MILIEU; SEPARATION. Now in the middle of his attempt to reach María before she dies, Efraín is overwhelmed by the beauty of the land he loves, and makes still another association with María, acutely aware of possibly losing her.

—. . . *¡en el cielo!* (P. 347) ("In Heaven!") SEPARATION; TEST. These are the words of Efraín's mother as she tells him he has arrived too late. Given the psychic nature of María's ailment, questions arise as to guilt related to this tragedy.

Braulio, José y cuatro peones más condujeron al pueblo el cadáver, cruzando esas llanuras y descansando bajo aquellos bosques por donde en una mañana feliz, pasó María a mi lado amante y amada, el día del matrimonio de Tránsito. Mi padre y el cura seguían paso ante paso el humilde convoy . . . ¡ay de mí! ¡humilde y silencioso como el de Nay! (Pp. 353–54) (Braulio, José, and four other men carried the body to the village, crossing those plains and resting in those forests where, on one happy morning, María walked by my side, lover and beloved, the day of Tránsito's wedding. My father and the priest followed the humble procession step by step—oh God, humble and silent as that of Nay!) MARÍA-MILIEU; SEPARATION. María actually died several weeks before Efraín's arrival. He becomes ill on hearing of her death. Later his sister, Emma, tells him of María's last days. Here he describes the funeral procession. This passage relates María to the natural setting, to Efraín's family, to the country people (Braulio and Tránsito), and to the noble-savage idyll (Feliciana, formerly Nay). In other words, this account brings together the factors to which Efraín has responded with sensitivity and the need of identification.

A pocas caudras de la casa me detuve antes de emprender la bajada a ver una vez más aquella mansión querida y sus contornos. De las horas de felicidad que en ella había pasado, sólo llevaba conmigo el recuerdo; de María, los dones que me había dejado al borde de su tumba. (P. 361) (I stopped a little way from the house, before beginning my descent, to see once again that dear home and its environs. Of the hours of happiness that I had spent there, only a memory remained; of María, only the things she had left me at the edge of her grave.) SEPARATION. This passage circles back significantly to the first selection used in the present commentary on *María,* where Efraín recalls the feeling of separation he felt on leaving the family home to study in Bogotá. There is no circular structure here in the sense of exact repetition. The circling—or, better, spiraling— involves repetition only with respect to the basic sense of separation. The expansion of this sense changes completely, since Efraín knows the loss is permanent.

Había yo montado y Braulio estrechaba en sus manos una de las mías, cuando el revuelo de un ave que al pasar sobre nuestras cabezas dio un graznido siniestro y conocido para mí, interrumpió nuestra despedida. (P. 362) (I had mounted, and Braulio pressed one of my hands in his, when the flight of the bird, which upon passing over our heads gave a familiar cry, interrupted our farewell.) OMEN. This final appearance of the bird of evil augury would appear ironic, even insulting, if such a reaction were not obscured by concern for the welfare of Efraín.

Estremecido, partí a galope por en medio de la pampa solitaria, cuyo vasto horizonte ennegrecía la noche. (P. 362) (Shaken, I left at a gallop through the loneliness of the pampa, whose horizon was blackened by the night.) SEPARATION. Efraín is driven away not only by the hopelessness of definitive loss but also by fear with respect to his own future. His ride across the plain is reminiscent of that test in which, hastening to bring the doctor to María, he sensed the plains disappearing. Now, in a similar situation, he rides toward a dark horizon.

The dedication "A los hermanos de Efraín" informs us that he died before the fictitious editor offered the edited memoirs for publication. However, there is no indication of the nature of his death.

In general, the narration maintains the integrity of a first-person narrator who characterizes himself in terms of sensitivity to the loss he suffers. The narrative voice speaks retrospectively—that is, from a point in time that is later than the events of the story. What Efraín says about a given situation is, therefore, influenced by subsequent events. In such cases, the effect is to enhance Efraín's sensitivity. There are moments in the narration when the voice of Efraín might better give way to some other narrative voice—in the story of Nay, for example. However, even when another person speaks, we are still aware that Efraín-narrator is addressing the message to us. Although the text act reader knows, on the basis of the dedication "A los hermanos de Efraín," that an "editor" is responsible for the text at hand and that he was encouraged by Efraín to fill in the places (in the memoirs) that needed supplementary information, the editor does not supply in his own right the information that Efraín, as a first-person narrator, could not have known. Rather, the narrative voice of Efraín fills in the gaps in various ways. Basically, it is also Efraín who sees what happens, but he sometimes depends on a report from someone else. Such instances may vary from his saying that he knows the situation on the basis of what he heard around the house (p. 130) to Emma's extensive report of María's last days. In all cases, the information reaches us through Efraín and is subject to interpretation in accord with his sensitivity. His account differs from a diary type of memoir because it includes recapitulations and extra-scene commentaries that would be out of place in a diary. Isaacs, as author, is not intrusive except in the account of the passage upriver. In an oblique way, this account may suggest something about *where* the narration takes place—not the scene of the action, but the location of the narrator when he is telling the story, looking at events retrospectively. If we concede—generously, I would say—that the narrator of this episode is Efraín, his description of the region (different from his beloved valley) may reflect his feeling of foreignness while he writes in some unfriendly milieu reached in his flight toward the dark horizon. However, this speculation brings us back to Isaacs, because we know he wrote the novel while holding a position away from his native Cauca. The intricacies of a tripartite narrator (author, fictional editor, and protagonist) insist that the narration be understood as three overlapping communication acts.

The most obvious difference between *histoire* time and *récit* time is the concentration within the *récit* on a few months, whereas the *histoire* time covers about twelve years. This concentration is basic to the characterization of Efraín in terms of his sense of loss. There are, of course, many less obvious—though not less useful—time differences between *histoire* and *récit*. Genette's "descriptive pause" (*récit* time indefinitely longer than *histoire* time) is very important in Efraín's characterization of himself. Summary is, of course, essential in providing information that Efraín could not have known by himself, as well as for more general narrative use. Ellipsis is useful in maintaining emphasis on a theme. There is a period of time, for example, when Efraín must have been doing something between his father's bidding him to come to his room and the actual moment of Efraín's entrance (p. 87). Scene, which corresponds more or less to *histoire* time, tends to exemplify certain characteristics of people in Isaacs's novel: María's tenderness, Carlos's frankness, the firmness of Efraín's father, or the gaucheness of Emigdio, for example. Almost always scene contributes to appreciation of Efraín's sensitivity and his anticipation of separation.

The field of experience in *María* is rather limited in the sense that incidents cannot be highly varied given the circumstances in which the characters live, and geographical variety is improbable because the basic conflict in the novel involves the threatened loss of a particular region. The Nay story and the Braulio-Tránsito idyll are metaphors of the María-Efraín love that enhance the meaning of the novel. The events that specifically affect Efraín and María all have the same general significance—they threaten separation. In this respect, they are interchangeable, so creating a synchronic impression; the diachronic axis of the story depends on the increasing dimension of actual separation—Efraín's trips into the countryside, then his departure for England, and finally María's death.

Efraín as narrator expands his sensitivity by having others, especially María, share it. There can hardly be any doubt that the reader, anticipated by the "editor" or by Efraín, is expected to weep tears that signal a sensitive reaction to idyllic love and to delicacy of human emotions. The Spanish-American identification with *María* as "tan nuestra" very likely goes deeper than simple familiarity with customs and/or with the New World landscape.[17] It probably involves, through the vicarious experience of Efraín's loss, a threat of separation from these phenomena. At the same time, if a reader—whatever his cultural context—accepts the conditions set forth in "A los hermanos de Efraín," the sensitivity of the protagonist is entirely credible and provides a basis for universal empathy as the protagonist's loss is transformed into experience through the codes that define his characteristic sensitivity.

6

Structuration of the Narrative Text

Ramón Meza's Mi tío el empleado

Ramón Meza y Suárez Inclán (1861–1911) is far from being one of the well-known novelists of nineteenth-century Spanish America, even though he has enjoyed the admiration of perceptive critics from his own time to the present. One of the first to admire his work was José Martí; most recently, Raymond D. Souza has pointed out *Mi tío el empleado* (1887) as the most artistically significant novel in nineteenth-century Cuba. Antón Arrufat provides the clearest statement of Meza's place in Cuban fiction.[1] In general, critical commentary on his work has emphasized *Mi tío el empleado* and has clustered around the 100th anniversary of his birth.[2]

Edna Coll lists six novels by Meza published between 1886 and 1891; a seventh title is listed without specific bibliographical information, but with the date 1878–79. Even her purposely limited descriptive comments reveal a predilection for *Mi tío el empleado*.[3] This preference among the critics combines with frequent references to the novel's satire of colonialism in Cuba. In an introduction to the edition used here, Lorenzo García Vega analyzes an ambivalent experience of familiarity on the one hand and distortion on the other.[4] This effect is characteristic of a kind of fiction that may be described as picaresque *costumbrismo*. In this regard, *Mi tío el empleado* is similar to the novels of Emilio Rabasa, which coincide chronologically with Meza's work. In any novel of this kind, the narrator-reader relationship is of fundamental interest because it is influenced by a picaresque code. It should be clearly understood that reference to a picaresque code does not mean that *Mi tío el empleado* is a picaresque novel. Rather, it means that certain characteristics generally associated with the picaresque genre activate a sense of the picaresque in Meza's reader.[5] Although there is much in *Mi tío empleado* that is picaresque, one could hardly identify a *pícaro*. Certainly the narrator does not perform that role, as he would in a standard picaresque novel. It is immediately obvious that some interesting relationships must exist between the picaresque code and the narrative position. With this connection in mind, it seems probable that a more complicated examination of sense-awakening codes may add substantially to the experience of Meza's narration.

The following observations on *Mi tío el empleado* will be based on two readings by Roland Barthes: the very well known *S/Z* and a less familiar—but for the present discussion, probably even more helpful—reading of Edgar A. Poe's "Valdemar."[6] The latter work is especially interesting because it exemplifies the usefulness of Barthesian codes even in an analysis so short that only a few of the lexias may be given specific consideration. Barthes provides an "actional analysis" between the two passages that are dealt with in detail. Of course, such an abbreviated treatment cannot be entirely satisfactory, since the pleasure of Barthes's commentary depends on the many connotations of the narrative text. Indeed, the structuration of the narrative text is the equivalent of the interrelating of senses awakened by different codes throughout the narration. Since any lexia may require reference to numerous associations, it is apparent that a complete Barthesian reading may be many times the length of the printed text treated. On the other hand, Barthes demonstrates, in his study of "Valdemar," that a truncated commentary may set forth fascinating insights with respect to the way the experience of the work takes shape.

Word choice is a treacherous endeavor when one is talking about the Barthesian process. The critic himself uses "textual analysis" to name what he does in a reading. In the present study, we prefer to avoid that term because it seems that Barthes's reading is essentially a way to read rather than a way to analyze. Certainly no one can deny that the product is an exhaustive analysis, of a very unusual kind. On the other hand, we have usually expected an analysis of fiction to be somewhat shorter than the text analyzed and to provide some kind of synthesis of the work. Barthes's procedure does no such thing. It emphasizes the richness—the pleasure, if you will—of the text by allow-ing the several codes to awaken multiple associations and by observing the intermingling of these associations.

Barthes's "textual analysis" is, however, exquisitely textual—textual in a *textile* sense. It is an interweaving. Let us return, for example, to the relationship of the picaresque code with the narrative position (Barthes's rhetorical code).[7] In *Mi tío el empleado,* the first-person narrator introduces himself as one of the people he has been describing in the pages immediately preceding. Then the picaresque code awakens our sense of the protagonist's and the narrator's role as learners facing an unfamiliar world; specifically, this effect is achieved in the narrator's description of a friend's buying a theater ticket—the detail indicates that the overall significance of his actions is totally unfamiliar to the narrator. However, the narrator is not an opportunist and, therefore, not a *pícaro,* nor does he remain a first-person narrator throughout the novel. The picaresque code is related to the rhetorical code but is not homologous with it. When the reader's senses are awakened by the picaresque code, they will most likely include the expectation of social satire, because the reader makes an intertextual association with a familiar picaresque work. The association shows that the picaresque is a social code (common knowledge). This rather simplistic example shows how Barthesian codes weave a fabric of experience that is not an interpretation of a written text held in hand but an enlargement of that text—the result of association with the already known. One could say, with good reason, that the picaresque factor is the dynamic force in the experience of *Mi tío el empleado;* it is equally reasonable, and probably more meaningful, to say that the interweaving of codes moves the experience of the text toward completing itself. A Barthesian reading, therefore, emphasizes process rather than accomplished fact; it is structuralist not in the sense that the critic discovers a pattern that is common to all fiction but in the sense that the reading itself creates the structure and is consequently an act of structuration.

In order to produce a commentary of acceptable length, some decision is necessary with regard to selection of passages. Meza's novel is composed of two parts. We will emphasize the opening and closing passages from each part, plus a selection from each part chosen because of its importance to the experience of the work. These text fragments will be referred to alphabetically: A, B, C, D, E, F. A

synthesis of the experience of the relevant portions of the novel will
appear between text fragments. Rather than confine these observations to the action code, as Barthes does in his study of
"Valdemar," we will try to show, in a general way, how the interweaving works.

Since this essay is written in English about a text that is written in
Spanish, English versions will be given when the lexias are quoted
separately. These English translations are more literal than elegant
because such treatment makes possible the clear numbering of lexias
in both versions. We propose to avoid comments suggested by differences between the two languages, and we intend to disregard place-
identifying references such as street names in Havana.

Interweaving begins with the title of the novel:

Mi tío el empleado (My Uncle the Bureaucrat).

a) If the narrator gave the novel its title, the narration must be in
first person, since it will be about "my uncle." Here we have the first
indicated relationship between narrator and reader. We shall call this
the communication code, or one of the aspects of such a code.
(Barthes distinguishes between a rhetorical code and a communication
code in a very interesting way.[8] The distinction is not particularly
important for our comments here. We will understand the communication code as including all suggestions of relationship between
narrator and reader, communications within the narrative, and
comments on the narrative itself.) The title is similar to a request for
attention in ordinary discourse—something like "Let me tell you about
my uncle the bureaucrat."[9]

b) The connotative code comes into play with the use of
"bureaucrat." This code consists of language that defines a character
(or possibly a situation) through a series of references that have a
cumulative effect. Bureaucrat suggests a type of employment and also
a particular mentality. Obviously, a government employee comes to
mind, but one thinks also of commitment to routine tasks and to
insignificant detail, whether or not the person is a civil servant. In
addition, "bureaucrat" is mildly derogatory insofar as it refers to
status. One thinks of characters of mediocre ability created by Dickens

or Pérez Galdós (here intertextuality begins) and very likely thinks of characterization in realist novels.

c) The narrator's invitation or promise to tell about this particular kind of uncle introduces a question (enigma code). Why does the narrator wish to write about an apparent mediocrity? We may even suspect some kind of mischievous intent.

The first part of the novel has its own title:

Cómo llegó mi tío a Cuba (How My Uncle Came to Cuba).

a) This secondary title continues the communication code as noted in the principle title. The narrator is now saying something like "First let me tell you how my uncle came to Cuba."

b) The title of Part One has an additional effect because it is the first instance of the action code. The first important act of the novel is that the uncle (and the narrator) arrive in Cuba. Minor actions constitute details of this arrival, but it is this act itself that constitutes the base for other actions that the reader puts together to make the story line of the novel.

The title of the first chapter is

De arribada (Arrival).

a) The chapter title is redundant insofar as it repeats the message of the title of Part One with reference to the first important action of the novel.

b) The position of the narrator (communication code) appears to change. Rather than a promise to the reader, "Arrival" seems more documentary, as if the narrator were looking at the event more objectively. Our sense of relationship with the narrator suffers a mild jolt, and we may wonder how consistent it will be.

Text fragment A (p. 7)[10]:

(1) *En los primeros días del mes de enero, uno de esos días hermosos, espléndidos, después de largo tiempo de lenta navegación* (2) *llegó a vista del puerto de La Habana el bergantín* Tolosa. (3) *Henchidas sus blancas lonas e impelido por fresco viento del noroeste, parecía que iba a estrellarse el buque contra los negros riscos de la*

costa; mas cambiando bruscamente de rumbo, dirigió la proa hacia el punto medio de la estrecha boca del puerto. (4) *El cielo azul sin que manchase su pura trasparencia la más tenue nubecilla; el mar azul también y con sus aguas tan diáfanas que a trechos permitían ver las manchas oscuras de los escollos; el sol, en medio del cielo derramando raudales de luz por todas partes;* (5) *la ciudad de La Habana, con sus casas de variados colores, con sus vidriadas almenas, con las torres de sus iglesias, con su costa erizada de verdinegros arrecifes ceñidos por blanca línea de espuma, con sus cristales que heridos por el sol lanzaban destellos cual si fueran pequeños soles, con sus vetustos tejados y empinadas azoteas, con los grandes murallones de piedra gris de sus fuertes asentados sobre dura roca cubierta de verdor:* (6) *¡ah! todo esto se presentaba a la contemplación de dos viajeros, que venían a bordo del bergantín, con cierto maravilloso atractivo de que no les era posible sustraerse.*

(1) (In the first days of the month of January, one of those beautiful, splendid days, after a long, slow voyage,)

a) The chronology code can be very important in the narrative experience. It is not clear in this lexia whether the reference to a specific calendar time is valuable as an indicator of time itself or as a means of evoking association with a particular season. The reader's sense of time and his sense of season are both awakened. There is a notable contrast between the specificity of "the first days . . . of January" and the lack of definition in "long, slow voyage."

b) Reference to the quality of these days may be connotative—not with respect to characterization, but to the general circumstance in which the arrival takes place. At the same time, the enigma code is operative because the narrator causes us to wonder if this particular kind of day has a special bearing on events to come. It would be impossible to say whether the connotative code or enigma code functions primarily in this case, and that is good because the indivisibility exemplifies the process of interweaving.

(2) (the brig *Tolosa* came in view of the port of Havana.)

a) The action code here provides the first detail of the first major event announced in the preceding titles (the arrival). It is interesting that the action is not related to a person except by previous awareness of the titles of the novel and of Part One.

b) The event also announces the place—or, rather, emphasizes it by specifying the city. The enigma code functions here because we wonder why this particular place. Multiple associations with literary treatments of a modern Havana are canceled out by the means of transportation.

(3) (With her white sails swollen and a fresh northeast wind driving her, it seemed that the ship was going to crash against the black cliffs of the coast, but, changing direction suddenly, she turned her prow toward the midpoint of the harbor's narrow entrance.)

a) If this work were a short story, it is possible that the enigma code might function here, suggesting the possibility of a tragedy. However, with the previous awareness of titles, and considering the length of the text, we accept this action as a detail of the arrival.

b) The connotative code arouses our sense of the narrator's innocence. The experience of nearing port is apparently new to him. It may not seem especially strange that a person be unfamiliar with this particular experience, but the point is that the reader's awareness of his innocence is aroused, no matter how natural that condition may be.

(4) (The blue sky without the slightest cloud to darken its pure transparency; the sea also blue and with water so diaphanous that at intervals it allowed one to see the dark outlines of reefs; the sun, in the middle of the sky, spilling torrents of light everywhere;)

a) The cultural code functions here. The circumstance described is familiar, in a literary sense, even to readers who have never actually witnessed a comparable scene. The perfection implied by the situation awakens a sense of well-being with a probable touch of excitement. This lexia illuminates the question raised in (1) a.

b) The term "cultural code" may prove to be unsatisfactory. Barthes points out that all codes are in fact cultural; they refer to the "already seen, already read, already made."[11] We might well say "already experienced." Still, Barthes uses "cultural" to identify that particular code that corresponds to "knowledge, or rather . . . human knowings, of public opinions, of culture such as is transmitted by the book, by teaching, and in a more general, diffuse way, by the whole of society."[12] However, "cultural code" rapidly becomes "cultural codes" as we recognize that the chronological code is really a cultural code and that the picaresque code is a cultural code applicable to the present study in much the same way that the scientific code is a cultural code important in Barthes's reading of "Valdemar."

(5) (the city of Havana, with its houses of different colors, with its glazed parapets, with the towers of its churches, with its coasts bristling with reefs circled by a white line of spume, with its window panes that, struck by the sun, sent out rays as if they were tiny suns, with its old tile roofs and steep *azoteas,* with the enormous gray-stone walls of its forts situated on hard rock covered with green;)

a) The cultural code suggests a particular kind of city, one that has weathered considerably and is to some extent hermetic. However, one aspect of the sense aroused by this lexia is more general—the reference to church towers and to the sun's reflection.

b) The two aspects of the experience described in (5)a relate to the connotative value of this lexia; the narrator gives the same importance to generally familiar things (church towers) and to more particularized details (forts, *azoteas*), so reinforcing the reader's sense of the narrator's lack of sophistication, (3)b.

(6) (ah, all this offered itself for contemplation by two travelers, arriving on board the brig, with a certain marvelous attractiveness that they could not resist.)

a) The communication code reinforces the sense of paradoxical proximity-distance that we noted in contrasting the title of the first chapter with the titles of the novel and of the first volume. The narrator's presence is strongly felt when he says "ah," but he seems farther away when he speaks of "two passengers." There is a kind of enigma suggested within the communication code, because we may ask whether or not this paradoxical position of the narrator promises irony.

b) The enigma code functions cautiously in its more familiar guise. Why the trip? What is the promise? And why is this panorama now irresistible? Attractive, certainly. But irresistible? The narrator is teasing us, holding something back.

Synopsis of Narration between Text Fragments A and B:

In this short space the narrator mainly provides information concerning the two passengers. The connotative code sensitizes the reader to their provincial background, their relative poverty, and their general lack of sophistication. A retrospective reference tells of their coming to Cádiz, where they boarded ship (action code).

Text fragment B (p. 9):

(1) *Quien mirase fijamente a estos dos viajeros podría tomarlos por hermanos; pero mejor informado, puedo asegurar al lector, que aquellos dos viajeros no eran otros que mi tío y yo.*
(2) —*Oye sobrino, ¿has visto si está en el mundo la carta de recomendación del primo?*
(3) *Así me dijo mi tío,* (4) *suspendiendo un instante la admiración que le producía la vista de La Habana, bañada toda por la luz del sol, al recordar que nos acercábamos ya al término de nuestro viaje.*
(5) *Me dirigí al camarote, abrí el baúl y me palpitó con fuerza el corazón: la carta no estaba donde la había visto el día anterior y todos los demás días.* (6) *Volví al derecho y al revés medias, bolsillos, mangas, y la carta de recomendación no aparecía.*
(7) *Alarmado mi tío con mi tardanza se presentó en las puertas del camarote,* (8) *y la revolución en que vió las ropas, y el apuro con que yo las registraba,* (9) *le hicieron comprender la fatal nueva antes de que yo pudiera desplegar mis labios.*
(10) *Jamás he vuelto a ver hombre alguno tan desesperado. Lo primero que hizo fué pegar un puntapie* (11) *que rayó la tapa del mundo, como llamaba él al baúl.* (12) *Después tiró al suelo el sombrero, lo pateó, se dió de puñadas en el estómago y vociferaba que yo era peor que un ladrón, pues que le había arrebatado su porvenir a un hombre honrado;* (13) *que entrar en La Habana sin la carta de recomendación, era dar lugar a que nos confundieran con tanta gente vulgar que entraba en ella todos los días. ¡Bonito papel harían nada menos que los Cuevas, los recomendados por el ilustre madrileño señor marqués de Casa Vetusta, sin poder acreditar que lo eran!*

(1) (Anyone who looked carefully at these two travelers could take them for brothers, but I, better informed, can assure the reader that those two travelers were none other than my uncle and myself.)

a) The communication code here informs us that the proximity-distance paradox, mentioned in A(6) and elsewhere, is clearly a characteristic of the narrator's position. We note the difference between "*these* two travelers," before their identity is revealed, and "*those* two travelers" as part of the identification act. The narrator feels closer to the scene in the first case than in the latter.

b) Confirmation of the first-person narrator, as suggested in the title, is joined with a detachment that is characteristic of the *pícaro*. We now expect a narrator outside the *récit*, telling his own story.[13]

c) The revelation of identity resolves a small enigma, of which there are many in *Mi tío el empleado*. Of course, readers are not so informed at this point in the novel, but they are aware that the narrator teases by withholding information.

(2) ("Listen, nephew, have you looked to see if the recommendation is in the world?")

a) For the first time spoken words are reproduced in the novel, therefore the communication code appears most important. We are aware that the narrator has chosen scene in place of summary.

b) The connotative code advises us that the uncle is not one to take responsibility on himself.

c) The strange phrase "in the world" initiates one of the small enigmas.

(3) (My uncle spoke to me thus,)

a) Here we have the communication code in the form of metalanguage. The reader knows perfectly well how uncle spoke to nephew, but the latter feels that he must confirm this obvious fact. It may be no more than an elaborate way of tagging the utterance, like "my uncle said." On the other hand, the narrator may be referring to the uncle's shifting responsibility to the nephew, in which case we have a combination of communication code and connotative code.

b) It is also possible that this case of language commenting on itself may be related to the enigmatic "in the world." Since the phrase makes no sense, the narrator may be advising the reader that his uncle really did say it.

(4) (suspending momentarily the admiration produced in him by the view of Havana, all bathed in sunlight, when he recalled that we were nearing the end of our voyage.)

a) The enigma code refers here to the expectation of something extraordinary in Havana. The sense of pipe dreams interrupted by reality combines the connotative code with the enigma code.

b) The uncle's apparently sudden realization that the voyage is nearing its end reaffirms our sense of his lack of responsibility, as in (3)a, and (2)b.

(5) (I went to our cabin, opened the trunk, and my heart came into my throat; the letter was not where I had seen it the day before and every other day.)

a) The action code is obviously important here, especially given the narrator-nephew's reaction to not finding the letter. The action itself does not appear to be of great importance unless the search for the letter should turn out to be a major theme.

b) The connotative code informs us that both uncle and nephew are dependent personalities, or in a situation where personal recommendations are the key to success.

c) The enigma code holds us in the midst of the mystery concerning the letter's location.

(6) (I turned everything inside out and outside in—stockings, pockets, sleeves—and the letter of recommendation did not appear.)

a) The connotative code indicates desperation on the part of the narrator, either because he considers the letter indispensable or because he fears the wrath of his uncle. In the latter regard, his character suggests that of the *pícaro* who suffers by being inferior to his master, or at least feigns that condition.

b) The picaresque code, already suggested by the nephew's narrative position and by the connotation of this lexia, here reinforces the sense of the picaresque through the chaotic circumstance in which the narrator finds himself. The *pícaro's* world is normally chaotic. He finds himself within it but in a state of ignorance, trying to observe his situation and make sense of it.

(7) (Alarmed by my delay, my uncle came to the doorway of the cabin,)

The action code carries the story forward, with specific reference to the search for the letter.

(8) (and the mess in which he saw the clothing, and the anxiety with which I was examining it,)

The picaresque code modifies the action code by emphasizing the chaotic state of the narrator's circumstance.

(9) (made him understand the fatal news before I could get my lips open.)

a) This lexia completes the apparently disastrous final act in the search for the letter.

b) The connotative code suggests a certain complexity in the uncle's character. He has seemed only partially aware of what is going on around him (his sudden awareness that the voyage is ending), but he is sensitive enough to deduce a negative conclusion. That is, at least, what the nephew-narrator tells us. If he were narrating as a person really within the *récit,* he would not be able to make this statement; we assume, therefore, that he has made this conclusion after the fact.

(10) (I have never since seen a man so desperate. The first thing he did was give a kick)

a) The connotative code indicates a volatile temperament, and the nephew's anxiety seems to be transferred to the uncle's outburst.

b) The kick itself becomes a symbol (of course, the reader does not know it at this point) of the uncle's frustration. This aspect of his personality accords well with his willingness to blame someone else.

(11) (that scarred the lid of the world, as he called our trunk.)

a) A small enigma is resolved here—earlier reference to "the world" meant the trunk. Given the fact that the nephew was looking for the letter among their clothing, the reader probably assumes that "the world" refers to the trunk. This assumption may be considered a step toward resolution, but the real revelation leaves no room for doubt.

b) The connotative code is important here because "world" is the name given by the uncle to the container in which he keeps his possessions. We sense the alienation of a person who has left one land in order to live in another, carrying his "world" with him, or all of his world that he is able to carry. At the same time, we are aware that the contents of the "world" are material (except for the implications of the letter). These conditions conform to our notions concerning the picaresque. We note, however, that the narrator-nephew appears to transfer his reaction to his uncle; therefore, the picaresque code reveals more about the older man than about the younger.

(12) (Then he threw his hat on the floor, stepped on it, hit himself in the stomach, and kept yelling that I was worse than a thief because I had snatched an honest man's future from him,)

a) The uncle's temper now seems caricatured in such a way that it shows a volatile reaction carried to an extreme, with no corresponding emphasis on specific cause. This temper promises to become a theme of the novel, as does the reference to his future (symbolic code).

b) The two thematic possibilities appear related to two different enigmas. The display of temper belongs to the micro-*récit* of the lost letter; the concern for his future apparently belongs to the novel's major question of how successful the uncle will be. At this point we are aware of three enigmas, of different extension and importance, that fit into each other. The shortest concerns the meaning of "the world," the second concerns the lost letter, and the third has to do with the uncle's career.

(13) (that entering Havana without the letter of recommendation was an invitation to confuse us with all the ordinary people that came to Havana every day. A fine figure we Cuevases would cut—we Cuevases, recommended by that illustrious *madrileño,* the Marquis of Rottinghouse, and unable to prove it.)

a) The first reference to a family name comes within a context of false pride, that is, the connotative code sensitizes us to the falseness by use of the marquis's name and by the uncle's contrast with "ordinary people" (we know his humble status).

b) The connotative code is close to the picaresque in producing a sense of the uncle's pretentiousness. This attitude is an appropriate one for the *pícaro's* master and might even be reflected in the *pícaro,* but we note that in *Mi tío el empleado* the narrator has disassociated himself from the ridiculous figure of his uncle. The prideful reference to the Cuevases' social status includes the nephew but is actually attributed to the uncle (communication code).

Synopsis of Narration between Text Fragments B and C:

The uncle, Vicente Cuevas, finds the letter in his own pocket, so completing the farcical portrait painted by his nephew and providing the real solution to the enigma of the lost letter. The new arrivals experience the confusion of the warehouse and wharves (again the chaotic world), pass through customs with a display of ignorance (again the picaresque code) and find lodging through a friend from home whom they meet by chance.

The first complicated event following this sequence has nothing to do with the main story line. Vicente Cuevas is made the butt of a practical joke, the kind played on a susceptible new arrival, particularly one that needs deflating (the mission to get a left-handed screwdriver, for example). This trick is the kind of measure Lazarillo de Tormes might use to get even with his master, but in Meza's novel the narrator-nephew does not conspire with the tricksters.

Both uncle and nephew secure employment through their cousin, Genaro de los Dées, to whom the marquis addressed his letter. The nature of the work is clerical, but its exact identity is not revealed—a fact that emphasizes the general sense of paper-shuffling. Several following episodes are related to this kind of work and are characterized by the employees' opportunism and ineptness. The action code lays out the series of events through which Vicente climbs the ladder of success and then falls. Late in the first part, a secondary series of acts deals with Vicente's proposal of marriage, which is rejected. The enigma code regularly brings to mind the question of whether or not Vicente will make his mark; however, there are smaller enigmas associated with several different episodes.

In the association between Don Genaro and Vicente, the latter tends to fit into the role of *pícaro* and the former into the position of master. Genaro exploits Vicente, but allows him enough success to keep him interested. The picaresque code functions through a distorted view of reality realized in dreams, through reference to inadequate education, and through insistence on interest in material gain. The connotative code becomes satirical by suggesting Vicente's self-deception. In order to reveal this character, the narrator-nephew must distance himself from his uncle.

At the end of Part One, a change of government in Spain threatens to disclose dishonest operations (unspecified) on the part of Genaro and employees. Genaro shifts the blame to the latter, but sees that his relatives, Vicente and nephew, get out of Cuba on a ship to Mexico.

Text fragment C (pp. 148–49):

(1) *¡Ah! un relámpago prolongado e intensísimo fue el postrero: tal pareció que La Habana se estremecía desde sus cimientos al recibir aquellos raudales de luz.*

Y luego quedó sumido todo en oscuridad profunda.

¡No la vimos más!

(2) *Oí que mi tío daba sendas puñadas sobre la gruesa banda del buque, luego dió una fuerte patada que resonó mucho sobre la hueca cubierta y exclamó:*

—*¡Infame!. . . ¡maldito D. Genaro!. . . ¡maldito seas!. . .*

(3) *Y por extraña coincidencia era éste el mismo instante en que el bote, que conducía a nuestro insigne protector,* (4) *el excelentísimo e ilustrísimo D. Genaro de los Dées, tocaba los duros peñascos de la costa.*

Y mientras entregaba el ilustre personaje puñados de monedas al botero, repetía gozoso:

—*¡Eh! salvado, toma, patrón; y además toma esto para que eches un trago a mi salud. ¡Ya no le temo ni a los doce apóstoles del Morro!*

(5)—*¡Demongo!. . . María santísima . . .* (6) *¿y los otros?*

—*¡Que se los lleve el diablo! ¿qué importa? respondió D. Genaro alzando los hombros.*

—*Vaya . . . pues, salud.*

—*¡Eh! gracias, adiós.*

(7) *El botero abandonó nuevamente la orilla y se internó en el mar.*

Y nuestro insigne señor aliviado ya de aquellos dos fardos que sentía gravitar sobre su pecho, respiró con satisfacción y desapareció muy pronto entre las torcidas calles de la ciudad.

(8) *¡Era todo un buen hombre el activo D. Genaro!*

(1) (Ah! The last lightning flash was long and very intense. Havana seemed to tremble on its foundations as it caught those torrents of light.

And then everything sank into profound darkness.

We did not see the city again!)

a) This lexia closes out the story (action code). The disappearance of the city is a figurative expression of their leave-taking. The figurative description is made more realistic by "we did not see the city again."

b) The communication code indicates a more intimate commitment on the part of the narrator than has often been the case. The use of "ah" brings him closer, and "we" is sharply indicative of his involvement.

c) The appearance of the city has assumed symbolic importance because it is related to the circumstance in which the protagonist and narrator find themselves. The variations in this circumstance con-

stitute a major theme of the novel. Contrast the present lexia with
A(5).

(2) (I heard my uncle hitting the heavy rail of the ship with his fist,
then he stamped his foot so hard it resounded all over the empty deck,
and he exclaimed:

"The scoundrel! That damned Don Genaro! Damn him!")

a) It may seem that the connotative code is functioning here to
suggest the character of Vicente; however, his temper has actually
become a theme of the novel, and it is more accurate to say that it is
the symbolic code at work.

b) Hidden from the reader of this essay, but quite apparent to the
reader of the whole text, are the details of Vicente's defeat. In the
confrontation of two rascals, he has lost out (picaresque code).

(3) (And by a strange coincidence this was the very moment when
the boat that was carrying our worthy protector,)

a) The communication code is important here because the
narrative situation changes. There is no way the first-person narrator
could know what happens to Genaro while he, the narrator, is on a
ship bound for Mexico.

b) The action code indicates what happens to Genaro, but, since
the narrative situation changes illogically at this point, we assume that
the narrator takes the liberty of reporting this action in order to introduce an ironic contrast that is begun by the reference to "our
worthy protector."

(4) (the most excellent and illustrious Don Genaro de los Dées,
was touching the jagged rocks of the east coast.

And while this illustrious personage was giving handfuls of
money to the boatman, he repeated joyfully:

"Eh! Safe. Take this, captain, and take this too, and have a drink
to my health. Now I'm not afraid even of the twelve apostles of El
Morro!")

a) The symbolic code becomes ironic here. Genaro, who really
does occupy a position of some importance, has been referred to by
Vicente, since early in the novel, as "most excellent and illustrious."
This exaggeration is a characteristic of Vicente and also is appropriately picaresque; however, it is also interesting as a theme of the

novel—that is, the theme of great hopes for the future, always exaggerated in the imagination of Vicente. Here the words are no longer Vicente's but his nephew's.

b) The action code continues the incident and emphasizes the character of Genaro.

(5) ("Demongo! Holy Mary!")

This lexia contains the tag word (Demongo) of Domingo, a boatman who is also the friend who helped uncle and nephew when they arrived in Havana. "Demongo" is part of his speech whenever he appears in the narrative. His identity is not revealed here in any other way. The irony of the situation is enhanced by the suggested presence of Domingo, who now is an agent in the "exile" of uncle and nephew.

(6) ("and the others?"

"The devil take them! What difference does it make?" Don Genaro answered, shrugging his shoulders.

"Well, I'll be . . . well, take care."

"Eh! Thanks. Goodbye.")

a) The boatman's concern contrasts with Genero's primary interest in self-preservation (connotative code).

b) The boatman's words "the others" refer to the other subordinates of Genaro who are in jail and who will presumably be punished for his misdeeds. This insight into Genaro's character, therefore, is accomplished at least in part by the action code, since his dismissal of his responsibility carries out the story. It also answers a question raised by another enigma, that is, what will happen to the people exploited by Genaro.

c) The irony of the situation includes an adjustment to a different level of irresponsibility, moving from Vicente to Genaro.

(7) (The boatman left shore again and went out toward the sea. And our worthy gentleman, relieved now of the two parcels that he had felt weighing so heavily on his chest, inhaled with satisfaction and disappeared very shortly among the winding streets of the city.)

a) The reference to two parcels requires some explanation. Genaro's arrangement with the boatman was to transport two parcels to the ship, not two persons. The narrator makes the reference to intensify the irony of this final passage. His barbs are aimed at both

Vicente and Genaro, with the narrator assuming a position superior to both.

b) Connotations relating to Genero's character are woven in with the action code through which we are told that the schemer disappears among the (significantly) winding streets of Havana.

(8) (The dedicated Don Genaro was every inch a fine man!)

The nephew-narrator wraps up his ironic passage with a terse statement in kind, apparently addressed to the reader. This destination is quite appropriate, since he appears detached from both Vicente and Genaro.

The title of Part Two is:

Cómo salió de Cuba mi tío (How My Uncle Left Cuba).

The title, if it is considered without reference to the narration, appears to be a suitable companion to the title of the first part; however, the reader knows that "my uncle" has already left Cuba unwillingly. The probability seems to be that the narrator, in naming Part Two, has in mind a larger plan than is yet apparent to the reader. We expect to learn more about the departure already described or, perhaps, to learn that he did not really leave. The enigma code functions in the title, therefore, since the title itself seems to run counter to the action code.

The title of the first chapter of the second part is

"Por la ciudad" (Around Town).

This title suggests very little to the reader. We left Vicente and his nephew-narrator on a ship bound for Mexico. Genaro was walking back into Havana, but his situation hardly suggests that he would be "around town." For these reasons we suspect a time lapse, even though there is no overt function of the chronology code.

Text fragment D (p. 154):

(1) *Unos seis años después de los sucesos con que termina la primera parte de esta narración, a las siete y media de una de esa noches serenas* (2) *en que la atmósfera que rodea a La Habana está*

*incesantemente renovada por vientos del nordeste que llegan a la
ciudad refrescados por las aguas del Océano, impregnados de sus
acres emanaciones y esparcen por toda ella una temperatura
agradable, deliciosa; una de esas noches en que el cielo está pròfun-
damente azul y sembrado de estrellas que lanzan sus vívidos e in-
termitentes fulgores sin que los empañe el más ligero celaje,* (3) *bajaba
por la calle de la Muralla una gran carretela, la cual revelaba a las
claras haber salido muy poco antes del taller, pues sus brillantes
charoles y el barniz de los rayos de sus ruedas reflejaban como un
espejo la luz* (4) *que a raudales se escapaba de lo interior de las tiendas
y de sus hermosas vidrieras iluminadas con profusión y ornadas con
gusto y con primor.*

(1) (Some six years after the events with which the first part of
this narrative ends, at half past seven on one of those peaceful nights)

a) The narrator immediately takes care of the time question raised
by the apparently illogical titles (chronology code). The lapse of six
years in the course of the narration makes practically anything
possible. Reasonably one might expect to find out how Vicente and
the narrator have fared through the years, but nothing in the titles
promises that information.

b) The exact time is set at half-past seven; however, its function
as an ambience indicator is made apparent immediately by reference
to the quality of the night. Compare with A(1)a.

c) The communication code informs us that the narrator is addressing the reader specifically and directly, orienting us for what lies
ahead.

(2) (when the atmosphere that pervades Havana is incessantly
renewed by northeast winds that come to the city freshened by the
waters of the ocean, saturated with their pungent emanations, and
spread an agreeable, delicious atmosphere over the whole place—one
of those nights when the sky is profoundly blue and sprinkled with
stars that spread their vivid and intermittent brilliance without even
the slightest cloud to darken them,)

a) The cultural code is fundamental here, evoking our sense of an
atmosphere that is familiar either through actual experience or
through aesthetic experience. Compare with A(4) a.

b) The comparison suggested above brings out a connotative
significance. The function of both lexias is more or less the same, in an

initial reaction, but the present lexia connotes the romantic quality of night.

(3) (a grand calash was going down Muralla Street clearly showing that it had left the shop only a short while earlier, because its shiny patent-leather fittings and its varnished wheel spokes reflected like a mirror the light)

a) We assume this action is meaningful because it is the first in the second part. As in Part One, the action code is functional before a person enters the narration. Compare with A(2)a.

b) The cultural code denotes luxury experienced in the newness of the vehicle, in the opulence of its fittings, and in the implication of light reflected in the general darkness.

(4) (that streamed from the interiors of shops and from the beautiful windows profusely illuminated and decorated with taste and skill.)

a) The cultural code intensifies our sense of city life with its accompanying excitement—an atmosphere of sophistication.

b) The title of the first chapter, "Around Town," now seems a logical choice for the apparent theme, but we are still unable to see a clear relationship with Part One. Obviously the enigma code functions here. The puzzle about the continuity of the narrative is combined with the more specific question of who will appear in the calash. Could it be Vicente? The nephew-narrator? Genaro?

Synopsis of Narration between Text Fragments D and E:

The owner of the calash is the extremely wealthy—and therefore greatly admired—Conde (Count) Coveo. Enigma and cultural codes join in developing the sense that no one knows or cares about the count's background. The cultural code triggers our reaction to conspicuous luxury, in a familiar satirical way. The general effect is reminiscent of the picaresque novel or of the Spanish *costumbristas* like Mariano José de Larra or Ramón de Mesonero Romanos.[14] The first-person narrator, however, has disappeared (communication code). The nephew does not appear in the action, nor does Vicente Cuevas. The narrator hints that the count is actually Cuevas; however, as is Meza's custom in the resolution of enigma, the rather broad hint precedes a clear revelation. In any case, even if the reader is aware of how the novelist handles these matters and, consequently, assumes that Coveo is Cuevas, there remains an enigma concerning how he acquired such wealth.

The first four chapters of Part Two are virtually synchronic so far as development of the plot is concerned. The actions are different in kind but similar in effect. They picture Count Coveo in different situations that exhibit his excessive spending, his basic insecurity, and his persistent hope that he will become a great man. The connotative code is very important; so is the cultural code, since the situations are typical of "high life." These situations, however, are exaggerated by the narrator so that they become satirical, and Count Coveo looks like a combination of fool and reprobate. The cultural code so far referred to as picaresque has changed slightly in this part of the novel and can be more accurately thought of as satire.[15]

Text fragment E (pp. 183–84):

(1) *Pesquisas matrimoniales* [chapter title]

(2) *Cuando despertó el señor conde, daba doce sonoros golpes, acompasadamente, el gran reloj del comedor.*

(3) *¡Siempre el mismo espectáculo; siempre la misma sensación! ¡Llena de luz de sol la persiana; henchido de tibio vapor el aposento; el mismo silencio, la misma calma y tranquilidad! Ni el más suave ruido se oía en toda la casa.*

(4) *El conde fijó su vista en los pliegues del fino lienzo de su mosquitero y quedó pensativo un momento.*

Sentía como si le hubiera puesto una enorme y pesada carga sobre el pecho.

Suspiró; y se sintió más aliviado.

(5) *—¡Oh! sí; me casaré, me casaré. Eso es lo que me falta.* (6) *Una mujer hermosa cuya sonrisa vea yo al despertarme, cuyos ojos iluminen este cuarto con más dulce claridad que la del sol, cuyo aliento perfume y vuelva más sutil esta enervante y pesada atmósfera. ¡Oh! sí, todo me falta, luz, aire, alegría; de nada me sirve esto si al par que yo no lo goza un ser amado. Un hermoso ángel cuyo rostro vea yo asomar por entre estos pliegues al despertarme y cuya mirada rebose de amor profundo y casto . . .*

(7) *Estos risueños pensamientos acudían con suma vaguedad a la*

mente del conde; mas de improviso quedaron interrumpidos (8) *por una traidora idea, que como nube negra oscureció el sonrosado horizonte en que su fantasía se abismaba.*

Su mirada quedó por un momento indecisa, vacilante; y luego riendo con malicia saltó de la cama:

—*¡Ah! sí, rica; eso es indispensable.*

(1) (Matrimonial Research)

a) These words constitute the title of the fifth chapter in Part Two. It represents an enigma because matrimony has not been one of the themes of this volume, and the reader wonders why such a title appears at this point.

b) The title has a connotative value that is likely to affect the reader in a kind of double-take reaction. Vicente Cuevas, in Part One, proposed marriage to a young woman whom he did not know but about whom he fantasized all the details of courtship. His exaggerated dreams caused him to make a fool of himself. The abrupt appearance of the matrimonial theme at this point may well strengthen the association of Coveo with Cuevas.

(2) (When the count awakened, the great clock in the dining room was rhythmically and sonorously striking twelve.)

a) The chronology code again seems to supply ambience—that is, it contributes to the general setting of the chapter.

b) The connotative code is effective because awaking at noon illuminates the character of Coveo. Similarly, the cultural implications add to the sense of luxury.

(3) (Always the same sight; always the same sensation! The blind full of sunlight, the bedroom full of tepid air, the same silence, the same calm and tranquility! Not even the slightest noise could be heard anywhere in the house.)

Although this lexia may contribute to our understanding of Coveo's character, the cultural code prevails over the connotative because we make multiple associations with awaking late on a sunny day in a situation where quiet produces a sense of loneliness. This already experienced situation, therefore, produces a familiar setting.

(4) (The count fixed his eyes on the fine linen folds of his mosquito net and remained pensive for a moment.

He felt as if an enormous and heavy burden had been placed on his chest.

He sighed and felt relieved.)

a) The connotative code obviously suggests a luxury-loving character. At the same time, the narrator is sufficiently omniscient (communication code) to indicate that all is not well.

b) The action code should not be ignored here, because we are presumably in the midst of a micro-*récit* in which the count's actions, though apparently insignificant, may be expected to constitute an important sequence (see also lexia 2).

(5) ("Oh, yes, I will get married, I will get married. That's what I need.")

a) Although this lexia represents a thought rather than an act, the action code is significant here because this notion supplies the basis for almost all that happens in the rest of the novel.

b) This statement illuminates the title of the chapter and also underlines the connotative value of the title. Coveo imagines a situation that seems desirable to him and immediately makes a decision that will presumably lead to its realization. Here is the paradoxical combination of dreamer and opportunist.

(6) ("A beautiful woman whose smile I see upon awaking, whose eyes light up this room more clearly than the sun, whose breath will perfume and refine this enervating, heavy atmosphere. Oh, yes, a pretty woman who gladdens with her presence and with her silvery voice, like a goldfinch in a gilded case, this lonely house. Ah, yes, I am missing it all, light, air, joy: none of it does me any good unless a beloved person enjoys it along with me. A gorgeous angel whose face I may see appear among these folds as I am waking up and whose expression radiates a deep and pure love.")

This extensive lexia is entirely connotative. It reveals the dreamer, and even suggests, through the quantity of trite detail, a person who envisions a pattern and will try to make reality conform.

(7) (These happy thoughts appeared with consummate vagueness in the count's mind, but suddenly they were interrupted)

a) The communication code places the reader in a special situation with regard to Coveo. We have become accustomed to an omniscient narrator, and there is no doubt, in the present instance, that he knows the count's thoughts. However, we have been appreciating the situation, in the preceding lexia, from the standpoint of the count. That is, we have not been observing him through the eyes of the narrator, but observing his situation through his own thoughts.

b) The punctuation of the preceding lexia is not clear. It appears to be a piece of spoken text, but the present lexia refers to the passage as Coveo's "thoughts." The effect is of interior monologue. Again we notice the fundamental change of narrative situation, as contrasted with Part One. In the first volume of the novel, the situation is not entirely consistent, but it is basically a first-person narrator telling his story. By this point in the second part, however, we are aware that this situation has been exchanged for an omniscience so pervasive that the narrator can concede the point of view, on occasion, to his protagonist.

(8) (by a teacherous idea that like a black cloud darkened the rosy horizon in which his fantasy was sinking.

His expression remained indecisive, vacillating, for an instant; then, laughing guilefully, he jumped out of bed.

"Ah, yes, rich; that is indispensable.")

a) The picaresque code is present in this revelation of deviltry. A heavier satire is effected by means of the contrast between the idealized dreaming in lexia 6 and the opportunistic slant of the last qualification. However, the rapid shift and the fact that the materialistic notion is accompanied by action, whereas the idealization is characterized by inertia, refer us again to the complex of attitudes and experiences associated with the picaresque.

b) It seems reasonable to accept the last sentence of this lexia as communicated in the same way as lexias 5 and 6.

Synopsis of Narration between Text Fragments E and F:

The rest of the novel deals mainly with the count's courtship of Clotilde, their wedding, and their life as leaders of Havana society. The connotative code emphasizes their preference for social extravaganza with little concern for human relationships. Attitudes and utterances are repeated or approximated to the point of symbolizing lack of taste and limitless materialistic ambition.

The narrator is generally, but not always, omniscient. The first-person narrator-nephew intervenes to explain how his uncle was called back to Cuba (following a favorable change in the Spanish government) to take over the position formerly held by Don Genaro, now returned to Spain. The nephew explains the broken relationship with his uncle by saying he can no longer tolerate the older man's combination of ineptness and opportunism. Metalanguage is fairly frequent, even to the point of recognizing the difference between *histoire* time and *récit* time.[16] On ending the narration of one incident, he says, "Todo esto ocurrió rápido, casi instantáneamente, en muchísimo menos tiempo del que hemos invertido en relatarlo" (p. 222). (All this happened rapidly, almost instantaneously, in much less time than we have spent relating it.)

The narrator-nephew's rejection of his uncle accords with the shift of emphasis from picaresque to satire. Coveo moves horizontally in society in Part Two. The upward struggle has been largely won. A convenient marriage is more important to his endless ambition than is attention to his bureaucratic job. The action code, therefore, emphasizes the courtship and marriage, returning to the picture of bureaucracy only to show Coveo resigning and going back to Spain now that his fortune is made.

The enigma code in this part of the novel concerns three aspects of the story. First, the identity of Coveo is definitively revealed after many broad hints. Second, there is a question concerning the outcome of the courtship. The resolution comes with the surprisingly ready consent of Clotilde—so ready, in fact, that it suggests a possible element of opportunism on her part. The third enigma is the appearance, on several occasions, of a beggar whose presence seems to disturb Coveo. This enigma is not resolved before his departure for Spain.

Text fragment F (pp. 292–93):

(1) *Mucho antes de llegar al Morro el vapor de las banderolas, volvió hacia el muelle; y el conde y Clotilde* (2) *pudieron descansar sus brazos adoloridos de contestar tantos saludos.*

(3) *Cuando el aire franco del mar, impregnado de salitre, acarició el rostro del conde, éste lo respiró con inmenso placer.*

(4) *Volvióse de espaldas hacia la boca del puerto, que iba cerrándose más y más, apartó la vista de aquella tierra que iba dejando rápidamente detrás y fijó su vista en medio de aquella línea, en que parecían tocarse el cielo y el mar,* (5) *como si hubiera por allí algún agujero que le permitiese contemplar algo que le entusiasmaba.*

(6) *Luego miró a su esposa y balbuceó:*

—Subiré pronto ... ¡es tan hermosa! ...

Y pasado un corto rato estiró los labios, alzó con desprecio los hombros y pensó:

No hay que contar con ella ... su frialdad la hace invulnerable ... es una linda muñeca ... y nada más.

(7) *Y Clotilde, recostada indolentemente sobre un gran sillón, componía las arrugas de su talle, arreglaba sus encajes y sonreía pensando en los triunfos que conseguiría en la nueva sociedad que iba a visitar, con su hermosura y sus riquezas.*

(8) *Desde los ásperos arrecifes cercanos al castillo de la Punta cuatro hombres veían angustiados alejarse con rapidez el vapor;* (9) *pronto quedó reducido a un punto: luego, nada se vio ya. Esos cuatro hombres eran D. Mateo, el canónigo, Domingo y González.*

(10) *—Se nos fue, murmuró muy conmovido aún el primero.*

—Buena nos la ha jugado, respondió el segundo.

Domingo secó con la palma de la mano una lágrima que asomó a sus párpados.

Y González reprimió un sollozo.

(1) (Long before reaching El Morro, the ship with the banners turned back toward the dock, and the count and Clotilde)

a) The action code provides a detail of the triumphal departure. A boatload of well-wishers has followed Coveo and wife for a short distance from land.

b) This lexia separates the couple from the environment with which we have associated them.

(2) (were able to rest their arms, which ached from so much waving.)

a) The communication code is important here. There is a difference between "were able to rest their arms" and "rested their arms." The narrator here does not simply state what they did; he reveals their attitude.

b) Especially since Text Fragment F is the last passage of the novel proper (there is an Epilogue), it is important to note once again the changing situation of the narrator with reference to his characters.

(3) (When the frank sea air, saturated with nitre, caressed the count's cheek, he breathed in with immense pleasure.)

The cultural code here again stimulates our awareness of a familiar situation. This lexia is complementary to lexia 1 in that it relates to the count's separation from his known setting.

(4) (He turned his back on the port entrance, which was gradually closing, looked away from the land he was rapidly leaving behind, and fixed his gaze on the middle of that line where sky and sea appear to touch,)

The action code reveals the count's separation specifically. This movement is his own act of departing; at the same time, his looking toward the horizon suggests great expectations.

(5) (as if there were, over there, some opening that might allow him to contemplate something that delighted him.)

The connotative code suggests, as it so often has, the uncle's constant expectation of greener pastures. We associate it with his willingness to solicit and accept any favor as fully deserved while considering any adversity as unjust.

(6) (Then he looked at his wife and stammered:

"I'll be up shortly . . . it's so beautiful! . . ."

And after a little while he pressed his lips together, shrugged his shoulders disdainfully, and thought:

No point in counting on her . . . her coldness makes her invulnerable . . . she is a pretty doll . . . and nothing more.)

a) The conversation code here is complicated. According to the information supplied by the narrator, Coveo spoke the words within quotation marks and thought those that came to him "after a little while." The latter communication resembles E(6). In that case, the narrator informs us, after the fact, that Coveo thought the preceding; in the present lexia, we are informed in advance.

b) It is interesting also to note another aspect of the communication: the narrator tells us that Coveo *stammered* the following words; he did not just say them. This statement gives the communication a connotative force that shows consistency in the characterization of the count. He has trouble expressing himself adequately. It is an aspect of Coveo's general ineptness.

c) Coveo's willingness to use people to his advantage is apparent here. Even his marriage, which is the main concern of the second volume, is now revealed as having no importance as an intimate human relationship.

(7) (And Clotilde, reclining lazily in a huge armchair, smoothed the wrinkles in her bodice, arranged her lace, and smiled, thinking of the conquests she would make, in the new society she was going to visit, with her beauty and her wealth.)

a) The cultural code here stimulates the notion of one's setting the stage to one's best advantage. The specific reference to clothing emphasizes her femininity.

b) The cultural code also has a connotative value in this lexia because Clotilde's concern for her physical appearance underlines Coveo's comment on her personality and accords with the narrator's revelation of her thoughts. She is a vulgarization of the renaissance *dama cruel*.

(8) (From the rugged reefs near Punta Castle, four men watched with anguish as the ship rapidly drew away;)

a) In addition to the obvious reference to the novel's final action, this lexia has a certain connotative value created by relating the locale to the mood of the characters. The roughness of the spot where they stand suggests their probable unhappiness with respect to the separation they are experiencing.

b) Even in this final episode, Meza indulges his taste for the small enigma. We see the figures before we know who they are.

(9) (soon it was only a dot, then nothing at all. These four men were Don Mateo, the canon, Domingo, and González.)

The action is complete, with the separation fully accomplished. The tiny enigma of their identity is resolved and we know they are four men who have reason to be grateful to Coveo.

(10) ("He has left us," the first murmured, still emotional.
"He did well by us," answered the second.

With the palm of his hand, Domingo wiped away a tear that came to his eye."
And González held back a sigh.)
The connotative code is operative at novel's end. The reaction of each man is related to his indebtedness to Coveo, and there is irony in each case. Don Mateo is Coveo's old teacher—an extremely poor one—who worked as his secretary in Havana, so achieving a degree of success he had never imagined. The canon has distinguished himself mainly by feasting at the extravagant dinners provided by Vicente and Clotilde. Domingo is probably the novel's most humane character. He helped Vicente as much as Vicente helped him, because Domingo was the friend who offered help early in the novel. González was the owner of the fleabag pension where uncle and nephew first lived in Havana. Both Domingo and González were given patronage jobs by Coveo.

EPILOGUE

The epilogue serves to resolve the enigma of the beggar who has appeared several times and caused a negative reaction on the part of Vicente. He is revealed as Don Benigno, a dedicated and honest civil servant who was fired in order to make room for Vicente Cuevas. The resolution of this enigma provides a final touch of irony by contrasting the tragedy of a competent person with the success of an incompetent opportunist.

Strictly speaking, it is impossible to write concluding remarks about the preceding commentary on *Mi tío el empleado,* because the commentary is an act in process—the act of structuring—and final comments assume a *fait accompli.* On the other hand, the act-in-process as it appears here is woefully incomplete, since it treats only a very small portion of the text in detailed fashion. The reader of this essay is asked to imagine a great deal of what appears between the selected text fragments; therefore, a few general remarks may help without aggravating the imperfection of our reading.

We have made use of five codes employed by Barthes in *S/Z:* action, enigma, connotative, symbolic, and cultural. We have also used three others, which may be thought of as additional independent codes or as three kinds of cultural codes: chronology, communication, and picaresque.

The action code refers to the series of events that are organized, in the reader's experience, to make the story. In *Mi tío el empleado,* these events are ample in number but are generally similar to each other because they are useful to the narrator, who wishes to make certain people look ridiculous and certain situations look absurd. The episodes, at the beginning of the second volume, that show Count Coveo in different places do not move the story forward, but they do accomplish a cumulative effect similar to that achieved by the other episodes. The comparatively static episodes are of special interest with respect to the picaresque and communication codes.

Given the episodic nature of the novel, the enigma code concerns not only the overall question of Cuevas's future but a number of *micro-récits* as well. Meza also favors withholding from the reader information that the narrator must reasonably have. This propensity is probably inherited from romantic novelists who created suspense in this way. (It is important to note, however, that *Mi tío el empleado* is by no means a romantic novel and, in fact, suffers from very little of the romantic persistence that characterizes much Spanish-American fiction of its time.) Revelations rarely come as a complete surprise, though the narrator sets them forth as if he had not previously offered any hints.

The connotative code is extremely important because it is largely responsible for characterizing Cuevas, the only one who is fully drawn, and for sensitizing us to his transition from a bumbling, opportunistic absurdity to a venal, pompous (though fundamentally insecure) fraud. Naturally, the connotative code also illuminates other characterizations. It is appropriate that Coveo's characterization stands out especially, and our reading certainly makes this kind of person the target of the narrator's satire. It is true, as others have suggested, that Meza's novel may be read as a criticism of colonialism in Cuba. Indeed, one knows that the Cuba referred to is a Spanish colony; however, the connotative code stimulates our sense of a certain kind of person rather than of a political status.

The symbolic code also refers often to the character of Vicente, showing the relationship of some personality trait to a theme of the novel. From the beginning, for example, his expectation of an enviable *destino* (the word is used repeatedly) is implanted as a basic characteristic, and it is also the novel's major theme. At first, we may think that *destino* refers to any kind of job that will provide satisfactory food and shelter; then it becomes apparent that it refers to a bureaucratic sinecure, since Vicente does not know how to do anything. Later, the symbol changes to "seré algo" (I will be somebody), a driving force that remains even after he has achieved wealth. It is through the symbolic code that we make the clearest association with colonialist exploitation. The connotative code illuminates the grasping, inadequate opportunist who is willing to use others to his own advantage; the symbolic code relates the characteristic most clearly to the protagonist's employment and, therefore, to the idea of colonialism.

The cultural code is the most general of all, and it is functional in *Mi tío el empleado*, as it is in all narration, because it evokes the already-experienced. The three specific cultural codes (chronology, communication, picaresque) are especially important in Meza's novel. References to time may be, in some instances, important mainly for ambience, but historical process (rather than mythic time) is essential to the revelation of Vicente's vertical movement in society. That is, time must pass so that Vicente may confront the various circumstances that he is able to exploit.

The communication code is important with regard to contact within the novel (the narrator informs us in what manner communication is effected between characters in the novel) and between the narrator and the reader. The latter is by far the more important because it is so closely related to the picaresque tone. The narrator is overtly aware of the process of narrating, as we see in numerous instances of metalanguage. The change from a speaker using the first person to a speaker using the third person is the greatest communication change within the novel. We know through the communication code that the narrator's relationship with the protagonist changes; we also know that it is never entirely consistent.

The picaresque code provides many of the novel's most pleasing moments. The sense of ridiculousness and unfounded ambition evokes the experience of picaresque tales. The discovery of what the world is like is an important factor in this experience, and, of course, Vicente's drive toward success is another. However, the dynamic factor of the novel (insofar as a single dynamic factor may be distinguished from the total structuration of the work) is the change, within the picaresque code, from the genuinely picaresque to satire. This process is appreciated in a complex of changes that includes the shift from first-person to third-person narration, the transformation of Vicente from unscrupulous rascal to powerful opportunist, and the termination of Vicente's vertical movement (assumed at the beginning of the second part), followed by his appearance in different contexts of Havana society as a wealthy man still trying to be somebody.

7

The Popular-Ethnic Sensitivity

Clorinda Matto de Turner's Aves sin nido

Aves sin nido (1889) is generally thought of as a landmark novel in Spanish-American Indianist literature. Thematically, it establishes a link between the noble savage of romanticism and the exploited native of realism. The author's concept of a novel also embraces characteristics of both romanticism and realism, not so much in combination as in uncomfortable juxtaposition.

Clorinda Matto (1852–1909) was born in the city of Cuzco; after her marriage in 1871 to José Turner, an English physician, she moved to Tinta, another town in the same province. It is important to know, in connection with the thematic concerns of her work, that much of her life was spent in a provincial environment. She was familiar with Lima, but her formation took place where she could witness the injustices denounced in *Aves sin nido* and in her other works, both literary and journalistic.

Early in her career, she began writing *tradiciones*, as a disciple of Ricardo Palma.[1] The nationalistic character of this genre coincided with her interest in creating a Peruvian literature. *Aves sin nido* is the first of three novels produced during an active career marked by political commitment and anticlericalism that eventually led to expatriation and excommunication.[2] The later novels reaffirm her interest in cultivating the "new" fiction (realism and naturalism), but *Aves sin nido* is the book responsible for her fame.

Studies of Clorinda Matto and her work generally agree on two points: first, that *Aves sin nido* is a novel of transition, and, second, that the author and her work deserve more attention than they have been given. It is true, certainly with regard to *Aves sin nido*, that many years of near eclipse followed an early period of attention; on the other hand, a review of the situation at this time reveals a substantial amount of interest in the author and her major novel. Francisco Carrillo says three editions appeared in 1889, in Lima, Buenos Aires, and Valencia. According to Carrillo, the Valencia edition was the one that circulated widely in Spanish America.[3] An English translation appeared in 1904.[4] Then came the period of neglect. The Valencia edition contains a "Juicio crítico" by Emilio Gutiérrez de Quintanilla that is especially important because his critical opinion is contemporary with the appearance of the novel. The essay serves as a bridge between that time and modern interest in the work.

The first modern edition of *Aves sin nido* appeared in 1948. It contains the essay by Gutiérrez de Quintanilla and also is the text used for a later edition by Fryda Schultz de Mantovani.[5] Three doctoral dissertations have been written in the United States on Matto de Turner, one of them during the years of neglect.[6] The most convenient general view of her life and works is found in Carrillo's study; the best analysis of *Aves sin nido* is Antonio Cornejo Polar's introduction to the Casa de las Américas edition.[7] From these studies emerges the idea of *Aves sin nido* as a novel of dubious artistic merit but of considerable interest in the history of Spanish-American literature and culture. Several factors related to the author and to the book combine to attract and hold reader attention. First, the author's crusading zeal is very apparent. Even if we had no biographical information, the novel itself would suggest much about her life and personality. Second, she is obviously aware of the act of making literature; her self-consciousness in this regard is an obvious characteristic of the novel. She thinks of *Aves sin nido* as a tool to be used for a social purpose, but it is nonetheless fiction. Third, she is acutely aware of being Peruvian, and this feeling reinforces her inclination toward realism; it is related to her exposé of what life is really like in the provinces. Fourth, *Aves sin nido* was burned, the author's house was sacked, her printing press was destroyed, and she was excommunicated and exiled. Obviously, what she had to say either infuriated or terrified somebody. Such a violent reaction lends special significance to the novel, and it is important, therefore, to analyze what Clorinda Matto wrote, and how she wrote it, in terms of the period when she created the work. And since the novel owes its fame largely to the author's defense of an oppressed ethnic group, an analysis should take into account the nature of the relationship between author and subject.

In line with the consideration of these questions, I propose to discuss *Aves sin nido* with part of my attention focused on an essay by Arnold Kettle about Charles Dickens and *Bleak House*.[8] The major point of the essay is that Dickens possessed a kind of "popular sensitivity" that differentiates him from "critical realists" in general. The present essay on Clorinda Matto is certainly not going to attempt a comparison between her and Dickens, nor will it force her into a mold more appropriate to another writer. Kettle's essay, however, does suggest some propositions that may illuminate the work of a socially committed novelist in such a way that the experience of reading the book may be more satisfying.

In order to orient the study of *Aves sin nido* with Kettle's essay in mind, it is necessary to consider briefly what his basic propositions are. First, he states his understanding of the difference between "Socialist Realism" and "Critical Realism":

> By *Socialist Realism,* in the field of literature, I assume we mean literature written from the point of view of the class-conscious working class, whose socialist consciousness illuminates their whole view of the nature of the world and the potentialities of mankind. By *Critical Realism* I assume we mean literature written in the era of class society from a point of view which, while not fully socialist, is nevertheless sufficiently critical of class society to reveal important truths about that society and to contribute to the freeing of the human consciousness from the limitations which class society has imposed on it.[9]

Obviously, Clorinda Matto is not a "Socialist Realist" (some would deny that she is any kind of realist), but insofar as her concept of fiction permits, she is a "Critical Realist." There is not the slightest doubt that she is "critical" in the sense defined by Kettle. However, he goes on to distinguish among writers of this group in order to point out the quality identified as "popular":

> Within the general environment of Critical Realism, it seems to me, there are certain writers who—though certainly critical of bourgeois society—remain in their overall sensibility essentially attached to the ways of thinking and feeling of that society. I would put Charlotte Bronte, Mrs. Gaskell, Thackeray and George Eliot within that category. . . . But their sensibility, for all its progressive aspects, seems

to me to be exercised, however critically, within the confines of petty-bourgeois feeling: it does not, even in the case of George Eliot (the best of them), burst the buckles of bourgeois consciousness, though it certainly strains them. Whereas, in a basic and essential way, Emily Bronte and Dickens and Hardy *do* burst the buckles. . . . The latter write from a point of view which can be described not merely in somewhat negative terms as critical but in positive terms as popular, that is to say expressive of the sensibility of progressive sections of the people other than the petty-bourgeois intelligentsia.[10]

Clorinda Matto deals with problems that contain an ethnic ingredient that is not a factor in Kettle's proposition. However, the ethnic factor combines with problems of right-versus-wrong in a way that makes an interesting issue of the author's sensibility. The story of *Aves sin nido* must be seen with some clarity before these matters can be discussed in detail.

The basic story material must be understood as extending over a period of time considerably longer than the plot of the novel. The locale is a small Andean town, Killac. One of the priests of the town, later a bishop, endows his parish not only with a large number of his own progeny but also with useful ideas about how to exploit the local Indians. Indeed, it is apparent that the church cooperates with the civil authority and the judiciary to take advantage of the *indígenas*. The standard form of extortion is to lend money to a peasant—whether he wants it or not—against the wool to be produced by the next shearing. The profit accruing to the lender may be as much as 500 percent. When the peasant cannot pay off his debt, the collector may take his property or even his children, the latter to be sold as slaves. The men of the church also abuse their female parishioners by taking them into the priestly households as servants who satisfy their sexual needs.

Juan and Marcela Yupanqui find themselves threatened by the imminent visit from the collector. Marcela appeals to Lucía, the wife of Fernando Marín, a man of substance and justice who, for business reasons, has come to Killac from the city. Through their attempts to aid Juan and Marcela, the Maríns incur the wrath of the local power consortium—church, civil authority, and judiciary. Agents of the consortium incite mob action against the Maríns. While defending the

Marín house against attack, Juan Yupanqui is killed and Marcela is mortally wounded. Doña Petronila, wife of the civil authority, and her son Manuel, a law student recently returned from the city, also defend the Maríns. Following the attack, the Maríns take in the wounded Marcela and her two daughters, Margarita and Rosalía. Shortly before her death, Marcela shares a secret with Lucía. Later, Manuel, greatly attracted to Margarita, promises the girl that, if Lucía is to be her mother, he will be her brother.

In Part Two, the power consortium chooses Isidro Champí, the parish bellringer, to be scapegoat in settling the Marín affair. Fernando Marín, now assisted by Manuel, undertakes Champí's defense, with some success. Marín then decides he must leave Killac—with Lucía, Margarita, and Rosalía—and Manuel carries out the final acts related to the salvation of Champí. The Marín family reaches Lima after a dramatic train derailment. Manuel soon follows. His proposed marriage to Margarita seems impossible because he is the son of a man who was responsible for the death of her father; however, Manuel overcomes this obstacle by explaining that he is really the son of the bishop. Then Lucía reveals Marcela's secret: Margarita is also the bishop's child.

The transformation of this material into the *récit* is characterized by three conditions that seem basic to all else that may be said about the novel.[11] They are concerned with (1) the conflict between romantic story and realist exposé, (2) the slim line of difference between effective balancing (of Part One and Part Two) on the one hand and dull repetitiousness on the other, and (3) the vacillation between objective narrating in a voice using third-person singular and the confidential tone of a voice using first-person plural.

In her "Proemio" to *Aves sin nido,* the author indicates clearly that she intends to write a novel that is more than a love story meant only to entertain. She believes the novel should show the vices and virtues of a people, condemning the former and praising the latter (p. 37). *Aves sin nido* does indeed do exactly these things. It does not eschew the love story, but does something in addition. Clorinda Matto's concept of realism seems to demand that she expose the evils of society and that she write certain descriptions in excruciating detail.

We learn, for example, on the first page of the novel, that the town square of Killac measures three hundred and fourteen square meters. The details become especially overwhelming when the course of action is interrupted in favor of describing a lady's attire. There are paragraphs that sound something like the commentary at a fashion show. In general, the combination of romanticism and realism indicates a rather hazy notion of the latter and a need to rely on romantic sensibility and plot conventionalities so that the author may feel certain that an interesting story is developing. This anxiety, although its results may be distressing to a present-day reader, attests Clorinda Matto's concern for the successful execution of her craft.

A similar concern is apparent in the problem relating to the two parts of the novel. Francisco Carrillo states categorically that Matto should not have continued the novel beyond Part One.[12] He contends, with considerable justification, that the problems are solved, by that time, about as well as they are ever solved. The virtuous have love and security; the evil have repented or consider themselves defeated. Antonio Cornejo Polar, on the other hand, sees the repetition of the problem in Part Two as an indication that the case of Juan Yupanqui is not unique, that the problem of injustice is collective and permanent, with the power consortium able even to prey on those Indians who have amassed a certain modest wealth.[13] This observation points to one of the most important aspects of the novel. By narrating the second case, the author reaffirms and strengthens her thesis. She also implies the general nature of the problem without insisting overtly on that point. In the interest of dispassionate evaluation, it should be noted that her parallelisms are not always convenient. The derailment of the train, for example, corresponds as a moment of dramatic intensity to the attack on the Marín's house in Part One. The railroad incident may have a certain functional value in emphasizing the isolation of Killac from the center of civilized behavior, but it certainly is not as important in the course of events as the attack is. The rather painful symmetry produced by the ironic twist in the Manuel-Margarita relationship (Manuel promises to be her brother, at the end of Part One; at the end of Part Two, they find out that he really is her half-brother) must be attributed to the author's romantic proclivity. It does appear, however, that she is keenly aware of making a novel and of using it for ideological purposes.

The awareness of making a fiction is apparent also in the narrative point of view. Basically, the narration is accomplished in the third-person singular by someone outside the events narrated. Occasionally this voice makes editorial comments regarding the people or events. For example, when Marcela first seeks aid from Lucía, the narrator advises us that one really has to see these poor people close up and hear their troubles in their native tongue in order to explain the sympathy they arouse (p. 41). Word choice plays an important role in coloring this comment. The poor people are "desheredadas criaturas" (abandoned children), their language is "expresivo," and the sympathy is created in "corazones nobles" (noble hearts). The last modifier is particularly important because it functions in the characterization of Lucía, and at the same time it advises the reader that if he is of noble heart he will react in a sympathetic fashion.

A second type of variation changes the narrative voice to first-person plural. The narrator invites us to see what some character is doing. For example, "Vamos a viajar por un momento en busca del Coronel Paredes, a quien dejamos sentándose a la mesa en casa de Teodora" (p. 149). (Let us go for a moment in search of Colonel Paredes, whom we left sitting at the table in Teodora's house.) The author uses this device to call attention to the simultaneity of events. The narrator finds it necessary, in order to maintain a logical sequence, to remind the reader that certain things happen while others are also taking place. The use of the "we" pronoun is not an invitation to the reader to participate in making the fiction; it simply guides his understanding. It does indicate again that Clorinda Matto was very aware of the act of making a novel, and, indeed, there are moments when she seems to stand away from and view it critically to be sure it is carrying her message. Given this emphasis, it should be helpful to examine three aspects of the novel that relate it to the society in which Clorinda Matto lived: (1) the historical situation and the main points of attack in the novel, (2) the characters as symbols, and (3) the imagery.

HISTORICAL SITUATION AND MAIN POINTS OF ATTACK

The action of *Aves sin nido* takes place over a period of time that includes the assumption of the presidency by Manuel Pardo in 1872. This event is mentioned in a conversation between Fernando Marín and Manuel, the law student (p. 156). Both men expect an improvement in the government of the country. Manuel Pardo was the country's first civilian president, so it was reasonable to expect some fairly basic changes.

For some twenty years following the achievement of independence from Spain, Peru had to withstand the clashing ambitions of its patriot leaders. Then, for most of the period 1845–62, Ramón Castilla maintained a state of relative equilibrium among the varous factions. Guano became a source of wealth and also of corruption. The Castilla years were followed by nearly a quarter century of instability. During the presidency of José Balta (1868–72), a United States citizen named Henry Meiggs turned his attention to building railroads in Peru. Meiggs was one of several nineteenth-century adventurers whose presence in Latin America was a mixed blessing, but he did make considerable progress in constructing a rail system. The influence of this enterprise probably explains the importance in *Aves sin nido* of the trip by train to Lima. The author uses the railroad to emphasize the isolation of Killac. The travelers must make a considerable journey on horseback before reaching the station. Once on the train, they appreciate it as a modern miracle, whizzing along at fifteen miles per hour. The derailment, however, destroys the illusion of convenience.

Balta was deposed and assassinated in a rebellion by the Gutiérrez brothers in 1872. These men were clannish militarists who feared losing their power. They very soon became victims of their own mistakes and of mob violence, but for a brief period they stunned the capital: "There was a feeling of emptiness in Lima. The people's distrust of the Gutiérrez brothers interrupted the life of the city."[14] The backlash was typical of a situation in which each side fears the other. It is referred to as a shameful incident in *Aves sin nido* and is associated in time with Marín's disgust with respect to Isidro Champí's being used as scapegoat for the attack on Marín's house (p. 130). The advent of Manuel Pardo's government must have seemed doubly welcome.

Aves sin nido has three important aspects as a novel of protest: (1) an exposé of how the Indian is exploited, (2) an argument that priests should be allowed to marry so they will not exploit native women sexually, and (3) a revelation of the difference between civilized life in the capital and relative barbarism in the provinces.

Indeed, the novel may be described as anticlerical quite as legitimately as it can be called *indigenista*. The third aspect is in the tradition of Sarmiento's *Facundo*. All three are obviously related to each other; however, it is the third that seems basic in the mind of the narrator:

> Juzgamos que sólo es variante de aquel salvajismo lo que ocurre en Kíllac, como en todos los pequeños pueblos del interior del Perú, donde la carencia de escuelas, la falta de buena fe en los párrocos y la depravación manifiesta de los pocos que comercian con la ignorancia y la consiguiente sumisión de las masas, alejan, cada día más, a aquellos pueblos de la verdadera civilización, que cimentada, agregaría al país secciones importantes con elementos tendientes a su mayor engrandecimiento. [P. 61]

> [It is our opinion that what goes on in Killac, as in all small towns in the interior of Peru, is simply one version of the savagery that always exists where the absence of schools, the lack of a good relationship with the clergy, and the manifest depravity of the few who exploit the ignorance and consequent submissiveness of the masses separate the people more and more from real civilization, whereas if they were integrated into it they would add to the nation elements capable of enhancing its greatness.]

Observations and statements supporting this proposition appear throughout the novel. "Real civilization" is found in cities, especially Lima. Given the historical situation, we may ask how the author can be so hopeful. The probable answer is that her solution to the problem is first of all education. Civic administration is secondary. Education in Lima even becomes a part of the novel's romantic element (p. 120). It is interesting that no specific political references appear until well into Part Two. This fact may indicate a growing awareness of politics on the part of the author. It is important to note, however, that the action of *Aves sin nido* occurs before the war with Chile (1879–83) and, of course, before Clorinda Matto's subsequent support of Andrés Cáceres, whose defeat by Nicolás Piérola led to the author's exile in 1895.

So far as the redemption of the Indian is concerned, obviously it depends on a more honorable authority, and that condition may be brought about by education. An active role for the Indian is not a point of emphasis, though presumably he might participate in a better educational process. The author's respect for the Indian culture is apparent, and good qualities of the Indian are revealed in several places; however, the possibility of improving his lot is slight, in his own opinion and in the author's.

The attack on the lascivious and unscrupulous priest is not so easily related to education. The Cura Pascual (Matto avoids the use of "Padre") is an ignorant man, but presumably he was subjected to an educational process at some time; his predecessor, who became bishop, could not have been entirely without education but was as culpable as Pascual. In a monologue following an interview with Pascual, Lucía Marín recalls having seen admirable priests in the city and concludes her observations with a disparaging use of the term "village priests"—the ultimate opprobrium in *Aves sin nido* (p. 49). Although the solution to the problems criticized in the novel may be deduced to be education, the experience of reading the novel insists on a difference between city life and small town life that is not necessarily and clearly related to schooling.

CHARACTERS AS SYMBOLS

Cornejo Polar has noted that family groups are of considerable importance in the novel because emphasis on them allows women to play an important role.[15] Therefore, it is Marcela who takes the family problem to Lucía Marín, and later it is Martina who pleads the case of Champí; Lucía is the angel of mercy who takes the initiative in the Maríns' involvement with the Yupanqui family; Doña Petronila, even though she is the wife of the *gobernador*, is a salt-of-the-earth type who defies her husband in order to be on the side of justice. In fact, women generically symbolize good against evil. Fernando Marín notes the feminine insistence on justice and mercy, and Lucía corroborates: "—¡Si también las mujeres fuesen malas, esto ya sería un infierno, Jesús!" (p. 164). ("If women were evil too, this would be Hell, dear Lord!")

To say that characters are used as symbols suggests that there is no individualization at all, which is not the case. Uniqueness is accomplished through a special set of interests and problems, as in the case of Manuel, or through the use of a single characteristic like Don Sebastián's byword, *francamente*, which he uses persistently and often illogically. Both men are also symbols, however, and belong to groups of characters that illustrate different aspects of the author's proposition.

Manuel belongs to the civilized urban group. Fernando and Lucía are the basic members of the group. They express their abhorrence of small-town customs (not petty matters, but questions of human rights and dignity). Their opposite numbers immediately label them "outsiders" and stir up the town's wrath against them. Manuel is a native of Killac, but has been away to study law. Upon his return, he is on the side of the Maríns and, like his friends, eventually decides to live in Lima.

Don Sebastián, Manuel's supposed father, is the most visible of the small-town powers. He is uncouth, ignorant, opportunistic, and, ultimately, a coward. His allies share these unlovely qualities in various combinations. His alliance with the Cura Pascual is based on their common insensitivity to the rights and needs of people who are less powerful than they. This characteristic places them in direct opposition to the enlightened city group. By novel's end, they have all been dealt with in one way or another. However, the experience of the novel informs us that they persist where they are; the Maríns and Manuel leave.

Interestingly, Don Sebastián does possess a certain basic kindness that earns the gratitude of his wife, Petronila. This fact provides an important element of shading in a novel that tends strongly to line up the categorically good people against the categorically evil. Petronila provides another shading because she is on the side of right even though she is not from the city. Of course, she is a woman, and that defines her as good. Her function in the novel is to provide a link between the city group and the small-town group. She is described as a diamond in the rough, a kind of woman completely unknown in the coastal area of the country (p. 64).

The Indian is seen through two families, Yupanqui and Champí, and also through comments made directly by the narrator. The Indian's general characteristics are fundamental decency and vulnerability to oppression. He functions as an object of interest from the standpoint of both the urban and the small-town groups. The symbols of enlightenment naturally emphasize the Indian's human qualities; the exploiting group thinks of him as little better than an animal. Throughout *Aves sin nido,* as the two groups react in their respective fashions, the reader experiences an ebb and flow of hope that the Indian's condition may be changed for the better. The Indian does very little of an active nature in this process. He appeals to the enlightened group and, in the incident of the attack on the Marín's house, comes to the defense of his advocates.

The fluctuation of power between the urban group and the small-town group is accompanied by an interesting sequence of observations, direct and indirect, concerning the Indian and his problems:

1. In the "Proemio," the author declares her affection for the "indigenous race," and mentions her first-hand knowledge of Indian customs. She points out their simplicity (in their customs) and refers to the tyranny under which the people live (p. 37).

2. In the narration of the initial scene between Marcela and Lucía, the narrator expresses deep compassion with a somewhat paternalistic tinge. In general, the emphasis is on the Indian's sensitivity, and specifically on Marcela's gratitude (pp. 41, 43).

3. Although the impression created by these early references encourages optimism, the narrator immediately reveals deep pessimism and pleads that God, in his goodness, may decree the extinction of the indigenous race, since it cannot recover its dignity or exercise its right (p. 44).

4. The second entreaty of Marcela intensifies her tragic situation, as she fears that her daughters may be sold into slavery (p. 59).

5. Fernando Marín recalls the sacrifice of Juan Yupanqui, who gave his life because of his gratitude—this in spite of the fact that "they say Indians are ungrateful" (p. 91). In the ensuing dialogue, Fernando and Lucía extend their observations to include the whole ethnic group. Lucía refers to the "rectitude and nobility" of the Peruvian Indians conquered by Pizarro; Fernando explains the effects of an inadequate diet; Lucía speaks of Juan Yupanqui as "unusual," and Fernando asserts that he is not at all unusual and follows with one of the novel's most interesting statements: ". . . si algún día rayase la aurora de la verdadera autonomía del indio, por medio del Evangelio de Jesús, presenciaríamos la evolución regeneradora de la raza hoy oprimida y humillada" (p. 92). (". . . if the day of the Indian's real autonomy should ever dawn, by means of the Gospel of Jesus Christ, we would witness the

regenerative evolution of the race that today is oppressed and humiliated.")

6. In Part Two of the novel, the plight of Isidro Champí's family reiterates and intensifies the experience associated with Juan and Marcela Yupanqui. Then the concern is again changed from individual to ethnic group, as Lucía Marín says: ". . . ¡Pobres indios! ¡pobre raza! ¡Si pudiésemos libertar a toda ella como vamos a salvar a Isidro!" (p. 176). ("Poor Indians! Poor race! If we could only free all of them as we are going to save Isidro!")

7. Fernando assures Lucía of Isidro's innocence, and she responds that she has never doubted it: ". . . sé que cuando hace algo malo el infeliz indio peruano es obligado por la opresión, desesperado por los abusos." (p. 187). ("I know that when the unfortunate Peruvian Indian does something evil, it is because he is driven by oppression or made desperate by abuse.") This affirmation of the Indian's quality parallels the dialogue on pages 91–92 of Part One.

8. Even after Champí gains personal freedom he has no hope for the group. Speaking with his wife, Martina, about the Indian's condition of virtual slavery, he says: "¡La muerte es nuestra dulce esperanza de libertad!" (p. 199). ("Death is our sweet hope of freedom!")

There is no indication at any point that the Indian, as an ethnic group or as an economic class, will undertake his own liberation. The experience of the novel indicates that his situation is close to hopeless. The novel does not rest on this point, however. Since the role of the Indian is relatively passive, the conflict in the narrative exists between the forces of urban enlightenment and those of provincial darkness.

IMAGERY

The most important image in *Aves sin nido* is the one contained in the title, of birds without a nest. It communicates a sense of being abandoned or lost, and its opposite signifies security and protection. In her "Estudio preliminar" to the edition used for the present study, Fryda Schultz de Mantovani notes that the title combines with the general recognition of the work as an *indigenista* novel to suggest the plight of Indian (p. 7). The use of the image, however, is more complicated than that, because several variations on it, used throughout the novel, correspond to the main aspects of the ideology that is part of the experience of reading the book. In several different ways, the meaning of the image relates to the use of characters as symbols.

The novel opens with a rhapsodic recognition of a perfect morning. The second sentence states that one's heart, "tranquilo como el nido de una paloma, se entregaba a la contemplación del magnífico cuadro" (p. 39) ("peaceful as the nest of a dove, surrenders to contemplation of the magnificent scene.") The natural situation in Killac leaves little to be desired. Just a few lines farther along, we are told that little gray doves with ruby eyes nest in the belfry of the church (p. 39). Personified bells also live there and weep for the dead as well as laugh for the newly born. From the very beginning, then, the novel's basic image is related to Christianity and to the life span. Thinking of *Aves sin nido* retrospectively, one is likely to recall Fernando Marín's association of the Indian's freedom with the Christian Gospel (p. 92).

When Margarita, the older Yupanqui daughter, is preparing to live with the Maríns as their godchild, she request that her parents bring her sparrow nests as a remembrance of home (p. 81). This variation suggests the home she is leaving, the possibility of transfer to another home, and also a certain humble simplicity (because of the variety of bird). Shortly afterward, following the death of Juan Yupanqui and the wounding of Marcela, Fernando Marín says: "Margarita, Rosalía, desde hoy esas palomas sin nido hallarán la sombra de su padre en esta casa" (p. 87) ("Margarita, Rosalía, from today on, these doves without a nest will find the shadow of their father in this house.") This use of the image signals his interest in protecting them. Just before Marcela dies, she refers to her daughters as "palomas sin nido" (p. 99) ("doves without a nest.") Her expression of the case is utterly desperate, but Lucía reassures her: "¡Tus hijas no son las aves sin nido; ésta es su casa; yo seré su madre!" (p. 99). ("Your daughters are not birds without a nest; this is their home; I will be their mother!") Here the image shifts from "doves" to "birds." It seems possible that this change might indicate some generalization of the reference; however, there is no immediate indication that the image refers to anyone but the two girls. Clearly, compassion and paternalism are shown here just as they are in the initial interview between Lucía and Marcela. Right at the end of Part One, Lucía excuses herself from a conversation with Fernando, saying that she is going to prepare a shelter for "las dos AVES SIN NIDO" (p. 109) ("the TWO BIRDS WITHOUT A NEST.") The reference is to Margarita and Rosalía; the words are capitalized for the first time.

In Part Two, Manuel enters the realm of the rejected when Lucía tells Margarita she must not marry the son of a man who is responsible for the death of Margarita's father. "Muda y temblorosa permanecía, como una azucena sobre cuyo tallo ha intentado posarse el ruiseñor sin haber plegado las alas, porque la debilidad de la planta le ha hecho continuar el vuelo en busca de mejor asilo" (pp. 147–48). ("[Margarita] stood mute and trembling, like a lily on whose stem a nightingale has tried to rest, but without having folded its wings, because the plant's frailness made it continue its flight in search of a better refuge.") The romantic tone of this variation should not be overlooked or taken lightly. The idyllic, youthful love of Manuel and Margarita is represented in romantic terms, and the import of this aspect of the novel is decidedly positive. It is good, and supports, albeit awkwardly, the position of the enlightened urban group. On the final page of the novel, after Manuel has informed Fernando of his true parentage, Fernando says: ". . . ¡no culpemos a Dios; culpemos a las leyes inhumanas de los hombres que quitan al padre al hijo, el nido al ave, el tallo a la flor!" (P. 211) ("Let us not blame God; let us blame the inhuman laws of men that rob sons of their fathers, rob birds of their nests, rob flowers of their stalks!") This variation includes Manuel among those victimized by the small-town power consortium. He is no longer their enemy only; he is also their victim. Lucía, realizing that the lovers are brother and sister, says: "¡Manuel! ¡Margarita. . . ! ¡AVES SIN NIDO. . . !" (P. 211) ("Manuel! Margarita! BIRDS WITHOUT A NEST!") The title image is repeated as the last words of the novel, capitalized just as they were near the end of Part One. The *aves sin nido* are no longer Margarita and Rosalía but Margarita and Manuel. The reference is not to an ethnic group but to individuals who have been robbed of their right to happiness by evil men. By effecting the change from Rosalía to Manuel, the narrator emphasizes two points of attack, economic exploitation and immoral clergy. To state it another way: variations in the use of the novel's title image, reinforced by imagery that communicates romantic sensibility and the benevolent splendor of nature, emphasize the conflict between civilization and barbarism, in the tradition of Sarmiento and many other Spanish-American writers.

In his remarks about the problems of the Indian as seen in *Aves sin nido,* Cornejo Polar states that Clorinda Matto does not see an economic solution in which the Indian would take an active role; she does not even speak of the ownership of land.[16] He attributes this oversight to the general lack of awareness, during that period of Peruvian history, with respect to such matters. The proposition has merit because she obviously was aware of economic problems, in terms of exploitation, even if she did not think in terms of economic solutions. Cornejo Polar emphasizes her insistence on education as a panacea.[17] In the experience of the novel, however, Christianity—unabused Christianity, that is—seems very important in any solution that may be effected. This religious factor is related to.the humane good will of the urban progressive group.

Questions concerning the improvement of the Indian's condition raise still other questions concerning the author's—or the narrator's— manner of relating to the group she is defending. In this connection, Arnold Kettle's essay on Dickens's popular sensibility can be very illuminating. Of course, Matto is not dealing with the "people" as Dickens is in *Bleak House;* she is concerned with an ethnic group, a fact that introduces other considerations. Nevertheless, seven characteristics of popular sensibility, defined at the end of Kettle's essay, offer a frame for discussing Clorinda Matto's popular-ethnic sensibility as experienced in *Aves sin nido.*[18] Kettle's requirements are that the novel be:

1. Realistic. (The fiction world should be related to the real world in such a way that reading the fiction will help readers cope with reality.) *Aves sin nido* is realistic in this sense because it describes specific incidents of injustice in terms of how the Indian is affected and of what motivates the abusive action. Its suggested solution— or solutions—may or may not be considered practical. In a present-day context, they appear rather ingenuous.

2. Critical. (Objectivity is not the point. The author must not be afraid of using his work to criticize society's evils.) Matto obviously is not afraid. She attacks the power consortium specifically and clearly. The novel sometimes comes close to being an essay. At times, a character sets forth a point; at other times, it is the narrative voice that states the case. The narrative situation of the novel indicates repeatedly that Matto is using the novel as a vehicle for criticism.

3. Non-abstract. (The novel should deal with people, problems, and solutions; it should not be a fiction based on a system of ideas.) One could hardly say that *Aves sin nido* is abstract. On the other hand, there are two characteristics that tend in that direction. First, the narrator's critical attack sometimes reveals an attitude that wants to say "What's wrong with Peru is . . ." In such cases, the narration becomes expository and the impact of real human experience diminishes. Second, the romantic factor in the novel tends to be abstract. It includes conventionalities that have meaning but are not realistic in the sense of the first characteristic in the Kettle list.

4. Non-metaphysical. (The characters should be "interdependent social creatures, historically placed," with "no tendency toward an underlying metaphysical pattern of interpretation.") Here again, *Aves sin nido* complies partially. In spite of the novel's romantic factor, the characters seem real and their actions are credible within the social framework of a place and time. However, they do become symbols in the sense that they reflect various aspects of the problem dealt with. The book is by no means an allegory, but the characters easily fall into groups.

5. Inclusive. (The novel should see "society from below rather than from above." This view will avoid the exclusiveness of the ruling-class or elite sensibility.) This characteristic is consummately important with respect to *Aves sin nido*. In the "Proemio," the author declares her love for the Indian culture. In the fiction text, Indian customs are spoken of as simple and admirable. The narrator describes Rosalía's tears as exactly the same as those shed by the children of kings (p. 50). This comparison may be more significant than it appears at first sight. Lucía and Fernando Marín receive members of the Yupanqui family into their own, without any reference to cultural difference. Except that we see Margarita learning to read, the girls act within the cultural pattern of their foster parents. It is important to point out that, in *Aves sin nido,* the elite sensibility does not belong to the ruling class; however, the assumption is that those with such sensibility should be the ruling class. Then, on the other hand, we have Fernando's mildly optimistic statement about the real autonomy of the Indian (p. 92).

6. Optimistic. (The novel should show confidence in "the capacity of men and women to make their world better.") *Aves sin nido* is

decidedly pessimistic, faith in education notwithstanding. There is no indication at all that the Indian will effect his own improvement. In fact, he sees no hope for himself. He plays an assertive role only in defense of his protector; he recognizes death as his best hope for freedom. Even when Fernando Marín speculates on the Indian's "real autonomy," this condition is dependent on the exercise of Christian faith. Some characters, especially Lucía, express hope in education, but the very structure of the novel indicates that there is no reasonable hope for change, and this structural function is emphasized by the narrator's despair (p. 44). Therefore, the novel is pessimistic with respect to the Indian's role, and also with respect to the possible effectiveness of his would-be redeemers.

7. Historically and linguistically based in existing manifestations of popular culture. *Aves sin nido* observes some ethnic customs, but always from outside. Even if we think of the non-Indians in Killac as, in some sense, "the people," still the view of them is from outside. As for language, Matto uses some typical expressions of both groups, mainly to add interest. In the case of the Indians, these expressions occasionally have cultural meaning; in the case of the small-town power consortium, they function principally as examples of ignorance or awkwardness. At the same time, the novel is national rather than cosmopolitan, and the author obviously intends it to be so. She is also apparently well disposed toward Indian culture. Therefore, *Aves sin nido* may be said to be based as required by this characteristic in the Kettle list, but this fact should always be considered in terms of the fifth characteristic.

Conclusions regarding Clorinda Matto's popular-ethnic sensibility should recognize three stages of Indian-oriented fiction, rather than two: (1) the idealized Indian or noble savage, as in Gertrudis Gómez de Avellaneda's *Guatimozín* and Juan León Mera's *Cumandá;* (2) novels of social protest that deal with social injustice toward the Indian, like Jorge Icaza's *Huasipungo* and Gregorio López y Fuentes's *El indio*. (3) ethnologically-based novels like José María Arguedas's *Los ríos profundos* and Rosario Castellanos's *Oficio de tinieblas* that are "inclusive" in the sense of Kettle's essay. A statement by Joseph Sommers defines the difference between the second and third stages: "Catalina Díaz Puiljá, the Tzotzil protagonist [of *Oficio de tinieblas*], represents a rarity in the Latin-American novel, which almost never succeeds in portraying convincing Indian individuals in the context of their own culture."[19] There is little question about *Aves sin nido* occupying a transitional position between the first and second stages—the position it is usually accorded. This assignment, however, limits—unfairly, I believe—the depth of the author's popular-ethnic sensibility. We should remember her expressed love for Indian culture; this feeling should be added to the knowledge that, as a child, she played with Indian children and spoke their language; then we should recall Lucía's ready acceptance of Marcela as a sister and, finally, add the attempts to portray both Marcela and Martina as women within their families. These portraits are not very successful, but they indicate a certain impulse toward the third stage.

It is also important to remember the author's statement that the novel should be more than a love story intended to entertain. In spite of this declaration, *Aves sin nodo* makes a great deal of the Margarita-Manuel story line, suggesting that the love story persisted in the author's mind as the basic ingredient of a novel. It seems likely that the Margarita-Manuel story flourished while the Marcela and Martina stories withered because Matto's narrative imagination was rather limited. Consequently, she emphasized the well-known, commonplace love story while failing to develop the more original and, therefore, more demanding popular-ethnic stories of the two Indian women.

The plight of the Indian is not the whole story in *Aves sin nido,* of course, or even the basis of the story. It is the catalyst, but, contrary to traditionally accepted notions, the conflict in the novel is between urban enlightenment and small-town obscurantism. In the history of Spanish-American literature, it accords more comfortably with the theme of civilization-versus-barbarism than with the theme of *indigenismo.*

8

Message and Meaning
Federico Gamboa's Suprema ley

Federico Gamboa (1864–1939) is generally and properly thought of as the leading naturalist among Mexican novelists. His most productive years in prose fiction extend from 1892 to 1913, coinciding roughly with the glory and decline of the Porfirio Díaz dictatorship.[1] Undoubtedly his best known novel is *Santa* (1903), a work that owes much of its fame to a sensationalist (for that period) story line—the fallen woman becomes a prostitute and continues her descent through several levels of her profession. This novel's reputation as a scandalous book (more recently shaded toward "camp") has tended to distract attention from its carefully developed story line and rich symbolic code. *Suprema ley* (1896) has also been obscured by its younger sister's flamboyant shadow. Its publication clearly antedates the author's supposed affirmation of a new religious faith in 1902—an act pointed out by Alexander C. Hooker, Jr., in his study of Gamboa, as a turning point in the novelist's use of naturalism.[2] The important difference seems to be that Gamboa was less pessimistic—possibly more idealistic—in the resolution of his later fictions. Whether or not a naturalist novelist must be committed to a pessimistic ending is a question that might be discussed at considerable length. The only relevance to the present study is that criticism of Gamboa's works often turns on the proposition that he was not really a naturalist. The choice of *Suprema ley,* rather than one of the later novels, makes consideration of a religious change unnecessary. There is no doubt that Gamboa was a practicing Roman Catholic, and he apparently did not take his interest in naturalism to be in conflict with his religious beliefs. With or without pessimism, religion is a factor in all his novels.

Studies of Gamboa have tended to deal with his life, the themes of his books, his view of society, and his understanding of naturalism. Analytical criticism has been less frequent.[3] A recent note by Emmanuel Carballo is a good example of contemporary ideas on Gamboa and his novels.[4] Basing his definition of naturalism on his reading of Joaquín Casalduero and Edmond de Goncourt, Carballo finds Gamboa deviating from the naturalist norm in several different ways: he considers him an observer of detail rather than an experimenter; he regards his religious concerns, moral judgments, and explicit preaching as inappropriate to naturalism; he believes Gamboa to have been naturalistic in themes but not in technique. Nevertheless, he thinks Gamboa was a good novelist, with a well-intentioned, bourgeois sensibility, who saw many of the sordid aspects of Mexican reality. The common people, for him, held a certain "exotic" attraction. Carballo says nothing about the naturalist novelist being less objective than the realist. He does note Casalduero's statement that naturalism proposes neither the study of characters nor of types, but of temperaments.

To a very considerable extent, *Suprema ley* accomplishes a study of temperaments. It would be difficult to eliminate the concept of "characters" from an analysis of the novel, because the temperaments, after all, are appreciated in terms of individuals. it is also worth noting that individualization (the discrete, human entity as against a social generalization) is evident in Gamboa as it is in Zola.[5] The tendency toward the study of temperaments (an application of a "scientific" theory) involves the choice of cases that illustrate the point. A delicate balance between the study of characters and the study of temperaments is maintained in *Suprema ley* by the special characteristics of the narrative voice(s). This function can be illustrated by using Roman Jakobson's model of the communication act.[6] There are variations in the sender that appear to be modifications or subdivisions of the omniscient narrator who is outside the story writing about someone other than himself. Such modifications alter the narrative situation and one may wonder, early in the novel, whether or not they contribute to a difference between the treatment of Julio and the treatment of Clotilde. It turns out that Julio is treated as the typical naturalist case but that Clotilde is not, and this difference is related to the balance maintained in the novel between study of character and study of temperament. Jakobson's model can be used to show how the variations function; however, it is necessary, first, to point out the differences between the basic anecdote and the developed plot of *Suprema ley.*

The plot emphasizes the emotional crisis of Julio Ortegal, an insignificant bureaucrat, and his subsequent moral and physical deterioration. Born late into a family identified by the long line of males who have held minor positions in the judicial system, Julio is pampered into ineffectiveness as an individual. He does all the things expected of him and, at the proper time, becomes a minor court official. Following the deaths of his parents, it occurs to him that maybe he should marry. The consequent choice is Carmen, an honest and unspectacular young woman; Julio marries her and they establish a household. Too little income and too many children keep them on the brink of economic desperation. Then Clotilde Granada is brought into court, accused of having murdered her lover. She is exonerated, but has been cut off from her family. Julio befriends her. His kindness and her gratitude lead them into an affair that destroys Julio's marriage and worsens his already weak physical condition. Clotilde becomes reconciled with her family; Julio dies of tuberculosis and of his inability to extricate himself from the trap of alienation.

The major *time* difference between basic anecdote and plot is that the latter begins when Clotilde is imprisoned. Information about the protagonists' earlier lives is supplied by the narrator, in different ways, after this fact. In addition to the time difference, two other factors in the plot development deserve special attention. First, Gamboa's use of detail creates the general ambience of the period and also underlines the meanness of Julio's life, by association with squalid surroundings. Second, the attitudes of Julio and Clotilde develop in such a way that they seem to fall into their love affair rather than seek it. The result is that this passion—the only extraordinary thing that ever happened to Julio—does nothing to enhance his self-esteem, since it is produced by accident rather than by design.

The Jakobson model of the communication act involes six factors, as follows:

A fiction text, of course, contains a very large number of communication acts. It seems reasonable, however, to deal with the total text in terms of the Jakobson model, and later to use the same model as a means of illustrating some of the important variations within the narrative process. First we will consider *Suprema ley* to be one huge communication act.

The sender-receiver line obviously deserves first attention, and particularly in view of the importance of the narrative voice(s) in maintaining the balance between character study and temperament study in the novel to be analyzed. The sender should be understood as three different but related entities, suggested by Wayne Booth: (1) author, (2) implied author, and (3) narrator.[7] The author of *Suprema ley* is rather clearly defined in the observations of Emmanuel Carballo, already referred to. Gamboa belonged to a conservative, traditionalist family. His father had fought against the Juárez government at the time of the French Intervention.[8] The novelist himself supported the Díaz dictatorship, though he was able to see many social problems of the time. He was a diplomat, and served as foreign minister in the Huerta government—the reactionary backlash against the government of Francisco Madero. As a diplomat, he learned to get along well with people, and became highly cosmopolitan in his awareness of literature. Carlos González Peña points out Gamboa's interest in new people and new things, in spite of his basically traditionalist attitude.[9] It is not difficult to imagine a receiver—a reader completely exterior to the text—with similar characteristics. This correspondence, however, is more relevant to an author named Federico Gamboa than it is to a novel entitled *Suprema ley*.

There are obvious points of contact between the author and the implied author, but it is important to note that the implied author may vary greatly in two or more novels by the same author. The implied author of *Suprema ley* believes that the established social institutions of his culture are good and that they exercise a potentially redemptive function. This function operates for Clotilde, but not for Julio—a difference that is perfectly credible as explained by the narrative study of the two temperaments. (Clotilde's separation from her family is basically accidental, and her orientation is always toward reunion. Julio, the mediocrity, is pulled into the affair by his need for some kind of distinction; separation from his family causes him to feel more guilt than regret.) The point is that *Suprema ley*'s implied author assumes there are forces in society that are capable of destroying established institutions. He is also aware of widely practiced vices like gambling and excessive drinking, and tends to regard them as foolish and futile. He obviously is well acquainted with the bureaucracy and is sensitive to its inadequacies.

The implied author is close to the narrator is *Suprema ley,* since the basic narrative position is outside the story. Narrator is different from implied author, however, because the narrator determines how the action is rendered (to borrow a term from Brooks and Warren); that is, the narrator controls the techniques of narration, though he may share the implied author's view of the reality portrayed. In dealing with the court officials, he is inclined to use a put-down that has a judgmental effect—for example, "El juez llegó a su hora, es decir, tarde"[10] ("The judge arrived at the usual time, that is to say, late.) He achieves a similar tone on certain occasions when he is narrating in third person, but actually in lieu of the person whose case he is revealing. In such cases, his language takes on a colloquial coloring through the use of cliché, as when he is describing Julio's selection of Carmen: "Carmen Terno se llamaba la vencedora, quien se acercaba a los veinte años, sana y limpia que era una gloria verla" (p. 17). (The name of the winner was Carmen Terno, almost twenty, so healthy and pure that she was a joy to behold.)

The narrator chooses to emphasize unpleasant details of the setting as a means of intensifying the ugliness of a situation. Julio's reaction after the seduction (near rape) of Clotilde is underlined by a description of the carriage in which it happened: "la agravante del coche sucio y mojado por la lluvia; un cristal roto, grasientos los cojines" (p. 287) (the exacerbation of the dirty carriage, wet because of the rain; a broken window, grimy cushions.) Although, in many instances, the third-person narrator seems very close to a character, there are times when he withdraws to a clinical position, examines the situation carefully, and even forecasts what a character will do later on: "Muchas ocasiones, cuando ya su drama carecía de remedio, achacó a esta condescendencia el origen de la catástrofe" (p. 97). (On many occasions, when the course of his drama could not be altered, he imputed to this condescension the beginnings of the whole catastrophe.) On p. 274, the narrator actually detaches himself to explain, with a "No digo . . . ," but this narrative position evolves within the same paragraph into a third-person exposition of Julio's attitude, stating the case as if the protagonist's thoughts were being transposed into the narrator's language. It is interesting to note that the narrator virtually concedes his role to the implied author and then reclaims it. Equally interesting, in the same passage, is another variation, one in which the narrator is obviously speaking *for* Julio, but it is doubtful that Julio would be *thinking* these thoughts (pp. 275–76). Rather, they seem to have turned into the thoughts of the implied author, stated as a proposition intended for examination in the naturalist manner. A similar investigative approach takes the form of a psychological exposition, later in the novel, with reference to Julio's and Clotilde's attitudes toward their love affair (pp. 423–28). In this case, the narrator uses the first-person plural to generalize some of his observations, then shifts to a third-person impersonal ("se") to create greater distance between himself and the characters.

We may think of an implied reader who fits into the "receiver" position in Jakobson's model.[11] This reader stays close to the narrator as he approaches or draws away from the characters, and is assumed to be ready to adapt to dialogue, pure narration, or exposition of a case. The reader presumably will join the narrator in judgmental attitudes. The characteristic of adaptability on the part of the reader is demanded by the nature of the contact. It is not enough to say that the contact is a bound series of printed pages called a "novel." These printed pages themselves include different forms of contact that anticipate different kinds of reaction. The *code,* on the other hand, tends to consolidate rather than diversify the reader's role. It is orthodox, literary Spanish of the period. The most important modification that may be called a sub-code is the occasional shading that has a judgmental or hyperbolic effect.

The most complicated problem is the *message.* Hooker says that the "fundamental concept" of *Suprema ley* is contained in a passage that incorporates the title.[12]

> El amor está lleno de sorpresas; preséntase cuando menos se le espera y bajo todas las formas; arrolla y domina; no conoce resistencias ni parentescos ni obligaciones; vence a todas las leyes, las divinas y las humanas, porque es él la suprema ley! [pp. 160–61]

> [Love is full of surprises; it presents itself when one least expects it, and it comes in all forms; it overwhelms and dominates; it does not recognize resistance or relationships or obligations; it conquers all laws, divine and human, because it is itself the highest law.]

These opinions are attributed to Berón, one of Julio's professional associates, who is given to delivering disquisitions of this kind. Indeed, it may be taken as a superficial description of what happens to Julio, but certainly not of what happens to Clotilde. Its function in the story is very interesting because it appears, not as a quotation, but as a report by the narrator of what Berón says. Immediately after this passage, the narrative manner changes back to dialogue, with Berón addressing Julio. The passage quoted is, in effect, a kind of summary of what Berón presumably said during part of an extended dialogue. It would be reasonable to think of Berón as the sender, Julio as the receiver, and the narrator's summary as the contact. This formulation changes the implied reader into a text act reader removed from the context of this subordinate communication act.[13] The narrative process focuses first on characterization, then on termperament, and after that, on characterization again.

The passage quoted is clearly a subordinate communication act and should not be taken as a substitute for, or summary of, the overall communication act that is *Suprema ley*. The message of the novel may be thought of as a series of propositions concerning the nature and power of love. Message is very different from meaning, which takes into account all aspects of the communication act.[14] The message is sent in many different ways—all within the possibilities, of course, of the contact. Thinking in terms of the power of love as a theme, the message appears in thirteen principal propositions:

1. The narrator reveals Julio's thoughts regarding the innocent love of childhood, followed by the disturbing presence of Clotilde in his reverie (p. 82).
2. A prisoner realizes the redemptive power of love. The narrator summarizes part of the prisoner's story of his life (p. 127).
3. The narrator analyzes Julio's attitude, pointing out his fear of the passion he senses, his ignorance of love, and his natural desire to experience it (p. 137).
4. In a conversation with Clotilde's father, Julio reveals—through the narrator's description—a morbid curiosity in Clotilde's past and a corollary desire to possess her (p. 147).
5. The "suprema ley" passage quoted above (pp. 160–61).
6. A reprise of a Biblical quotation by Berón, remembered by Julio,

that gives scriptural authority to the notion of *femme fatale* (p. 170).

7. Clotilde's wishful thinking (her thoughts reproduced in third person by narrator) finds a refuge in her religious training and concludes that Julio will leave her alone and return to his family (pp. 251–52).

8. In a discourse on the disappearance of love, the narrator indicates the effective end of the Julio-Carmen marriage (pp. 262–63).

9. In a reverie (reported in the intimate third person by the narrator), Julio recalls the Garden of Eden story and contemplates his guilt (pp. 276–78).

10. The narrator sets forth Clotilde's attitude after she is deeply involved in the affair with Julio (again the intimate third person approaches interior monologue). She knows she loves him, recognizes her guilt, but still cannot believe that a person will be condemned to hell for having loved, even though the love be illicit (p. 304).

11. Julio breaks ties with his family completely in order to save his love affair (narrative summary, p. 376).

12. In conversation with Berón, Julio, fearing separation from Clotilde, changes the "suprema ley" statement: "—Es una equivocación, Licenciado; la única suprema ley es el dolor!" (p. 474). (It is a mistaken idea, Licenciado; suffering is the highest law.)

13. Julio, now alone, explains to a poor watchman how Clotilde's confession to a priest put an end to their love affair, and says he cannot understand how a priest can prohibit love (pp. 534–35).

The meaning of the communication act depends on the message conveyed in these thirteen propositions and on all the other aspects of the model, including the context. There is a context within the communication act itself and a context outside the act. The latter takes into account the complex society of the middle years of the Díaz dictatorship, during which the author was a member of the establishment. The interior context takes into account the attitudes of the implied author as expressed by the narrator and of the reader who corresponds to him. The relatively new interest in psychology is an important factor in this context, as is the skeptical view of bureaucracy combined with acceptance of an orderly, if repressive, political organization. This context also incorporates the ambience of the city at a particular time in its history, including its entertainment media as well as its home life.

If the series of passages on the theme of love may be taken as the message, this message has meaning only in terms of the context and the way the message is sent. The meaning seems to depend to a great extent on variations in the narrative procedure that affect the characterization and the study of temperament. This phenomenon can be illustrated by describing a series of subordinate communication acts.

The basic presentation of Julio Ortegal takes place in the first chapter, beginning in an office setting and using the narrator's knowledge of his past to furnish all the information needed (pp. 12–21). Substituting particularities of the case in the Jakobson model, we have this scheme:

> *context:* characterizations
> of Julio's co-workers
> *message:* Julio's biography

sender: narrator
close to implied ————————————————— *receiver:* implied
author   reader interested in
                                                                         bureaucratic types

> *contact:* summary
> *code:* standard Spanish
> for period and author's
> social milieu, with some
> derogatory expressions

This passage is a normal procedure used by realist and naturalist novelists as a basis for characterization. The ambience is established before the biographical section begins. The "code" indicates the narrator's (and the implied author's) lack of respect for the protagonist. The message contains information that suggests Julio's temperament—a mediocrity frustrated without even being aware of his frustrations. Although the language occasionally suggests a closing of the gap between narrator and protagonist, the scornful tone maintains an emotional separation.

The essential information regarding Clotilde Granada's past is presented in a very different way (pp. 43–47). It is revealed in the course of examination by Julio, following her arrest.

context: questioning in
court by Ortegal
message: Clotilde's
illicit love

sender: Clotilde;
narrator's para-
phrase of Clotilde
———————————————————————
receiver: Ortegal; im-
plied reader interpret-
ing paraphrase

contact: summary and
scene
code: standard Spanish

Whereas the presentation of Julio is objective, with great distance between the narrator and Julio, the presentation of Clotilde places her in a give-and-take situation with another character. Scene and summary alternate, in contrast to the predominance of summary when Julio is first presented. The passage analyzed here is more a study of character than of temperament, as far as the woman is concerned. On the other hand, Julio Ortegal's response as receiver reveals an interest that is overtly sympathetic but that suggests he is aware of dealing with an unfamiliar kind of person. This reaction not only serves to set forth his own temperament but also, because of this sense of unfamiliarity, focuses attention on the temperament of Clotilde. When the narrator paraphrases in third person, condensing Clotilde's words, he seems closer to her than he is to Julio, in the latter's introductory scene, specifically because the code does not include derogatory expressions.

The presence of the implied author is felt more intensely in the interpolated story of Apolonio, a convicted murderer. He is a member of the lower class, a victim of the social framework that defines his position, his values, and his fate. In addition to the experience of this story in its own right, we appreciate its influence on Julio's reaction to Clotilde's plight, since he is close enough to see all the horror of Apolonio's execution and the time immediately preceding it. Apolonio has no interest in religion, but a priest leads him into confession by asking him to tell the story of his life (pp. 125–30).

context: situation
preliminary to
Apolonio's execution
message: Apolonio's
biography

sender: Apolonio   *receiver:* priest and
and narrator   implied reader

contact: summary
and scene
code: standard Spanish

Major interest in this passage focuses on the sender. When the narrator's third-person voice substitutes for Apolonio's part of the dialogue, it is not in the nature of a paraphrase of his presumed words, but more like an exposition and commentary on his life. In the presentation of Julio, the narrator was separated from the protagonist by his feeling of disrespect. In the case of Apolonio, the narrator is separated by an objective position that is almost clinical. He seems to explain to an implied reader what life is like for poor people like Apolonio, bringing out points that Apolonio would not make if he were simply talking about himself. Apolonio's speech is hardly differentiated from the narrator's explanation—nothing more than a diminutive, like "cervecita" (p. 125), for example. The language of the narrator himself changes as much or more in a few instances when he moves toward paraphrasing. However, this tendency never really takes hold, so Apolonio's story becomes a case history—not an unexpected phenomenon in a naturalist novel. In the present case, the Apolonio episode, taken as a whole, contributes to the characterization of Julio by supporting his inclination to help Clotilde.

Julio is pushed closer to the brink of disaster when Clotilde's father asks him to receive and deliver to Clotilde a monthly allowance to be sent by her father. Again Julio's temperament comes into prominence as he experiences a sense of power cloaked in the rhetoric of helping someone (pp. 141–47).

> *context:* Julio ill from Apo-
> lonio episode and association
> of it with Clotilde's fate
> *message:* Agustín Granada's
> version of Clotilde's story

sender: Granada ———————————————————————— *receiver:* Ortegal
and narrator   and implied reader

> *contact:* dialogued interviews
> —scene with intercalated
> summary
> *code:* standard Spanish;
> Granada's is flowery

The sender role is dominated by Granada. Naturally, Julio speaks. What he says does not constitute part of the message unless we turn the model around every time the dialogue changes, so making Julio an alternating sender. Preserving the sense of the interview taken as a whole, the narrator's intervention serves only to abbreviate the dialogue. Granada's "sub-code" (his courtly speech) is a very important part of the meaning of the passage because it enhances Julio's appreciation of the circumstance as extraordinary. That is, Granada's manner is impressive to Ortegal. The context shows him in an extremely vulnerable position.

Once exonerated, Clotilde lives with the Ortegal family until she realizes the nature and extent of Julio's interest in her. Then she establishes a residence of her own. After going to her new quarters, she takes account of the situation, recognizing Julio's passion, her own love for him, and the related problems (pp. 247–53).

> *context:* Clotilde, separated from
> others, evaluates her situation
> *message:* Clotilde's reaction
> to new environment

sender: narrator
close to implied ———————————————————————— *receiver:* im-
reader   plied reader

> *contact:* narrator's analysis, plus
> questions that could reflect
> Clotilde's thoughts
> *code:* standard Spanish

This passage is remarkably different from the early presentation of Clotilde. Here she is not in contact with another character, and the narrator's analysis tends toward the clinical. Some occasional questions may be taken to reflect or paraphrase Clotilde's verbal formulation of the problems before her. If this sender identification were developed in the narrative process, Clotilde might well become the receiver, in a kind of conversation with herself. However, this possibility remains only a suggestion, and the questions are equally plausible as formulations set forth by the narrator and then answered or discussed by him, with the direction clearly toward the implied reader rather than toward a character in the story. The effect is that attention is focused on the aspects of the problem rather than on the plight of an individual. This passage is the most intensely clinical point in the treatment of Clotilde. Subsequently, the narration emphasizes her character rather than her temperament, and builds toward her reconciliation (or redemption).

When Julio's affair with Clotilde becomes flagrantly apparent, the situation of the deserted wife and children takes on added importance in the story. The adherence of both author and implied author to established institutions makes the survival of the Ortegal family (without Julio, of course) almost a foregone conclusion. The instrument of salvation is the devotion of the first-born, Julito, to his mother. There are many details and several useful passages that might be pointed out in this connection, but a very short and significant one is the first description of the relationship (p. 347).

> *context:* Julio gives money to family, but otherwise ingores them
> *message:* Julio reads to his mother

sender: narrator ————————————————————— *receiver:* implied reader

> *contact:* summary
> *code:* standard Spanish, imperfect tense

The particular value of this passage is in a detail of the message. The narrator uses the imperfect tense to describe what habitually went on in the Ortegal family at this time, and pictures Carmen sewing while Julito studies or reads her a serial novel, "de esas que conmueven a las mujeres y a los niños por lo enmarañado de la trama y lo bien parada que a todos tiros queda la virtud" (p. 347) (one of those that move women and children because of the entanglements of their plots and how well virtue bears up under all attacks.) There is, therefore, another (subsubordinate) communication act described by the narrator, one in which Julito is the sender, Carmen is the receiver, the contact is a melodramatic novel, the code is unknown, the context is an abandoned mother and son, and the message is whatever the contents of the novel may be as Julito reads it. We know only what the narrator says about it, but that is enough to identify a familiar kind of text. It is interesting that what happens to Carmen and her children in the rest of *Suprema ley* is remarkably similar to the kind of novel the narrator describes in this passage. The effect is that Julio is separated from his family in more than one way—that is, the story of Julio follows a naturalist line while the story of his family relates an idealized, virtue-rewarded situation. It makes the Julio-Clotilde study look even more like a case history.

The disruption of the family and the virtue of the mother-son relationship are emphasized in a brief passage in which Julito describes the ceramics school to which he has been admitted (pp. 358–59).

> *context:* Julito seeking gainful
> employment
> *message:* description of school
>
> *sender:* Julito ——————————————— *receiver:* Carmen
>
> *contact:* scene
> *code:* standard Spanish

Julito's enthusiasm is reassuring to Carmen and indicates his maturity. An aspect of secondary interest is the usefulness of the passage as an indication of the implied author's ideas about education. Julito's enthusiasm is founded on the practical, job-oriented nature of the school. There is no derogatory shading by the narrator, so it seems safe to assume that a point is being made about education. However, it is worth noting that the narrator, in this case, allows a character to state the case. It is not easy to find him so relaxed in explaining the Julio-Clotilde relationship. More frequently he seems anxious to control the differentiating lines between his two characters. The present scene, of course, emphasizes the alienation of Julio by focusing on the growing maturity of his son. In combination with the much earlier comments derogating Julio's profession, it suggests that the latter might have fared better as a tradesman. However, his temperament would never have permitted it.

The plot crisis (not necessarily the major point in the study of characters or temperaments) comes when Clotilde's Aunt Carlota arrives in Mexico City to act as intermediary between Clotilde and her family. Her arrival immediately spearates the lovers, since Julio cannot spend nights with Clotilde, and threatens an eventual break. The basic communication of this change is a letter from Agustín Granada to his daughter (pp. 480–86).

> *context:* Carlota and Clotilde
> alone in latter's home
> *message:* Clotilde's father's
> proposed reconciliation

sender: Carlota ————————————————————————— *receiver:* Clotilde
reading letter

> *contact:* letter
> *code:* histrionic Spanish

The code is more important here than in any of the other passages analyzed. The exaggerated emotions expressed in the letter place the Clotilde-family relationship in a class with the saga of Julio's wife and children. Julio is left unredeemed and, apparently, unredeemable.

After Clotilde makes the final break with Julio, he goes to the neighborhood of her house. A sleepy watchman is the only person available for company, so Julio tells him his story (pp. 531–36).

context: Julio separated from
Clotilde and from family
message: Julio's view of
affair (reprise)

sender: Julio _____ *receiver:* watchman
and narrator   and implied reader

contact: scene and summary
code: standard Spanish

The words actually spoken by Julio are little more than introductions
to the narrator's summary of what Julio talks about. The predominant
theme is Julio's need to justify his actions and to blame someone for
his most recent loss. If the communication act were stated with the
dialogue reversed, that is, with the watchman in the sender position,
the message is the only other component of the diagram that would be
changed. The watchman's role in this passage is to emphasize the
absurdity of Julio's position. The watchman has a common-law wife
and some children. He is attached to them and does not see anything
complicated about the conjugal relationship. Julio's discourse simply
bores him.

The extraordinary factor that entered Julio's life has vanished. He
is out of contact with the institutions of the world he lives in.
Spiritually, he is destroyed. There is a suggestion of possible reconciliation with his family, but his physical demise comes before that can
take place.

Consideration of the series of propositions concerning love as the
overall message of *Suprema ley* seems accurate and, at the same time,
very inadequate. It is not sufficient, for example, to explain Julio's
dilemma by saying that he is the victim of the power of love. In fact,
the experience of the novel emphasizes his insignificance more than
the power of love. The dynamic factor in the novel (the principal
factor in the transformation of basic anecdote into developed plot) is
not the definition of the role of love but the changing idiosyncrasies of
the sender. The passages examined in terms of the Jakobson model
indicate that the sender varies in such a way that the distance between
narrator and character at times may indicate a clinical evaluation or at

other times may reflect a more personal involvement. A few differences in the code (far fewer than might have been advantageously used) contribute to the effect; basically, the sender variation sets Julio apart from the others. He alone is not saved by some form of reconciliation. Gradually, the experience of the novel involves awareness of Julio as a mediocrity whose emotional inclinations are unknown even to himself. The force that leads to his destruction is not the power of love—or certainly not as it is explained in any of the propositions made in the novel—but his deep need to stand out from the mediocrity that identifies him. To the extent that this need expresses itself in a bizarre love affair, the message of the novel is indeed the series of propositions concerning love. On the other hand, it might be better to say that the message is an alternating personal and clinical view of Julio, in which the clinical aspect becomes dominant.

There are moments in the novel when the view of Clotilde is also clinical, and the experience of the work admits briefly the possibility of alternating views of two characters, balanced against each other. However, Clotilde achieves reconciliation, and reasonably so within the context of the novel as a whole. It might be possible to think of her as a case study, but it is much easier to think of Julio in this way because, gradually, his plight becomes more important than his person—the study of a temperament is more impressive than the character study of a man named Julio. This development is the meaning of the communication act, because it synthesizes the experience of the novel.

9

A Process of Aesthetic Regionalism
Gonzalo Picón-Febres's El sargento Felipe

Gonzalo Picón-Febres (1860–1918) dedicates his major novel, *El sargento Felipe* (1899), to the "honorable and industrious people of Venezuela, the real victims of our civil wars."[1] The reference, as exemplified in the novel, is to those people who are caught up in civil strife against their will and against their best interest. Specifically, Felipe Bobadilla is a small farmer who is modestly but comfortably well off. The historical setting is the time of Matías Salazar's rebellion against the dictator Antonio Guzmán Blanco. Felipe is conscripted and becomes a sergeant in the government forces. During his absence, his property and his family are destroyed. The author's prose style and the general tone of the novel indicate that, although the book may be dedicated to a relatively unpretentious sector of Venezuelan society, it is addressed to a more sophisticated audience, one that would appreciate the combination of fine writing with the portrayal of regional customs.

The *criollista* tendency is strong in *El sargento Felipe*—that is, the inclination to emphasize typical, regional customs, thus distinguishing Spanish-American culture from cosmopolitan, Europeanized society. The experience of the novel, however, becomes more complicated than the appreciation of local color. The rural factor takes on a bucolic quality similar to some *modernista* poetry. At the same time, Felipe's tragedy relates him to the Martín Fierro archetype. These two conditions suggest two necessary components of a satisfactory analysis of the novel: (1) a consideration of the story structure to see how the archetypal suggestion is communicated, and (2) an examination of

175

the relationship between the bucolic mode and the regionalistic mode. Two stanzas from *Martín Fierro* introduce Dillwyn Ratcliff's discussion of *El sargento Felipe* in his *Venezuelan Prose Fiction*.[2] They assert, plaintively, that the protagonist once enjoyed the good life, only to have his home destroyed during his enforced absence. Ratcliff later spends considerable space on the regionalistic scenes that seem to have attracted most readers of Picón-Febres's novel: the tavern that is the source of both drink and song, a rural wedding, the village priest who enjoys dancing, the harvest, a threatened fight at a party, and, above all, the arrival of the military recruiters.[3] It is significant, however, that Ratcliff's comments, which are more descriptive than analytical, begin with a reference to the Martín Fierro figure, a more fundamental aspect of *criollismo* than the typical scenes. It is reasonable to speculate that Picón-Febres, because he advocated a "national" literature, was very aware of portraying the typical scenes while subconsciously conforming to a Spanish-American archetype.

Pedro Orgambide and Roberto Yahni, in their excellent essay on *Martín Fierro,* point out that the narrator-protagonist frequently states that his own fate is typical of many.[4] This generality accords with the dedication by Picón-Febres, and Ratcliff cites similar cases in Venezuelan literature.[5] The stories of Martín Fierro and Felipe Bobadilla share several characteristics: both men enjoy comfort, a home life, and a sense of independence; they are separated from this situation by a circumstance exterior to their needs and aspirations; the original situation is destroyed during their absence; on returning, they find no way to recover what has been lost. The protagonists respond to the new situation in different ways, but with similar significance. Martín Fierro chooses exile and goes to live among the Indians. (Reference here is to the first part of *Martín Fierro,* which is the fundamental story. The second part, his return, repeats many aspects of the first, transforming the story into an appreciation of a basic social change—the disappearance of a way of life.) Felipe kills his specific enemy and then kills himself—a denouement probably influenced by the author's awareness of naturalism. The protagonist's vengeance is exercised on a specific person, but his real enemy, like Martín Fierro's, is society. Both protagonists resemble the scapegoat archetype; they suffer in place of society rather than in place of the king. The importance attached to their sense of independence, in their original situations, lends greater significance to the fact that they are society's victims. Their stories are told—and seen—within a framework of the nineteenth century, and the scapegoat is translated from a mythic mode to a low mimetic mode (the terminology is borrowed from Northrop Frye).[6] This transition into the commonplace emphasizes the regional, folkloric customs pictured in *El sargento Felipe*.

Although the novel's similarity to *Martín Fierro* is its most important *criollista* characteristic, the typical scenes probably arouse initial awareness of the book's regionalistic character. All critics mention these scenes. Ratcliff notices both factors. Kessel Schwartz considers it a historical novel and also notes the folkloric scenes.[7] Rafael Di Prisco, referring to Gonzalo Picón-Febres along with other Venezuelan novelists of the nineteenth century, says that their work is more useful for a history of ideas than for its contribution to a literary tradition.[8] However controversial this judgment, it indicates the importance of the novel as social commentary. *El sargento Felipe* expresses the author's disgust with regard to the constant unrest in Venezuela, and his intrusions into the narration make the point clear. The novel does indeed suffer from such intrusions and also from occasional melodrama and schmaltz. However, Picón-Febres does not cause characters to speak his lines; he places them in a situation that communicates his position. This situation is defined not only by the events that occur but also by the narrator's prose style.

Mariano Picón-Salas says that Picón-Febres, in his novels following *El sargento Felipe,* becomes so concerned about eloquent style that the orator dominates the novelist.[9] He refers to the rural freshness of *El sargento Felipe,* but fails to note the beginnings of stylistic elaboration. There are, in fact, two prose styles in the novel. One establishes the bucolic quality of Felipe Bobadilla's basic situation. This mode is hardly surprising for the period and especially in the work of an author who had written Parnassian poetry.[10] Static portraits of idealized rural life are not at all exceptional in *modernista* verse. Picón-Febres accomplishes a similar impersonal view of Felipe's situation by using the imperfect tense to describe his daily activities, thereby making his good life appear general rather than specifically relevant to a single character. Later, the narration becomes more specific with reference to the course of events. The style then is not poeticized by rhetorical devices, though it might be accused of overstatement.

With these general observations in mind, it is possible to appreciate, by examining the narrative structure, how the Martín Fierro archetype is developed and communicated to the reader. Tzvetan Todorov, in *Littérature et Signification,* explains the operation of *micro-récits* in *Les liaisons dangereuses:* "Le récit entier est constitué par l'enchainement ou l'emboitement de micro-récits."[11] Each of the *micro-récits* is composed of elements that can be classified under a limited number of generic titles. Todorov then makes a table of "propositions" that shows their paradigmatic and syntagmatic relationships. In the case of *El sargento Felipe,* it is helpful to observe how two *micro-récits* function in a manner similar to arithmetic addition, making a sum that is the *récit* as a whole.

	Felipe owns a farm.	Conditions of war may destroy the farm.	Matías & F.'s family may save farm.	Property lost during F.'s army service.
+	Felipe has a family.	Don Jacinto plans to seduce Encarnación.	Matías wishes to marry Encarnación.	Matías burns F.'s home, trying to harm Don Jacinto.
=	Felipe enjoys a good life.	Military conscription removes F. from control of situation.	F. murders Don Jacinto.	F. commits suicide.

The statements made in the preceding diagram indicate the story of *El sargento Felipe* when they are read horizontally. That is, the syntagmatic (diachronic) component of the novel is apparent when the scheme is read horizontally. However, the three horizontal lines do not represent a 1-2-3 sequence, but a 1-plus-2-equals-3 sequence. This structure, therefore, differs from that of *Les liaisons dangereuses,* as analyzed by Todorov, and it seems probable that the difference is caused by the fact that society, not an individual, is the real antagonist in *El sargento Felipe,* as well as by the presentation of Felipe as a recognizable archetype closely related to a major social problem in Spanish America. The *récit* of *Les liaisons dangereuses* is based on the actions and reactions of two people with respect to each other.[12] It is interesting to note that Todorov's "propositions" are in terms of actions and the consequences of these actions. The "propositions" in the schematic representation of *El sargento Felipe* tend to refer to general circumstances as frequently as to specific acts. This difference seems reasonably in accord with the appreciation of society as enemy. For the sake of clarity, each horizontal line of the scheme should be seen in some detail. In the top line, Felipe owns a farm (circumstance) that suffices for his material welfare. Rumors of civil war (circumstance) threaten this material comfort because the country people know that conscription is arbitrary and a man may be taken from his home without notice. Felipe knows that, during his absence, his nephew Matías may be able to take care of the farm with the help of Felipe's wife and daughter (circumstance). However, while he is away, marauding soldiers steal or destroy much of this property (series of acts that, because they are not performed by any of the main characters, take on the quality of a general circumstance rather than function purely as an act in the *récit*).

The middle horizontal line must be understood as concurrent with the top line, not as subsequent to it. In addition to the farm, Felipe has a wife and daughter (circumstance) who share with him a satisfactory family life. This happy situation is threatened by Don Jacinto's relentless pursuit of daughter Encarnación, who seems inexplicably interested in him (circumstance). Felipe's nephew, Matías, would like to marry Encarnación, but she finds him unattractive (circumstance). When Matías discovers Encarnación and Jacinto trysting in the kitchen of Felipe's house, he locks them in and sets fire to the place (act). Jacinto escapes and assumes the role of rescuer, taking Encarnación and her dying mother into his home.

The bottom horizontal line is the sum of the other two. Given the ownership of his farm and the pleasure of his family, Felipe enjoys a good life (circumstance). Then he is conscripted into the military forces of Guzmán Blanco (act). When he is discharged, he returns to the scene of his former good life and murders Don Jacinto (act). Then he jumps off a cliff to his own death (act).

The acts, as different from the circumstances, are concentrated mainly in the bottom line. The most notable exception is the last "proposition" of the middle line, which refers to Matías's incendiary act of vengeance. It would be possible to place a circumstance rather than an act in this position, by referring to his state of jealousy; however, the statement of the act is important in identifying Don

Jacinto as a specific object of vengeance. It is logical, of course, that the bottom line should consist mainly of acts (albeit of a passive nature, in the act of conscription). This line represents what the protagonist does. The top line and the middle line represent, for the most part, circumstances that lie behind the acts of Felipe. This structure, therefore, communicates a basic circumstance that forces Felipe to act in a certain way.

An examination of the vertical columns suggests that a generic identification should be found for each of the four. The first column on the left represents Felipe's basic condition, one of security. The second column represents his anxiety, or the threat to his security. The "propositions" of the third column indicate hope—that is, of possible alleviation of the threat. The fourth is the line of defeat, or ultimate loss. Therefore, the following relationships may be noticed:

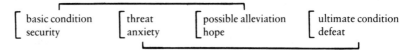

$$\begin{bmatrix} \text{basic condition} \\ \text{security} \end{bmatrix} \quad \begin{bmatrix} \text{threat} \\ \text{anxiety} \end{bmatrix} \quad \begin{bmatrix} \text{possible alleviation} \\ \text{hope} \end{bmatrix} \quad \begin{bmatrix} \text{ultimate condition} \\ \text{defeat} \end{bmatrix}$$

The basic condition relates to hope that it may be maintained. In much the same way, the ultimate condition relates to the threat that it will be realized. In the nature of things, we experience a logical reversal, since the basic condition necessarily precedes hope, and anxiety necessarily anticipates realization of the ultimate condition. One way of looking at the above relationships produces an a-b-b-a effect because the basic and ultimate conditions are of a factual nature, whereas threat and possible alleviation are anticipated situations. This view suggests that a proportion may be stated in the following manner: basic condition : threat : : ultimate condition : possible alleviation. This statement is quite valid so long as it is considered only with reference to the paradigmatic (synchronic) axis of the novel, that is, the vertical columns. However, it destroys the logic of the syntagmatic (diachronic) axis, that is, the horizontal lines. It is possible of course, to state it this way: basic condition : threat : : possible alleviation : ultimate condition. The problem then arises from the suggested similarity between basic condition and possible alleviation, and also between threat and ultimate condition. These two pairings state: fact : psyche : : psyche : fact—an unproductive formulation. We are faced, therefore, with an apparent paradox, unless we return to the earlier statement of relationships, which makes use of intercalation:

| basic condition | threat | possible alleviation | ultimate condition |

In his analysis of *Les liaisons dangereuses,* Todorov is able to state a pure proportion by saying, in effect: desire : rejection of desire : : acts : rejection of acts. But it must be remembered that he is dealing with sequential *micro-récits* in which acts are more important than circumstances.[13] He notes that the *récit* he is dealing with may be called "psychological," and a different kind of *récit* might not be the same. In the case of *El sargento Felipe,* the importance of circumstance, in the *récit,* alters the case and emphasizes the function of the novel as a statement concerning society.

Since the statement of ratio and proportion suggests some kind of paradoxical relationship between diachrony and synchrony in *El sargento Felipe,* it is illuminating to view the diagram of "propositions" in terms of circumstance and act. In the same three-line-and-four-column chart, the distinguishing terms "circumstance" or "act" may be substituted for the "proposition" in each section.

	circumstance	circumstance	circumstance	circumstance? act?
+	circumstance	circumstance	circumstance	act? circumstance?
=	circumstance	act	act	act

The consistency of circumstance, in the first column, is appropriate since it indicates that two aspects of the basic condition add up to Felipe's total basic condition. Columns two and three indicate that two circumstances add up to an act. It is exceptionally interesting that the top and middle "propositions" of the fourth column may be called either "circumstance" or "act," depending on the perspective in which they are seen. In the preceding discussion of the three horizontal lines, this duality was noted, and it was also apparent that whereas "circumstance" seems more apt with respect to the top line of column four, "act" is the better choice in the middle line of column four. This difference seems reasonable because the top line is more indicative of the social situation, the middle line more indicative of Felipe's private life; therefore, the ultimate condition, in the top line, naturally expresses itself more in terms of a circumstance, and the ultimate situation of the middle line is more an act. The bottom line, once the total basic situation is expressed as a circumstance, consists of acts, with the paradigmatic and the syntagmatic representations coinciding in the protagonist's suicide.

The termination of vertical lines two, three, and four in actions related to the protagonist shows how the total *récit* is moved forward by the acts of Felipe. His acts, however, determine only his personal fate; they do not alter the circumstances that produce the acts. The murder of Don Jacinto, however justifiable it may have been, really does not reach the heart of the matter. Column four reveals that the ultimate condition in each *micro-récit* is a combination of circumstance and act, with act more emphatic in the *micro-récit* that is more personal. The ultimate condition in the third line is pure act and purely personal. The combined consideration of column four and line three shows (1) that Felipe acts as the result of circumstances, but not with direct relevance to them, and (2) that the paradox noted in the statement of ratio and proportion is confirmed by the overlapping of "circumstance" and "act" in two "propositions." The two *micro-récits* reach ultimate situations that refer to both society and individual; the ultimate situation of the total *récit* is a purely personal act, but one that signifies frustration with respect to Felipe's function in society. The archetype, therefore, becomes apparent because he stands out against a background of circumstance, but at the same time it is inevitably related to the circumstance, and within it he is unable to maintain his basic situation.

The difference between the structure of *récit* in *El sargento Felipe* and the structure of *récit* as Todorov analyzes it in *Les liaisons dangereuses* does not refute the logic of either formulation. Todorov is quite aware of possible differences, and points out that his analysis could have the effect of separating the actions from the characters. The psychological nature of *Les liaisons dangereuses* precludes this effect. In Todorov's study of the *Decameron,* the problem is not important, because in Boccaccio's stories the character is usually only a name to which actions may be attached.[14] In the case of *El sargento Felipe,* the separation is avoided by taking account of the arithmetical addition of *micro-récits* that shows the relationship of circumstances to acts. These circumstances are essential to the revelation of Felipe as an archetypal character, and they are equally related to his acts.

It seems there must be at least four kinds of *récits* that may be characterized by four kinds of repetition. One is the reflection of the protagonist's acts in the acts of an *alter ego,* as in the case of Martín Fierro and his friend Cruz. A second is a double *récit* in which the second part of the novel repeats essentially the *récit* of the first part in order to emphasize the message, as in *Aves sin nido.* Sometimes the second part of a narrative, in a third kind of repetition, may correspond to the first part while enlarging the significance or the field of reference. The second part of *Martín Fierro* is a reasonable example; Agustín Yáñez's *Al filo del agua* is an even clearer example. These three kinds of repetition complicate the description of structure by reference to *micro-récits,* because it should be understood that such repetitions are not themselves *micro-récits;* they are made up of *micro-récits.* The fourth kind of repetition is the relationship of *micro-récits* within a total *récit* that is not repeated or reflected as a total phenomenon. Both *Les liaisons dangereuses* and *El sargento Felipe* belong to this fourth category. Repetition of this kind corresponds rather closely to Brooks and Warren's "complication."[15]

There is a difference, of course, between sequential *micro-récits* and intercalated *micro-récits.* The first structure is analogous to a compound sentence in which clauses of equal value add successively to the message of the sentence. The intercalated structure is not analogous to any kind of sentence one is likely to hear; however, an analogy is not illogical. The sentence would consist of parallelisms or appositives for each of its components, and would conclude with a summary statement. Such a sentence—if it were actually uttered— would resemble a satire on the kind of dual phrasing sometimes associated with the oral expression of the American Indian. It might be absurd, as a sentence; on the other hand, it is illustrative as a logical suggestion. The nature of *récit,* in sophisticated narration, is highly complicated, and various incidences of *récit* are intensely idiosyncratic. It is interesting, however, that the two structures of *récit* considered here may be compared logically—though not practically— to two structures of a sentence. They show how the grammar of narrative discourse may be related to linguistic structure without being an exact replica of it.

In another essay concerning the nature of narrative, Todorov uses the *Decameron* to illustrate the use of linguistic concepts in a reciprocal function with the study of narrative. In other words, if linguistic concepts are useful to the description of narrative, that description may also contribute to the wealth of linguistic concepts.[16] The main point of interest with respect to *El sargento Felipe* is the notion of two types of episodes in a narrative that describe states of equilibrium or of disequilibrium: "The first type will be relatively static and, one might say, iterative; the same kind of actions can be repeated indefinitely. The second, on the other hand, will be dynamic and in principle occurs only once."[17]

Todorov relates these two types of episodes to two parts of speech—adjectives and verbs. Episodes of equilibrium are "adjectives"; episodes of disequilibrium are "verbs." It is necessary to explain that substantives do not appear, because "the substantive can always be reduced to one or more adjectives." Once this condition is accepted, the concept of narrative adjective and narrative verb is useful in describing the *récit* of *El sargento Felipe*. Since its structure is of a particular kind, its idiosyncrasies will naturally alter the concept in some way.

If the original representation of the *récit* of Picón-Febres's novel is enlarged, it may be seen as follows:

	basic condition	threat	possible alleviation	ultimate condition
	Felipe owns a farm	Conditions of war may destroy the farm.	Matías & F.'s family may save farm.	Property lost during F.'s army service.
+	Felipe has a family.	Don Jacinto plans to seduce Encarnación.	Matías wishes to marry Encarnación.	Matías burns F.'s home, trying to harm Don Jacinto.
=	Felipe enjoys a good life.	Military conscription removes F. from control of situation.	F. murders Don Jacinto.	F. commits suicide.
	equilibrium	disequilibrium		equilibrium
	narrative adjective	narrative verb	narrative adverb	narrative adjective

It is helpful to think of a "narrative adverb," in the case of *El sargento Felipe,* rather than of verbal moods, as Todorov does with reference to the *Decameron.*[18] The "narrative verbs" in the two *micro-récits* of Picón-Febres's novel have already been identified as circumstances rather than acts; in terms of the parts of speech, they are verbs, but verbs that communicate modes of being rather than actions. In their synchronic dimension, they make an entirely reasonable particularization of their summation, which is expressed in an act that Todorov might describe as "obligative," since it is not willed by Felipe but is required by society. In their diachronic dimension, on the other hand, the "narrative verbs" must be modified by their "narrative adverbs" in order to reveal the individual forced into conflict with society, an essential aspect of the Martín Fierro archetype. It is important to note that, on the summation line of the grid, where acts predominate over circumstances, the "narrative verb" is an act not willed by Felipe and the "narrative adverb" takes the form of an act for which Felipe is responsible. However, the act of military conscription really has much of the quality of circumstance since it is not willed by Felipe but is actually performed against his will and best interest. Then Felipe's "optative" act—to use Todorov's term—functions as a modifier to the circumstance created by conscription. Felipe's murder of Don Jacinto, since it could not possibly resolve or even fully avenge Felipe's tragedy, has more the value of hope than of accomplishment. Therefore, in spite of the fact that these propositions constitute acts in the summation line, one really modifies the other. Together, the two columns labeled "threat" and "possible alleviation" contain the acts or circumstances of disequilibrium. They specify the change effected between the equilibrium of fortunate to the equilibrium of tragic, with reference to Felipe, corresponding to the trajectory of the archetype.

Although the particular characteristics and ordering of events in Picón-Febres's *récit* indicate the archetypal quality of Felipe Bobadilla, they are not the only narrative techniques that contribute to this effect. The novel may be described as written in two modes, bucolic and realistic, that are determined mainly by differences in the narrator's prose style. The realistic mode, generally speaking, corresponds to the story of Felipe as defined by specific time and place—the story of an individualized human being. The bucolic mode, on the other hand, is more general in its signification. Its style imparts a sense of happy continuity in a special manner of living, and suggests an idealization of rural customs found in the work of some *modernista* poets, notably Julio Herrera y Reissig and Leopoldo Lugones. The universalized quality of the bucolic mode emphasizes the appreciation of Felipe as archetype, especially because it pervades the opening pages of the novel, where the protagonist's basic condition, the initial equilibrium, is established.

The first twenty pages of the novel contain narrative that is generalized, primarily by using the imperfect tense and the impersonal "se" construction. These forms create the sense of Felipe's habitually performing certain chores, observing his surroundings, relishing the good life. The person is clearly Felipe, but he is not related to any specific point in time. Political references, for example, do not appear in these opening pages. It is the sense of continuity that predominates, and the narrator occasionally enhances the effect of the imperfect tense by using the verb *soler* to indicate customary action. The use of impersonal "se" further generalizes the situation (it means something like "one" or impersonal "you" in English). It tends to combine Felipe with the bucolic situation and, therefore, to de-specify him further.

Extremely rich metaphor intensifies the idealized bucolic scene. This quality of Picón-Febres's style might possibly be thought of as romantic exaggeration; however, an apparent insistence on the beautifying adjective, rather than on the sensitivity-producing modifier, corresponds more closely to *modernismo*. Felipe wakes up "En cuanto el alba comenzaba a deshojar sus frescas rosas en las puertas del Oriente" (p. 1) (As soon as dawn started dropping its fresh rose petals at the doorways of the Eastern sky.) The narrator mixes humble customs with the beauty of nature—for instance, Felipe's fastening on his knife, saying prayers, and awakening his wife, and the dark green canopy formed by the leaves of the banana grove, the orange trees that whiten their surroundings with blossoms. Even the morning chores acquire an unexpected beauty—the "delicious ring" of milk hitting the pail, and Felipe's mouth watering as the fresh milk foamed, "white as untouched snow" (p. 4). The first chapter of the novel (twelve pages) is narrated entirely in this mode and deals with Felipe's home life.

The second chapter, still in the same mode, takes him to the *pulpería,* the country store-tavern. This ambience provides a transition into a less idealized world, one in which conflicts exist, but the same sense of generality is maintained until page twenty, where, already within the world of problems, the situation is related to time: "Una noche la pulpería estaba llena, y la conversación giraba al rededor [sic] de la política" (p. 20). (One night the *pulpería* was full, and the conversation concerned itself with politics.) The subsequent dialogue establishes the historical context as the time of Matías Salazar's uprising in Carabobo. Except for Felipe, the speakers are not identified by name, but they concur in their fear of losing property to armed marauders. Speech acts are attributed and qualified by verbs in the preterite tense: "vociferated the storekeeper," "boasted the first man who had spoken" (p. 23). Felipe fits naturally into this context, but the fact that he is the only named speaker makes him stand out even in this less idealized situation—less idealized, that is, than in the bucolic passages, which by their nature make Felipe a special kind of person. The episode in the *pulpería* effects a transition from the bucolic mode to the realistic, or *criollista.*

The sense of generality is created mainly at the beginning of the novel, although it is experienced less intensely in a number of other places—for example, to describe the people's hiding from the soldiers (p. 77). However, Picón-Febres consistently maintains Felipe in an emphasized position, and the *modernista* style sustains the impression of beneficent bucolic life as a utopia from which the protagonist has been removed. Examples abound, but a typical passage describes the rural ambience when Felipe is away: "El campo todo se veía como cubierto por un baño de espléndida blancura, pero blancura inexpresable, semejante a una gasa de espuma espolvoreada de átomos de sol" (p. 187). (The fields seemed bathed in a magnificent whiteness— an indescribable whiteness, like voile powdered with atoms of sunshine.) These lines are as significant for what they do not say as they are for what they actually state. The idyllic situation serves as background for the culmination of the threat to Felipe's domestic tranquility (the second horizontal line in the original diagram). Although the ugliness of daily life is always implicit, the narrator encourages his reader to suspend that reality momentarily and to substitute for it a magnificence that is really "inexpresable"—a qualification that suggests the improbability of Felipe's bucolic existence. It suggests that the utopia from which the protagonist is removed never really existed but still constitutes an opposition to the social forces that cause Felipe to act against his best interest.

The realistic mode, in *El sargento Felipe,* ranges from matter-of-fact, unadorned narrative summary to scenes in which the peculiarities of rural speech are represented phonetically. Its effect, in general, is to portray rural customs—manners and values—from the viewpoint of a sympathetic outsider. Occasional touches of humor never approach caricature. This realistic-*criollista* mode produces a very unusual effect when it functions in contrast to the *modernista*-bucolic mode. Both modes deal with a rural situation—presumably the same situation in both cases, even though it may look different according to the narrative mode prevailing in a given passage. The bucolic mode is cosmopolitan in the sense that its significance is generally the same throughout western culture. The *criollista* mode is regionalistic. The difference, therefore, is similar to the city-versus-country contrast that appears frequently in Spanish-American fiction; on the other hand, the contrast acquires a different significance, since both cosmopolitanism and regionalism portray rural scenes. This variation on a generally accepted dichotomy produces a certain defamiliarization, because both modes contribute to the characterization of Felipe.

The two narrative modes of *El sargento Felipe* anticipate readers familiar with both manners of expression—quite reasonably so, in view of the publication date. The defamiliarization occurs in the association of both narrative modes with Felipe's character and with the rural setting. More commonly, one would expect a representative of cosmopolitanism to be in conflict with a representative of regionalism. Instead of developing such a conflict, Picón-Febres emphasizes the archetypal quality of his protagonist by contrasting the bucolic Felipe with the *criollista* Felipe. He is clearly the protagonist even within the *criollista* frame of reference. This special designation makes more plausible his role within the bucolic frame. Felipe's similarity to the Martín Fierro archetype is apparent in both narrative modes, and it is especially convincing because he is appreciated both as individual and as archetype in two different representations of the rural situation. The narrative structure is the basic factor in this development because it is responsible for the interrelated functions of circumstances and acts. The synchronic dimension of the novel contains, paradoxically, a change from circumstance to act. The bucolic mode confers a utopian value on the circumstance, and this value intensifies the novel's specific protest even as it generalizes the problem through the archetypal characterization of Felipe. As a complement to the structural organization, Picón-Febres's prose style differentiates between the general and the specific by using *modernista* imagery in contrast to unadorned exposition. The contrast, however, is in a sense paradoxical; like the period to which it belongs, *El sargento Felipe* is a combination of two apparently antagonistic tendencies, *modernismo* and realism. The combination embellishes *criollismo* and transforms it from genuine realism into a stylized version of rural customs—a version that is improbable but recognizable. Felipe is the protagonist-corollary of this representation.

10

Conclusions

Relationships among the Critical Approaches

When a particular analytical procedure proves to be useful in answering a question or resolving a problem raised by a given narrative text, we may then wonder if the same procedure might provide new insights when applied to a different narrative text, even if the latter has not suggested the same question or problem. To put it another way, an analytical procedure may answer a question before it is asked. This apparently flippant observation, if taken seriously, is one way of describing the kind of literary criticism that enhances the experience of fiction. It may be useful, therefore, to speculate on how the procedures used in the foregoing eight chapters might function if applied to the seven other novels analyzed in this study. Naturally, detailed analyses must be avoided for reasons of time and space. Therefore, the speculative nature of the following observations should be kept in mind.

Analysis of one aspect of the narrative process in *Guatimozín* (how the transformation of *histoire* to *récit* relates to the use of scene-versus-summary) shows that there is a difference between the *histoire*-to-*récit* transformation, on the other hand, and the history-to-*histoire*-to-*récit* transformation, on the other. Application of the same procedure to the seven other novels would point out the importance of the historical record (the facts of history) in each novel: first, whether or not history is an active element in the work; second, if it is active, to what extent it operates as a vital part of the narrative process, and what the nature of its function is.

The study of scene-versus-summary is interesting because it illuminates one of the principal means used by the narrator to enhance the significance of the historical record (insofar as it is important in each novel) as human experience. Specific historical events are factors of varying importance in *Amalia, Martín Rivas, Aves sin nido,* and *El sargento Felipe.* Any importance in the other three novels would have to be shown through more careful analysis than the present speculations permit.

Among the four novels cited above, *Amalia* is the one in which history is most important. The *histoire* differs from history in two ways: first, the people of fiction live along with historical personages, and second, the author has already interpreted history, according to his own ideology, in the *histoire.* The author does not have to fill out the historical information as in Avellaneda's characterization of Guatimozín, since the most developed characterizations are fictional. We also discover that Juan Manuel de Rosas, whose tyranny is a pervasive factor in the novel, really is of little importance as a character in the *récit;* his function is to define the ambience of repression. Narrative summary, when he does appear, emphasizes his vulgarity to the point of caricature. The analysis would also find a relationship between narrative summary and certain non-narrative, documentary material inserted by the author. In this instance, the anxiety of the implicit author becomes apparent.

The analysis would show that historical references in *Martín Rivas* and *Aves sin nido* are not of fundamental importance. They identify the chronological setting of the stories and may in some way contribute to the general atmosphere of the narrative. It makes little difference whether the references occur in scene or in summary. They are not otherwise important except for the rather strange association of love and liberty in the case of Rafael San Luis, Martín Rivas's friend. This case, however, involves the use of a historical circumstance as a technique of characterization, and is one of the aspects of transforming *histoire* to *récit.* In *El sargento Felipe,* the condition of civil war is important, but the specific moment is less so. Analysis would show that reference to specific historical facts occurs mainly in passages of summary; the more general effect of civil strife is appreciated in both summary and scene, a quality that makes the circumstance more intimately functional (more "human") than the recorded fact.

A projection of this analytical procedure onto the nineteenth-century novel in Spanish America, taken as a whole, suggests several probabilities: that many historical novels include documentary or semi-documentary material that is not intrinsically narrative but is related to narrative summary; that this non-narrative material decreases as the cultivation of the history-to-*histoire* step of transformation increases; that many novels refer to historical events without using these events as essential elements in the narration; that authors are generally more comfortable using scene with invented characters than with historical characters.

The principles of Brooks and Warren's *Understanding Fiction,* as used in the analysis of *Amalia,* promote awareness of the actual making of the *récit.* This awareness is different from the Barthesian notion of structuration of the text because it isolates problems instead of maintaining the narrative sequence, and views the narrative phenomenon from the standpoint of an author in the act of narrating rather than from the standpoint of a reader in the act of experiencing the fiction. To some extent, the critic emulates the author and confronts a series of requirements inherent in the narrative process. There is a certain ambivalence involved in this reader function, since reader cannot be author. This analytical procedure, therefore, is somewhere between the kind of procedure in which the analyst follows the development of the narrative and the kind of procedure that analyzes the text as a *fait accompli.*

The Brooks and Warren principle of "Complication" is especially important in explaining the narrative appeal of *Amalia* because it defines the narrative as a story of intrigue. This emphasis is of course closely related to the identification of Daniel as hero (Brooks and Warren point out that characterization is best effected through action). An interesting contrast may be noted if the same principles are applied to *Guatimozín.* Avellaneda effects "Complication" through a series of incidents that might appear, at first, to be very similar in function to those of *Amalia.* The difference is that the complicating scenes of *Guatimozín* are conventionalized. Many of them could be from any romantic historical novel if the characters' names were changed. (This condition is also true with regard to the love story line of *Amalia,* but not true of the intrigue line.) Since the character of Guatimozín is developed through a combination of his conventionalized actions and summary narrative, he turns out to be a conventionalized hero—interesting as a kind of period piece, but less vivid than Daniel. The author has conventionalized exotic material. One of the factors that rescues Avellaneda's novel for reader interest is pointed out by Brooks and Warren's question, "Whose story is it?" Guatimozín's, of course, but the narrator associates the young man with Moctezuma in such a way that they share a single function. Moctezuma's historicity adheres to Guatimozín.

The act of striking into the story, as Brooks and Warren put it (in the terminology of Genette, we might refer to the point in the *histoire* where the *récit* begins), may be indicative of how the author will confront other problems. The initial events in all eight novels are moments of crisis or of significant change in the lives of central characters. In the case of *Martín Rivas,* the drawing-room episode initiates a process of adequate "Complication" that never becomes very exciting. Analysis would probably show that Martín's characterization is seen largely through his actions, and that he is an honorable but not very colorful man—a personality that matches the quality of the events that produce complication of the conflict. Insight of an entirely different kind might be produced by a similar analysis of *Aves sin nido.* The very beginning of the novel suggests that the author senses that her description of the town requires realistic details; it also suggests a possible emphasis on the milieu. The first event focuses on an Indian woman who is not the protagonist, and this fact raises the highly relevant question, "Whose story is it?" Analysis would probably show that it is extremely difficult to say that *Aves sin nido* is anybody's story; however, one might feel a certain tendency to single out Lucía Marín in this connection. She could not possibly be considered a protagonist in the sense of suffering the injustice that constitutes the basis of the narrative. She is, on the other hand, the sympathetic observer and frustrated redeemer. This position relative to the message of the novel coincides with its generally didactic tone.

Mi tío el empleado, María, and *Suprema ley* all begin at a point of radical change in the life of the protagonist, and analysis would probably show that the narration proceeds to place events at the service of characterization. Most readers would likely consider *Suprema ley* the most interesting story, basing their judgment on the degree of curiosity regarding how it is going to turn out. That interest probably is created by the complexity of Julio's characterization.

Efraín in *María*, on the other hand, is identified by the nostalgic sentimentality that is experienced from the first scene. The Brooks and Warren type of analysis would probably suggest the intensification of this quality, but very likely would not point out the shadings that become apparent through use of the codes of characterization, as in the chapter on *María*. The ridiculous aspects of Vicente Cuevas's personality are apparent in the first episode of *Mi tío el empleado*. Analysis according to the Brooks and Warren principles would probably reveal a series of similar incidents that indicate the author's interest in the satirical representation of a personality type rather than a full characterization or an intricate story line. It would also invite attention to the variable narrative voice.

With respect to the problems of "Conflict" and "Complication," an analysis of *El sargento Felipe* would indicate some confusion of focus. Felipe himself is the overall object of attention, and the incidents that "complicate" the conflict build toward his ultimate tragedy. However, his daughter would probably be seen as more central to the action in these episodes than is Felipe. For this reason, a similarity to *Aves sin nido* emerges (with respect to "Whose story is it?"). On the other hand, an important difference must be noted— Felipe, unlike Lucía, could never be seen as an agent of redemption or reform. His exterior relationship to many of the narrated events would appear to coincide with an aspect of his characterization, which causes Felipe to be appreciated in a general bucolic sense. The analysis would note, in this connection, that the opening scene of the novel serves to create the ambience rather than to recount a specific event.

The principles of Brooks and Warren, applied in general to the genre during the period studied here, would probably indicate more interest in story-telling than the authors are usually credited with. Very likely it would reveal a frequent tendency to develop a love story tangential to a major plot line—like Eduardo and Amalia, Matilde and Rafael in *Martín Rivas*, the triangle involving Tecuixpa in *Guatimozín*, and Manuel and Margarita in *Aves sin nido*. As the century advances, characterization would probably seem more important, with the events of fiction designed to serve the revelation of character. Narrator control would probably appear rather rigid. In spite of an occasional interesting narrator situation as in *María* or a variable one as in *Mi tío el empleado*, the novels are most likely to appear to be told by a clearly exterior determining agent.

Use of the model tentatively proposed by Floyd Merrell has the effect of illuminating the nature of fiction, showing both standard characteristics and individual differences when several works are considered. Such a procedure may be thought of primarily as a definition of narrative rather than as a convenient method of analyzing a given work. On the other hand, it is also useful from the more casual reader's standpoint because it brings into consciousness the deeper significance of the narrative conflict, and does so in such a way that the meaning of a novel may be considerably altered. To put it another way, if a reader once applies the model to a novel, he may then continue to think of the model advantageously—without actually setting out the phenomena in a carefully made diagram—as a means of penetrating more deeply into the significance of other novels.

In *Amalia,* for example, we become aware immediately of a conflict between safety and danger. This contrast is almost immediately associated with a political situation involving the Rosas' tyranny. Later the conflict may appear to be order-versus-anarchy. It is probable, however, that these contrasts may be best expressed as security-versus-fear. It is debatable whether or not this polarity constitutes a valid axiological contrast; it may be that the only truly axiological contrast is life-versus-death. Indeed, life-versus-death or reunion-versus-alienation may be taken as more fundamental metaphors of security-versus-fear; however, security-versus-fear seems to be the most basic polarity that identifies the situation in *Amalia.* Still other metaphors seem real enough but less fundamental: freedom-versus-tyranny, safety-versus-danger, anarchy-versus-order, refinement-versus-coarseness (as suggested by Viñas in his commentary on Mármol's novel). All these metaphors for the same basic conflict find expression in the narrative process; their metaphoric quality identifies the synchronic dimension of the novel.

It may be possible to build significantly on the notion of security-versus-fear. It might be reasonable, for example, to think of a diagram like the first figure in the chapter on *Martín Rivas.* Under the headings "security" and "fear" we could imagine the terms "shelter" and "flight." Under "security," "shelter" would refer to the state of European refinement mentioned by Viñas; "flight" would signify a condition of non-involvement. Under "fear," "shelter" might refer to physical protection and "flight" would signify exile. In such a formulation, we might postulate that physical protection is to the concept of non-involvement as exile is to the security of European refinement. On the praxemic level, the contrast between non-involvement on the one hand and exile on the other might be seen as a way of describing the diachronic dimension of the novel. The kind of refuge represented by non-involvement would possibly be seen as modified by the state of anarchy; the notion of exile would be modified by the expectation of the kind of security suggested by the European refinement idea. A possible mediation might be found in the promise of Lavalle's intervention.

It should be pointed out more clearly than ever, in view of the preceding paragraph, that such casual use of a model is an act appropriate to the thought process of an interested reader. It is not meant to demonstrate—and even less to prove—a theory; its use is the encouragement of insightful reading that will make the experience of a novel more satisfying.

Regarding basic contrasts, it is readily apparent that the polarities of reunion-versus-alienation and ultimately of life-versus-death constitute the axiological contrast in *María* and in *Suprema ley.* In two of the novels in which political practices are important, *Aves sin nido* and *El sargento Felipe,* the contrast of security-versus-fear provides a reasonable base for speculation. *Guatimozín* offers a special problem. Given the circumstances of the Spanish conquest of the Aztec empire, one might suspect that here too the security-versus-fear contrast might work well; however, the issue is confused by a suggestion of the noble savage notion. The latter naturally refers to a contrast of innocence-versus-sophistication, but the pairing does not really fit the situation, because the native Mexicans are not innocent even though they are certainly seen as very praiseworthy. They are clearly very sophisticated in political matters and in human relationships. One might consider the contrast of acceptance-versus-treachery or, since Cortés is not wholly evil (and so possibly not to be reviled by a term as strong as "treachery"), acceptance-versus-egocentricity might provide a good starting point.

Mi tío el empleado is not a promising case. This novel's episodic nature indicates that the model referred to here might be more useful with reference to separate episodes than to the whole novel. Nevertheless, there is an obvious conflict between honesty and chicanery that applies to the whole novel. An idiosyncrasy of this work is that the narrative situation would make narrator (nephew)-versus-protagonist (uncle) a metaphor of honesty-versus-chicanery. Another metaphor becomes, ironically, failure-versus-success, because of the novel's satirical character.

It is difficult to imagine whether or not the use of Merrell's tentative model would suggest any general characteristics of the Spanish-American novel during the last century. It might be enlightening, of course, to see how frequently the reunion-versus-alienation and the security-versus-fear polarities might be useful in dealing with two kinds of novel. Whatever the possibility of generalizing, analysis would certainly point out some interesting contrasts. One would find, for example, that Emilio Rabasa's *Novelas mexicanas,* which are similar in many ways to *Mi tío el empleado,* are not analogous to it with regard to the failure-versus-success metaphor. The honesty-versus-chicanery contrast is analogous, but Rabasa's rascals, although temporarily successful, ultimately end in failure.

The analytical process applied to *María* is useful for showing how a characterization is effected rather than for observing all aspects of the transformation of *histoire* into *récit.* It is especially useful if a characterization is the dynamic factor in this process, or if a character is attractive to the reader for whatever reason—puzzling or empathetic, for example. Analysis of the narrative situation according to text act theory is not a necessary step in using codes of characterization. In the case of *María,* it is especially enlightening because the narrative situation is an important part of the characterization of Efraín. It might also be important—in a different way—to an analysis of the characterization of Vicente Coveo in *Mi tío el empleado;* an examination of the narrator-nephew's responsibility to the narration as a whole and to the protagonist in particular might be productive. An analysis of the narrative situation in *Aves sin nido* could possibly illuminate the characterization of Lucía Marín, since she appears to have a strong reformist motivation and it is known that the author shared this inclination. (Worth noting, in this connection, is the likelihood that such an analysis of the Lucía characterization might not suggest itself unless the Brooks and Warren question of "Whose story is it?" were asked beforehand.)

It might be enlightening to note instances of relationship

(association code) between Lucía Marín's concern for the exploited Indians and her belief that the provincial power elite is less than civilized. With regard to the suggestion code, it must be remembered that Clorinda Matto was not a very subtle author; however, the equation of feminity with justice and kindness (the directness of her assertion varies) is worth considering in this connection. The novel contains no prophetic symbol like the black bird in *María,* but variations on the idea of "aves sin nido" have a kind of prophetic function, and also may be of interest in analyzing the relationship between Lucía and the narrative voice. The confirmation code might be seen in Lucía's decision to adopt the two orphan girls. This revelation of gentle concern underlines her social protest. Among the narrative elements that might be called "intensification," clearly the attack on the house refers to duality mentioned with regard to the association code.

In the case of an entirely different characterization, Daniel in Mármol's *Amalia,* the same system of codes still promises to be helpful. The association code might bring out the combination of personal concern and political position as causes of his actions. The suggestive code would refer mainly to the constant threat of repression—sometimes overt but always implied. The prophetic code would probably be composed chiefly of the actions of María Josefa, an important personality who is not fully characterized in the novel. She is a kind of omen throughout the story. The confirmation code might refer to Daniel's sweetheart. He is primarily the swashbuckling hero, and Eduardo is the male protagonist in the love story, but references to Daniel's sweetheart reveal another side of him, like a reversal of the procedure in *María,* where certain actions of Efraín confirm his masculinity as the complement to sentimental tenderness. The intensifying factors are probably the moments when Daniel is at his cloak-and-dagger best.

Application of the same series to the other novels would probably indicate, in *El sargento Felipe,* an association of Felipe and the milieu reminiscent of *María;* an idealized and rather trite hero in *Guatimozín;* confirmation of the basic conformist in Martín Rivas; and confirmation of Julio Ortegal's mediocrity (*Suprema ley*) in his need to distinguish himself, the most complicated characterization in the eight novels studied.

If these codes were applied to a large number of novels of the past century in Spanish America, it seems likely that recognizable social types would appear more frequently than full characterizations, that many protagonists would reflect the author's ideals or goals, and that characterizations would be more complex toward the end of the century. Whatever the convenience of this set of codes, however, it should be understood that they were invented for application to a particular case. There is no reason why one or all should not be changed in order to illuminate a different novel. A contrast code, for example, might be useful in the case of Daniel; it would show his character in opposition to Eduardo's and possibly to others. The pleasure of looking at characterization this way derives from the fact that we experience events in the order of the *récit* and, at the same time, appreciate the interrelationship of several different functions that contribute to the characterizing process.

The use of codes in the study of *Mi tío el empleado* is much closer to the exposition of Roland Barthes. There is no reason why the reader should not identify any codes that might be appropriate to a given work; they have only to refer to narrative functions that activate fields of association. On the other hand, it seems that four of the Barthesian codes might be taken as common to all narratives: action (proairetic), enigma (hermeneutic), connotative, and symbolic. The cultural codes are no less valid, but may vary, in a detailed sense, depending on the particular text. "Scientific" is one of the cultural codes in Barthes's reading of "Valdemar"; "picaresque" is equally meaningful in the reading of Meza's novel; and similar changes should be expected in other cases.

This kind of reading is equivalent to the active experience of structuring a narrative text; it is not the *post facto* study of what has already been experienced. It is like the Brooks and Warren procedure to the extent that it cultivates awareness of the text in the making; however, the Brooks and Warren process interrupts the experience of structuration by isolating problems, whereas a Barthesian reading maintains structuration inviolate. It is unlikely, of course, that many complete readings of the Barthes variety will be published, especially of novels. It is also true that such a reading is likely to interest primarily the person who is noting the function of the codes (the reader of the text); with a few notable exceptions, extensive written commentaries of this kind are not likely to interest large numbers of readers.

In the case of *Mi tío el empleado,* the Barthesian process is especially helpful because it emphasizes the relationship of enigmas that vary in importance, and because it shows clearly the transition from picaresque to satire. In the case of *Amalia,* it seems probable that Daniel's role would be emphasized by the action code and, of course, by the enigma code. In this connection, we should note that action is awareness of what has happened—the reader puts together the events in the process of reading; enigma is anticipation of what is going to happen. (An interesting way of appreciating the Barthesian process is by comparison of this definition with the meaning of Genette's "analepse" and "prolepse.") Action code and enigma code make the adventure aspect of *Amalia* very apparent. The picaresque code, of course, should be abolished or exchanged for something else— perhaps a "repression" code. It might be a code that sensitizes the reader to the pervasive role of the strong man in Spanish-American culture.

The connotative code would probably be the most revealing in an application of this critical procedure to *Guatimozín, Martín Rivas,* and *María* because of the importance of characterization in each case. A cultural code activating association with the noble savage idea might be useful in analyzing *Guatimozín;* it would be interesting to see how active this notion is in the novel, even though it obviously is not the novel's basic definition of the native Mexicans. In the case of *Martín Rivas,* it might be possible to specify a code that would refer to the kind of honesty found in Martín and in Edelmira.

The symbolic code would be very important in appreciating the structuration of *María,* and not simply because of the black bird. The association of María with the region is a theme suggested repeatedly by Efraín's putting the two together, and references to the idylls of Nay-Sinar and of Braulio-Tránsito have symbolic value related to the association of María with the region. In *Aves sin nido,* the symbolic code would probably show variations on the title to be very important; the theme of redemption would be highlighted by the symbolic code in *Suprema ley;* in *El sargento Felipe,* the bucolic effect might be pointed out by the symbolic code, or "bucolic" might itself be a cultural code. There may be a certain similarity between the symbolic code and the cultural codes in some instances, as suggested here in the case of Picón-Febres's novel—it may be seen in the idea of pervasive repression in *Amalia* and the theme of civil war in *El sargento Felipe,* as well as in the social protest of *Aves sin nido.*

It seems likely that application of the Barthesian procedure to a large number of novels throughout the century would show, as in the case of the Brooks and Warren procedure, more emphasis on storytelling than the novelists have usually been given credit for. The enigma code could be very important in the earlier novels, though it might show considerable ingenuousness in handling suspense. Interesting similarities among novels might become apparent through observation of cultural codes (and sometimes symbolic codes), like the pervasive awareness of the dictator's presence, or civilization-versus-barbarism.

The adaptation of Arnold Kettle's essay, used as an analytical procedure in the chapter on *Aves sin nido,* can be illuminating only in dealing with novels that may possibly be characterized by "popular sensitivity," according to Kettle's definition. The plight of the working class (or of some other non-elitist, exploited class) must be an issue of protest. Only one of the seven other novels studied here (*El sargento Felipe*) comes close to satisfying this requirement. Application of this scheme of analysis, therefore, is not likely to be productive except to the extent that it might emphasize some interesting characteristics of each novel. *Guatimozín,* the only other novel that deals with the Indian, certainly does not see him as exploited. The native American is presented as elitist, from an elitist point of view. However, the fact of his defeat by the intruder sets the stage for exploitation in the future.

There could hardly be any question about the anti-popular slant of *Amalia.* Although there is no clearly defined exploited class, the sense of the novel is that the common people side with Rosas (analysis might show that they are deceived by him) and are therefore on the less admired side of the dichotomy pointed out by Viñas. The novel's emphasis consequently would appear to be strongly elitist. This attitude is related to the civilization-versus-barbarism distinction in a way that would be contrary to Kettle's third requirement.

Martín Rivas places emphasis clearly on the individual. There is some attention to differences between upper and lower middle classes, but individuals represent the best values in both situations. It might be argued that individuals might profit from reading the novel, as in Kettle's first proposition, but there is no indication of possible collective change. It is hardly surprising, of course, that emphasis should be heavily on the individual in nineteenth-century fiction, and that appears to be the case generally in the eight novels studied. *María,* which is above all else the characterization of the narrator, shows his embarrassment with regard to slavery and his patronizing friendship with some other workers. It is doubtful, however, that reality is viewed from their standpoint at any stage of the narration. *Suprema ley* is also a highly concentrated case study and probably includes only one incident that would be interesting in terms of the Kettle analysis. Julio tells his troubles to a watchman, at the end of the novel, and the workman's attitude reflects the narrator's idea of a "popular" understanding of Julio's problem.

Mi tío el empleado is a denunciation in humorous terms. The object of criticism is more caricature than character; he may represent a social phenomenon but hardly a social class in any sense that would satisfy an ideological critic. The protagonist of *El sargento Felipe* comes closer to representing a popular class than anyone else in the seven novels studied in addition to *Aves sin nido.* However, even in this case, consideration of Kettle's propositions would probably elicit negative responses except for the second requirement.

In general, it seems likely that a search for "popular sensitivity" in the nineteenth-century Spanish-American novel would show that there was not much of it. The lower middle class might be seen rather frequently as the object of redemptive intent. The importance of individuals would almost certainly predominate, and they would rarely be from the most humble sectors of society. There are novels of protest, but usually of a specifically political rather than social nature. Investigation would probably show occasional flurries of commitment that would satisfy Kettle's first requirement. The second might find even more cases of satisfaction. Although some probably would fulfill satisfactorily the third and fourth, it is practically certain that none would satisfy the remaining three.

There are enough passages, easily remembered, in novels other than *Suprema ley* to suggest that use of the Jakobson model might be a generally worthwhile experiment. One readily thinks of, for example, the disquisition by Moctezuma in *Guatimozín* on the tradition to which he belongs; the reappearance of the first-person narrator in the second part of *Mi tío el empleado;* the summarizing letter to the protagonist in *El sargento Felipe;* Rafael's comments on Santiago society in *Martín Rivas;* the account of María's funeral by Efraín's sister; the two different episodes in which Rosas appears in *Amalia;* the pleas of the two native women in *Aves sin nido.*

In the analysis of *Suprema ley,* the model is applied to passages that suggest initially some alteration in the sender. The procedure then is to note this variation and see what happens to the other components of the model. The application may show that one of these components is more revealing than the sender phenomenon itself. Emphasis on the sender is not a requirement for using the model. The initial suggestion might be made with reference to any of the six components. We might speculate, for example, that variation in contact would be revealing with respect to the question raised in the chapter on *Guatimozín*—that is, the relationship of scene-versus-summary to the transformation of history to *histoire* to *récit.* This possibility assumes, of course, the understanding of "contact" as in the essay on *Suprema ley.*

For quite different reasons, the sender provides the initial suggestion in both *María* and *Mi tío el empleado.* In the first case, the narrator's characterization of himself clearly invites attention to his role; however, it seems likely that other components—context, for example—might change in even more surprising ways. The sender in *Mi tío el empleado* changes from a first-person usage to a third-person, with numerous suggestions of ambivalence on the part of the narrator. In *Amalia,* it might well prove enlightening to think in terms of the receiver, since we generally assume that the author had both his contemporaries and future generations in mind.

Context is the most suggestive variable in *Martín Rivas,* for two reasons: first, the difference between the drawing-room stasis of the first part and the movement of the latter half; second, the contrast between the world of the Encinas and the world of the Molinas. Context might be attractive also in *El sargento Felipe,* as the protagonist moves from his bucolic paradise into a more realistic frame. On the other hand, the code changes in agreement with this variable context, and it might be the component to watch first. It is also possible that code might be the key component in *Aves sin nido.* The nature of the sender raises some questions in analyzing this novel, and it might be interesting to begin with code variations and see if there are corollary changes in sender and, of course, in the other components.

Thinking of Spanish-American novels in general during the last century, it seems probable that sender-receiver relationships would be rather standard; extraordinary cases probably would be unintentional more often than planned. Contact, as understood here, would probably show a growing awareness of technique in the course of the century. Different contacts might be used frequently, but the earlier novels (and many of the later) would likely show a poor sense of balance with respect to variety in the form of the contact. The overall context of many novels would be an imitation of France, with Hispanic names added. As for the contexts when the model is applied within the novel, they might well reflect individual situations rather than societal ones. This speculation, however, is highly tentative; it could itself become an interesting study. The code would generally give the impression of being self-conscious; it would usually be exceedingly literary, with deviations carefully signaled by the author.

It should be understood that the ideas of Tzvetan Todorov used in the chapter on *El sargento Felipe* are extracted from a much more complicated formulation and adapted to the analysis of a single novel. It is quite likely that a different emphasis, with respect to Todorov's exposition, might be more useful in the analysis of a different novel.

The primary effect of the Todorov studies used here is to illuminate the nature and function of the episodes that make up *récit.* Along with consideration of these characteristics of a fiction text, it is helpful to take into account the phenomena that Brooks and Warren call "Complication" and "Pattern and Design" (repetition). In the application of these principles—of Todorov or of Brooks and Warren or of both—to a given novel, emphasis naturally falls on the story line itself (on the action and enigma codes, in the Barthesian procedure), but it is possible that other characteristics may be highlighted as a result of the analysis—for example, the archetypal quality of Felipe Bobadilla in *El sargento Felipe*. In these two functions (the natural emphasis and the incidental discovery), we find a clear difference between the use of a fiction text for the exposition of a theory and the use of a theory for the analysis of a fiction text.

Todorov's studies as used here are therefore helpful for two reasons: first, to show how a given *récit* corresponds to or differs from the Todorov formulations and, second, to see if such an analysis points out aspects of the work that might otherwise be overlooked or not fully appreciated. A reasonable beginning-point would be to formulate a schematic notion of the *récit's* structure by making a general statement of (1) the initial situation, (2) the act that changes the basic situation, (3) the counteraction that would presumably be the second component of the narrative conflict, and (4) the new situation created by the action of (2) and (3) on (1). In the case of *María,* the general statement might be made as follows: (1) Efraín wishes to hold close the woman-region he loves; (2) he offers himself to her; (3) his hope of fulfillment is threatened; (4) he is bereft of the woman-region.

A second step in this procedure could be examination of the *micro-récits* to determine whether or not they repeat the overall pattern described above, or whether they are in some other way related to the whole and to each other. In the case of *María,* the structure might be seen in two different ways: first, as a series of several *micro-récits,* and second, as a progression of two *micro-récits,* with the second much shorter and much more intense. The first view of the structure sees *María* as a series of incidents in which three steps of the four-step sequence would be repeated, with the fourth suspended except in Efraín's anxiety. The second view—and probably the better—appreciates the four steps in the section of the novel that ends in Efraín's departure for England; then the four steps are repeated in a more intense *micro-récit* beginning with Efraín's loneliness in England and ending with his ultimate loss of María and the region with which she is associated.

The third step in the analytical procedure might be to ascertain whether or not the pattern of *récit* illuminates any other aspect of the novel. Speculation on this point is virtually meaningless since it amounts to forecasting the unpredictable; nevertheless, one would certainly keep a watchful eye on the meaning that the Nay-Sinar story could take on in such an analysis. Thinking of *Suprema ley,* in view of what we have already noted about that novel, we might wonder if the Todorov-inspired procedure might emphasize the difference between the characterization of Julio and that of Clotilde. The total *récit* might be seen as (1) Julio settled in mediocrity, (2) Julio seeks exceptionality, (3) society execrates Julio, (4) Julio lost in alienation. Although this statement appears acceptable for the *récit* as a whole, it is not at all certain that it applies to the *micro-récits.* One could consider the possibility of an entirely different set of propositions concerning the total *récit,* with two intercalated *micro-récits,* one focusing on Julio and the other on Clotilde.

It is doubtful that speculation concerning the other novels would add to the foregoing observations. Clearly, all of them could be analyzed this way, and the idiosyncrasies already discovered in each work would naturally provide interesting objects of attention—for example, the serialized character of *Amalia,* the picaresque quality of *Mi tío el empleado,* or the question of who is the central character in *Aves sin nido.* Similarly, it is impossible even to make an intelligent guess about what unexpected appreciations this procedure might effect if applied to large numbers of nineteenth-century Spanish American novels. The basic applicability of the procedure is obvious so long as the selected novel has a diachronic dimension. The analysis presumably would show that dimension and, at the same time, point out the synchronic dimension. We may assume that all nineteenth-century novels have both dimensions, and significant speculation on the use of this procedure stops at that point.

Although the analyses in the eight principal chapters of this study show the appropriateness of certain procedures in illuminating different problems or questions, the speculations that make up this concluding chapter suggest repeatedly that relationships exist among the procedures themselves. In fact, these speculations recall suggestions of such relationships in earlier chapters.

If the critic (reader) is not confronting a specific problem, is there a single preferred point from which he may initiate a general elucidation of a novel in such a way that the analysis invites the application of different procedures? There may be no such simplistic beginning, if one thinks in terms of a rigorously exact theoretical proposition; on the other hand, it may be possible to specify such a point of departure if one thinks of satisfying a practical need. This need may refer to discussion of a fiction text among any two or more readers, or even to an analytical reading by a single person.

It is best to think first of a narrative that is unequivocally diachronic. Fiction texts that do not qualify in this regard should be considered separately. With respect to nineteenth-century novels, a reasonable description of the narrative structure might posit a diachronic line of (1) moment when *récit* cuts into *histoire*—(2) statement or insinuation of conflict—(3) development of the conflict—(4) climax—(5) denouement. These components are in syntagmatic relationship; the sequence is not logically reversible; one component cannot take the place of another. A synchronic (paradigmatic) line could be thought of as intersecting the diachronic line in the middle—that is, at the point of the third component (development of the conflict), because the events that serve to develop the conflict are functionally metaphoric. It is possible that reference to names, places, and times may give these events a diachronic appearance; on the other hand, the effects they exercise on the development of the conflict are probably homologous (even though the intensity of the effect may vary). These characteristics of the events that make up the third component suggest the paradoxical joining of diachrony and synchrony.

The first component of this scheme (moment when *récit* cuts into *histoire*) immediately refers to Gérard Genette because it is conveniently expressed in his terminology and one associates this specific act of beginning with the larger narrative situation, which must take into account the relationship of the narrator to characters, time, and place of narration. In all probability, if the reader is acquainted with the analytical procedures used in this study, the suggestion of Genette will first invite association with Brooks and Warren's definition of striking into the story. The next association may be with Wayne Booth's exposition of the Narrator role, and then with text act theory and with Jakobson, so bringing into focus the actual role of the reader in the narrative process.

Obviously, one does not make extensive analyses using all these procedures at the moment of beginning a reading; on the other hand, it is very natural that any given analytical process may suggest another. As soon as the initial association relates Genette to Brooks and Warren, a reader's awareness is likely to include both the latter's principle of "exposition" and the former's explanation of the difference between *récit* time and *histoire* time. Naturally enough, this aspect of narrative transformation suggests the Brooks and Warren formulation concerning summary, narrative, scene, and analysis, and also a long tradition of theory concerning this phenomenon. A detailed analysis may ensue and take any of several directions, or the complex awareness may do no more than sensitize a reader for a fuller appreciation of the fiction text in hand.

There is a difference between analysis of a fiction text taken as a *fait accompli* and an analysis that functions from the standpoint of the text-in-the-making. A practiced awareness of any critical procedure naturally moves a reader toward the second position—that is, of experiencing the text in the process of becoming. Nevertheless, some procedures seem to encourage one position more than the other. Barthes's codes, for example, tend to stress the text-in-the-making position; Jakobson and Todorov encourage the *post facto* analysis. This difference becomes quite evident on consideration of the second component of the narrative scheme (statement or insinuation of conflict). Whatever the point of beginning, certainly the conflict must be the basis of the story. The action and enigma codes of the Barthesian procedure are suggested immediately. An interesting contrast becomes apparent in the qualifying analysis of Kettle's essay, a clearly *post facto* explication. The function of Barthes's codes naturally must incorporate all the codes, and therefore a reader's sensitivity is enlarged to include the whole narrative process. The Barthesian procedure is particularly useful in emphasizing the phenomena that would, in another terminology, be called style and characterization. The connotative code, which is largely responsible for characterization, becomes associated with the action code and recalls the Brooks and Warren assertion that characterization is best effected through action. The statement of conflict may also suggest Brooks and Warren's fundamental question, "Whose story is it?"; the same inclination also brings to mind Genette's notion concerning the fundamental action of which the *récit* is an expansion.

The third component of the plot design may be regarded as the heart of the matter because it refers to the series of events that develop the conflict. It is possible that emphasis on how these events function may distract attention from something as important as the narrative position—that is, the awareness of who is speaking and who is seeing. However, if a reader associates these questions with an analysis of the episodes, his sensitivity to the act of narrating becomes multidimensional. Todorov's exposition of *micro-récits* is certainly suggested by this stage. Primarily, Todorov's analysis is likely to be useful in a *post facto* reading, but association of his ideas with awareness of the narrating voice and the observing eye tends to activate the process. It is the Barthesian procedure, of course, that interweaves best the several operations of narration in process. The Brooks and Warren principle of "Pattern and Design" points out the functionally repetitive nature of the incidents in series; this quality, naturally enough, suggests their synchrony, and the consequent association is with Merrell's proposed model, which emphasizes the metaphoric (synchronic) expression of the basic contrast.

The fourth component (climax) may suggest resolution of conflict, or illumination of enigma. Brooks and Warren identify a difference between climax and "key moment." The latter may or may not be the same as climax; it is the point in the *récit* where a reader feels he has grasped the full meaning of the narrative. In a case where climax and key moment do not coincide, a question naturally arises as to whether one or the other corresponds to the resolution (even if only apparent) of the conflict and also to the paradoxical joining of synchrony with diachrony. Moving then to Todorov's idea of episodes of equilibrium and episodes of disequilibrium, it seems that the third and fourth components of the five-point design might be episodes of disequilibrium and that the first and second (taken together), as well as the fifth, might be episodes of equilibrium. The Brooks and Warren suggestion of a difference between key moment and climax, however, renews concern about the meaning of the *récit,* and this problem may well bring up the Jakobson model again.

Such an interweaving of theories certainly could not be

satisfactory to anyone who espouses a single theory (or procedure) as the right one. The associations mentioned here—and others not mentioned—more likely will interest readers who place the text itself in the central position and seek all ways of appreciating its meaning fully. The interrelationship of theories then becomes an attractive, though always secondary, phenomenon. The simple five-point scheme serves as an opening step. But an opening step to what? To most nineteenth-century novels, certainly. But can it be useful in analyzing recent novels that appear to eliminate or minimize the diachronic dimension?

Much recent narrative tends (the qualifying nature of "tends" is important) to be synchronic-metaphor-paradigmatic—that is, *système*. It seems reasonable to think that this tendency may be related to an increasingly comprehensive cultural frame of reference, one that includes more than the ideas generally thought of as typifying Western culture. History, in Western culture, is basically diachronic—a straight line. It may include ideas about cycles of various kinds, but Western people do not live as if caught in circular time. It seems natural that, if people live on a chronological continuum, they will expect narration to be diachronic. One may hypothesize that narration of the opposite tendency will flourish and endure to the extent that non-Western concepts influence or replace Western concepts. Criticism that assumes a diachronic dimension obviously cannot deal affirmatively with narrative that is purely synchronic. Very little of the latter exists, of course, but the tendency toward it mitigates the usefulness of criticism that depends heavily on diachrony. The opposite kind of criticism would necessarily be considered highly specialized until Western cultural concepts are no longer the norm. Meanwhile, it seems convenient to assume some starting point—a general design—similar to the five-component formulation used here. When a narrative deviates sufficiently to make this design preponderantly negative, some other formulation must be proposed, with simple negativism (saying what a particular narrative is not) avoided as much as possible.

In the analysis of nineteenth-century novels in which the diachronic dimension is readily apparent, use of the five-component design may lead to multiple theoretical references that constitute a kind of structuration of the analysis—that is, one experiences the interrelationships in the act of interrelating. The convenience of the basic design as a starting-point in the analysis of a particular narrative text suggests the possibility of its usefulness in appreciating more fully the meaning of the nineteenth-century novel in Spanish America, generically speaking. The idea may appear far-fetched, but it may also be helpful if it is regarded as a beginning-point only.

The *histoire* of the genre so defined by time and place might include all novels written after Fernández de Lizardi (who may be thought of as belonging to an earlier period) and up to some point very likely past the turn of the century. In a more general sense, of course, the *histoire* might be thought of as the entire history of the novel. Point One in the design might be associated with the publication of *Amalia;* earlier fiction would correspond to Brooks and Warren's "Exposition." Insinuation of the conflict (Point Two) could well be the contrast between European refinement and American coarseness (also with an element of vitality), pointed out by David Viñas and referred to in the first chapter of the present study. The development of this conflict (Point Three) would involve all the important novels of the time and place, and also a large number of the less important ones. The metaphoric expression of the conflict would include several thematic oppositions: civilization-versus-barbarism, noble savage–versus–social problem, beneficent land–versus–threat of alienation (or physical danger). Another metaphor contrasts the differences between stylistic elegance and *criollista* homely expression. It is important to note an occasional tendency to invert these values, granting the quality of beneficence or uprightness to the coarse-vital component of the basic contrast. Such a switch might in fact signal Point Four of the design; however, there appears to be some relationship between this switch and the elegance–versus–homeliness metaphor that refers to prose style (*El sargento Felipe,* for example). In Picón-Febres's novel and in Gamboa's *Suprema ley,* as a further example, there is an apparent joining of refinement and homeliness. Even if this phenomenon does not correspond satisfactorily to the fourth point as a moment of climax, it may serve well as the point where diachrony and synchrony appear to join in this account of one phase of the novel's history—a *micro-récit* in the story of a genre. The denouement (Point Five) might be described in several different ways, generally more relevant to the history of the novel as a whole than to the nineteenth-century novel in Spanish America. In terms of the latter it may be best to say that the denouement corresponds to a transition from the sense of refinement to vanguardism.

Notes

1. A number of novelesque works were written during the colonial period, and there are considerable arguments for calling some of them novels. There is no question about *El Periquillo Sarniento,* since it is obviously narrative fiction and accords with a commonly recognized generic definition, the picaresque. The strongest competitor for the distinction of first American novel is, in my opinion, *El siglo de oro en las selvas de Erífile* (1607), a pastoral novel by Bernardo de Balbuena. On this point, see José Rojas Garcidueñas, "La novela en la Nueva España," *Anales del Instituto de Investigaciones Estéticas* 8, no. 30 (1962): 57–78. The generic identity of this novel is unquestionable. True, the narrative thread is slender, but that is characteristic of pastoral novels. One might object that its theme is not sufficiently "American." In that case, we identify a clearly American theme as a necessary component of the American novel. This apparent requirement is significant in our consideration of the novel's development in nineteenth-century Spanish America.

2. The pícaro's first name is a double diminutive, Pedro-Perico-Periquillo, that means "parrot." It refers to the boy's clothing, an inelegant combination of green and yellow. Sarniento is a play on the family name Sarmiento. By changing the "m" to "n," the author gives the name the same root as *sarna* (the itch); hence "the itchy (or mangy) parrot."

3. Such lapses complicate the problems of literary history. A generational approach is helpful in this regard, and the studies by both Arrom and Goic (see bibliography) are enlightening. Such studies may be based on the interests and artistic canons of writers born within specific periods; dates of publication are not important. Goic, for example, places Villaverde in the generation of 1837 (born between 1800 and 1814), and defines the generation specifically and satisfactorily without concern for the publication date of the whole work. We may agree with his generational definition and still ask if it is not also significant that a novel so characterized should be finished and published completely during a period when a different generation would, presumably, be dominant.

4. With reference to this phenomenon, see Susana Zanetti's comments on local color in *María,* in Mirta Yáñez, ed., *La novela romántica latinoamericana,* p. 527.

5. "Mármol: Los dos ojos del romanticismo," in David Viñas, *Literatura argentina y realidad política,* pp. 125–40.

6. Fernando Alegría's use of the term "realismo romántico" is enlightening in connection with this combination. He divides the romantic novel into

213

five categories: (1) political novel in Argentina, (2) sentimental, (3) historical, (4) idealization of the Indian, and (5) romantic realism. A subsequent chapter is entitled "Naturalist Realism." There is much to be said in favor of this scheme, particularly if one is willing to look at the novel of the last century synchronically. *Martín Rivas* belongs to "romantic realism," a perfect classification of the novel. Alegría's terminological system, however, risks minimizing the importance of *costumbrismo* in categories other than "realismo romántico." Fernando Alegría, *Historia de la novela hispanoamericana*.

7. R. Anthony Castagnaro, *The Early Spanish American Novel*, pp. 42–44.

8. Alegría, *Novela hispanoamericana*, p. 88.

9. It is interesting to note some ambivalence in this regard. Alegría dismisses the scene as trite and uninteresting (ibid., pp. 87–88); Castagnaro finds it fascinating—superior to the portrait of Buenos Aires in *Pot-pourri*—and speculates that Paris was, at that time, closer to Cambaceres's heart than was Buenos Aires (Castagnaro, *Early Spanish American Novel*, p. 122).

10. Hubert Herring, *A History of Latin America*, p. 730.

11. An interesting Marxist discussion of this period, with emphasis on *modernista* poetry, may be found in Francoise Pérus, *Literatura y sociedad en América Latina: El modernismo*. See also "La novela naturalista hispanoamericana" by Luis Iñigo Madrigal, in Ricardo Vergara, ed., *La novela hispanoamericana*, pp. 71–94.

12. Castagnaro (*Early Spanish American Novel*, p. 125) writes in some detail of Cambaceres's style. Especially interesting in his comment concerning "a staccato-like intensification of his nervously-paced style through the intermittent appearance of prepositional and adverbial phrases."

13. Kessel Schwartz, *A New History of Spanish American Fiction*, I, 110.

14. Schwartz calls Vargas Vila "a kind of modernist-naturalist," (ibid., p. 140).

15. One of the investigators to recognize the significance of this novel is Juan Loveluck. See his *"De sobremesa, novela desconocida del modernismo,"* *Revista Iberoamericana* 31, no. 59 (January–June 1965): 17–32. A more recent, comprehensive study of the novel is Héctor H. Orjuela's *"De sobremesa"* in his *"De sobremesa" y otros ensayos sobre José Asunción Silva*, pp. 11–45.

CHAPTER TWO

1. Emilio Cotarelo y Mori, *La Avellaneda y sus obras*. Among the studies that emphasize biography, Rafael Marquina's *Gertrudis Gómez de Avellaneda* is of interest because of its Cuban source. More recently, Raimundo Lazo, another Cuban scholar, has published *Gertrudis Gómez de Avellaneda: La mujer y la poetisa lírica*.

2. Kessel Schwartz cites an article by Edith Kelly, "La Avellaneda's *Sab*

and the Political Situation in Cuba," in *The Americas* (1945): 303–16. (See Schwartz, *Spanish American Fiction,* I, 385.) In 1961, Helena Percas Ponseti published "Sobre la Avellaneda y su novela, *Sab*" in *Revista Iberoamericana* 28, no. 54 (July–December 1961): 347–57. Alberto J. Carlos—complaining, interestingly enough, that *Sab* was being ignored while *Guatimozín* received more attention than it deserved—published "René, Werther y *La Novelle Héloise* en la primera novela de la Avellaneda", *Revista Iberoamericana* 31, no. 60 (July-December 1965): 223–38. An edition of *Sab* was published in 1973 by the Instituto Cubano del Libro with a lengthy essay by Mary Cruz on Avellaneda and *Sab*. This study—"*Sab*, su texto y su contexto"—is by all odds the most analytical with reference to Avellaneda's process of making a novel.

3. Concha Meléndez, *La novela indianista en Hispanoamérica*, pp. 75–78.

4. Meléndez, ibid., p. 78, cites four editions: Madrid: D. A. Espinosa, 1846; Valparaíso: Imprenta del Mercurio, 1847; Mexico City: Imprenta de Juan R. Navarro, 1853; "y otra vez en México en 1887." The Navarro edition is the one used here; references to it will be made by page number, parenthetically, within the text. The English translation was made by Mrs. Wilson W. Blake (Mexico City: F. P. Hoeck, 1898). Meléndez mentions this version; a copy of it is in the library of Pedro F. de Andrea in Mexico City. In the preface, Helen Edith Blake (so signed) says she knows of only two copies of *Guatimozín* in Mexico City. She also notes that Lew Wallace's *Fair God* has been called a plagiarism of *Guatimozín*, but that examination shows that both novels are based on the history of the conquest by Bernal Díaz del Castillo.

5. Meléndez, *Novela indianista*, pp. 75–77.

6. Cotarelo y Mori, *Avellaneda*, pp. 128–29.

7. Meléndez, *Novela indianista*, pp. 75–76; Cotarela y Mori, *Avellaneda*, 131–32.

8. Wayne C. Booth, *The Rhetoric of Fiction;* see especially pp. 154–55.

9. Cleanth Brooks and Robert Penn Warren, *Understanding Fiction*, p. 667.

10. Gérard Genette, "Discours du récit", *Figures III*, pp. 127–29.

11. Ibid., p. 75. For Genette, the basic verb in the *Odyssey* is *Ulysses returns to Ithaca;* in Proust's *Rememberance* it is *Marcel becomes a writer.*

12. The subtitle is inaccurate. Agustín Iturbide used the title "emperor." (Maximilian of Austria also used the title, but after the publication of *Guatimozín*.) Cuauhtémoc was the last emperor of the Aztecs.

13. Cotarelo y Mori, *Avellaneda,* p. 128.

14. Meléndez, *Novela indianista*, p. 78.

15. These words present some difficulty in English. One version is, "Am I on a bed of roses?" The approximation will probably suffice, but the Spanish used here is less commonplace: *Tálamo* is a nuptial bed; *flores* is the generic word for flowers.

16. J. Lloyd Read, *The Mexican Historical Novel, 1826–1910* p. 77.

CHAPTER THREE

1. For more discussion of this point, see any edition of *Facundo, o la civilización y la barbarie,* by Domingo Faustino Sarmiento. The point is made in Sarmiento's text itself; however, a good introductory essay, by Raimondo Lazo, may be found in the "Sepan Cuantos" edition (Mexico City: Porrúa, 1969), pp. ix–xxxv.

2. Juan Carlos Ghiano speaks of this matter in his "Prólogo" to the novel, p. xi. All references to Ghiano's analysis of the novel and to the narrative text will be to this edition, and will be cited parenthetically within the body of the present essay.

3. The essay may be found in David Viñas, *Literatura argentina y realidad política,* pp. 125–40. The same volume contains another relevant essay, of somewhat lesser importance, entitled " 'Niños' y 'criados favoritos' de *Amalia* a Beatriz Guido a través de *La Gran Aldea,*" pp. 81–121.

4. Alegría, *Novela hispanoamerica,* pp. 35–38.

5. Brooks and Warren, *Understanding Fiction,* especially pp. 644–68. References to this book will appear parenthetically in the text of the essay, identified by the initials "BW".

6. See Viñas, "Mármol."

7. Ibid., p. 133.

8. José Mármol, *Amalia* (Havana: Casa de las Américas, 1976), "Prólogo" by Trinidad Pérez, pp. vii–xlvii: see especially p. xxxi.

9. Jacques Barzun, *Classic, Romantic, and Modern,* p. 80.

10. I am using "message" as in the Jakobson diagram of a communication act. See Robert Scholes, *Structuralism in Literature,* pp. 24–27.

11. Fryda Schultz de Mantovani, *Apasionados del nuevo mundo,* p. 36.

CHAPTER FOUR

1. Alegría, *Novela hispanoamericana,* pp. 48–50. For specific reference to *Martín Rivas,* see pp. 53–54.

2. The expression "gente de medio pelo" offers a problem of translation. "Lower middle class" is probably the best approximation. The Molinas might be described as vulgar, with moral standards that have a low threshold of vulnerability. However, individuals are capable of great moral strength. The portrayal of this one family does not justify the same kind of generalization that can be made about the Encinas and their friends.

3. Interesting, in this connection, is an essay on another novel by Blest Gana, *Durante la reconquista,* by Mireya Camurati, "Blest Gana, Lukacs, y la novela histórica," *Cuadernos Americanos* 197, no. 6 (November–December 1974): 88–99.

4. Alegría, *Novela hispanoamerica,* p. 51. Alegría makes the observation as follows "El lector chileno entra a las novelas de Blest Gana como a un museo histórico donde las figuras, al verse reconocidas, comienzan a agitarse en la sombra y a revivir una curiosa paradia de gestos y actitudes que aún pueden identificarse en el Chile de hoy."

5. The text used for this study is the eleventh edition by Zig-Zag, Santiago, 1967. Cedomil Goic, in *La novela chilena*, p. 184, cites twenty-two editions in Spanish, sixteen of them published in Santiago. The most recent cited by Goic is the ninth edition by Zig-Zag, Santiago, 1963. Assuming there was a tenth by Zig-Zag, a total of twenty-four are accounted for by 1968. Goic also cites an English translation by Mrs. Charles Whitman (New York: Alfred A. Knopf, 1916).

6. Raúl Silva Castro, *Alberto Blest Gana (1830–1920);* Hernán Diaz Arrieta, *Don Alberto Blest Gana;* Hernán Poblete Varas, *Genio y figura de Alberto Blest Gana.*

7. Goic, *Novela chilena,* devotes one of eight chapters to *Martín Rivas* (pp 33–49). The corresponding bibliography, with comments on some items (pp. 184–87), is as thorough as the analysis itself.

8. Ibid., p. 34.

9. Ibid., p. 185.

10. Floyd Merrell, "Toward a New Model of Narrative Structure," in *The Analysis of Hispanic Texts: Current Trends in Methodology,* eds. Mary Ann Beck, et al., pp. 150–69. Where necessary, references will be made parenthetically by mentioning the author and page number, e.g. (Merrell, 151). The model is provisional and has been altered since the publication of this article.

11. Roman Jakobson and Morris Halle, *Fundamentals of Language,* pp. 91–92. See also Scholes, *Structuralism,* pp. 20–22.

12. Brooks and Warren, *Understanding Fiction,* pp. 644–68.

13. Cedomil Goic notes this tempo and says that in this slow first part, as well as in the more rapid second part, the tempo corresponds to the developing love of Leonor for Martín. Goic, *Novela chilena,* p. 40.

14. For a brief general statement concerning the complexity of the symbol, see J. E. Cirlot, *A Dictionary of Symbols,* pp. 144–45.

15. It may be coincidence that "fiesta" is important in Merrell's analysis of "La cuesta de las comadres," the story by Juan Rulfo that serves as the example of his proposition. On the other hand, it may well be that any axiological opposition, as defined by Merrell, is characterized by some aspect of creation-alienation-regeneration. Merrell's references to the fiesta are on his pp. 158, 162–63, where he refers to Mircea Eliade, *The Sacred and the Profane,* pp. 87–88.

CHAPTER FIVE

1. *María,* edited and with introduction by Donald McGrady (Madrid: Editorial Labor, 1970); *María,* introduction by Enrique Anderson Imbert (Mexico City: Fondo de Cultura Económica, 1951); *María,* introduction by Daniel Moreno (Mexico City: Porrúa, 1967). References will be made to the McGrady edition unless otherwise indicated, and page numbers will be given parenthetically in the text. McGrady's edition carries the authority of his having compared the editions in which the author himself made changes.

2. Seymour Menton, "La estructura dualística de *María*," *Thesaurus* 25 (1970): 1–27.

3. I refer to the Russian formalist's *fable* or Gérard Genette's *histoire*, that is, the chronological series of incidents that is transformed into a literary narrative. See Scholes, *Structuralism,* p. 165.

4. See Menton, "Estructura," pp. 21–22.

5. These are the terms used by Gérard Genette to define the nature of narrative. *Histoire* (story) is an abstraction referring to the basic events in chronological order. *Récit* means the work of fiction as we read it, transformed by many techniques that change the order of events, prolong some in relation to others, establish narrative points of view, and so forth. *Narration* is the narrative situation, the means by which the *récit* is presented. See Genette, "Discours du récit." In *María,* regionalism is intimately related to the transformation of *historie* to *récit* because it is an essential factor in defining the narrative situation.

6. Winifred Bryan Horner, "Text Act Theory: A Study of Nonfiction Texts" (dissertation).

7. On the recoverability of intent, see particularly ibid., pp. 22, 51–52, and 96; and the reader in text act theory, see pp. 93–96.

8. The following modification of Roman Jakobson's communication act model (see "Linguistics and Poetics," in *Style and Language,* ed. Thomas A. Sebeok) may be helpful on this point:

First Stage			Second Stage		
narrative voice	context message contact code	text reader or real reader		context message contact code	text act reader

(Note: Horner assumes a text reader who is inherently within the communication act, a real reader who exists in approximately the same time and space, and a text act reader who is removed in time and/or space. See also, in this connection, an essay by Mieke Bal, "Narration et focalisation," *Poétique* 29 (February 1977): 107–27).

The model, adjusted specifically for *Mária,* might look like this:

| 1st-person protagonist via fictitious editor | Romantic period &
New Worldism
Efraín's loss
summary &
scene
lyrical Spanish | Efraín's siblings | | Romantic period in
historical perspective
Efraín's loss
novel
old-fashioned
Spanish | present-day reader |

The principle factor to be considered is the context. Since the second-stage context is a fair indicator of what the second stage experience is like, it is important to understand that it may signify only a patient acceptance of romantic foible. However, if the first-stage communication act is the "sender" of the second-stage act, then the second-stage context is related to the whole first-stage act in the same way that "Romantic period & New Worldism" is related to "1st-person protagonist via fictitious editor." Therefore, the expected reaction of "Efraín's siblings"—as part of the first-stage act—influences the meaning of the second-stage context, guaranteeing a degree of sensitivity that accords with Efraín's sense of loss. (It should be understood that I am using only Jakobson's basic model of a communication act, not his ideas regarding literary particularity. See also the essay on Gamboa's *Suprema ley* in the present volume.)

9. The dedication appears in the McGrady edition of *María*, p. 47, and in many others. The term "hermanos" has an extended meaning that includes the kindred spirits of Efraín. The sense of the dedication vacillates between the specific and the general meanings.

10. Porrúa edition (see note 1, above) pp. xxix–xxxi.

11. Ibid., pp. 1–2. This piece also appears in a Mexican edition of Isaacs' *Poesías* (Mexico City: Angel Pola, 1907), pp. 175–77. It is the first piece in a section entitled "Prosas," which are *about* Isaacs, except for this first selection.

12. Genette, "Discours du récit," p. 75. For Genette, the basic verb in the *Odyssey* is *Ulysses returns to Ithaca;* in Proust's *Remembrance,* it is *Marcel becomes a writer.*

13. The fictitious editor may be considered the "text reader" or the "real reader"—following Horner's theory—depending on whether he is thought of as being within the fiction text or outside the fiction text. He may be thought of as within the narrative text act if the dedication "A los hermanos de Efraín" is taken as part of the narrative text act. So far as the importance of the context is concerned, the choice makes little difference because there is no important time lapse between the experience of the text reader and that of the real reader. On the other hand, acceptance of the dedicatory statement as part of the narrative text act enhances appreciation of the intended reader's reaction, and also makes Efraín's death a part of the narrative text act, thereby effecting a satisfactory division between Efraín and Isaacs.

14. Roland Barthes, *S/Z: An Essay.*

15. McGrady edition of *María*, p. 37; Menton, "Estructura," 15–20.

16. On this point see Barzun, *Classic, Romantic, and Modern,* especially pp. 16–62, on Sir Walter Scott.

17. José Juan Arrom says, "La historia de María se enlaza tan íntimamente con el medio, resulta tan de nosotros, que para lograr una nota exótica Isaacs se ve obligado a interpolar el cuento de Nay y Sinar." *Esquema generacional de las letras hispanoamericas,* pp. 167–68. This appreciation underlines the combination of María as a person with her surroundings. The characterization makes it impossible for her to project an exotic quality.

CHAPTER SIX

1. Edna Coll has provided the most extensive bibliography of and on Meza, in *Indice informativo de la novela hispanoamericana: Las Antillas,* pp. 343–45. Coll cites an original publication and two republications of Martí's *Mi tío el empleado:* Novela de Ramón Meza:" (1) *El Avisador Cubano* (New York), 25 April 1888; (2) *El Fígaro* (Havana) 17, no. 46 (1901): 538; (3) *Cuba y América* (Havana) 21, No. 7 (13 May 1906): 102–3. Souza's evaluation is found in his *Major Cuban Novelists,* pp. 9–10, 101. Arrufat's essay, "Ramón Meza y la novela cubana del siglo XIX," is in *Cuba en la UNESCO* 2 no. 4 (December 1961): 184–203.

2. See Coll, *Indice.* Note especially the issues in honor of Ramón Meza of *Cuba en la UNESCO* 2, no. 4 (December 1961). Coll's bibliography should also include the introductory essay by Lorenzo García Vega in the 1960 edition of *Mi tío el empleado* (Havana: Dirección General de Cultura, Ministerio de Educación), pp. v–xvii.

3. Coll, *Indice,* pp. 343–44.

4. García Vega, introduction cited in note 2, above.

5. The notion of picaresque as used in the present study depends largely on Claudio Guillén's generic definition in *Literature as System.*

6. Roland Barthes, *S/Z: An Essay* and "Textual Analysis of a Tale by Edgar Poe," *Poe Studies* 10, no. 1 (June 1977): 1–12.

7. Association with the picaresque suggests the phenomenon of intertextuality, which will be amply apparent, with respect to the picaresque, in the course of this reading. Exposition of further intertextuality is the purpose of José Lezama Lima's "Ramón Meza: Tersitismo y claro enigma," in his *La cantidad hechizada,* pp. 215–25.

8. See Barthes, "Textual Analysis," especially pp. 5 and 11.

9. See Mary Louise Pratt, *Toward a Speech Act Theory of Narrative Discourse,* on narrative discourse and natural narrative.

10. Page numbers used in the text will refer to the edition of the novel cited in note 2. I have corrected obvious typographical errors and inconsistencies.

11. Barthes, "Textual Analysis," p. 10.

12. Ibid., p. 11.

13. See Genette, "Discours du récit," especially pp. 254–59. The fact that the narrator of *Gil Blas* (Genette's example) uses the first person does not mean that he is a second-degree narrator (functioning as narrator within the *récit*). Actually he is a first-degree narrator (outside the *récit*) telling his own story.

14. Meza was an accomplished cultivator of the *costumbrista* sketch. See the chapter on him in Emilio Roig de Leuchsenring, *La literatura costumbrista cubana de los siglos XVIII y XIX,* vol. 4, *Los escritores,* pp. 239–48.

15. The change is interesting in connection with Robert Schole's definition of fictional modes. See his *Structuralism,* pp. 132–38.

16. See Genette, "Discours du récit," pp. 127–29.

CHAPTER SEVEN

1. A *tradición* is a narrative sketch based on a historical event or on a legend. Ricardo Palma is given credit for having invented the genre. His followers were numerous, in Peru and in other Spanish-American countries.

2. After the destruction of her house and press, Clorinda Matto left Peru. There is some doubt as to whether she was deported or left as a result of her own decision. See Francisco Carrillo, *Clorinda Matto de Turner y su indigenismo literario*, p. 17.

3. Ibid., p. 27.

4. *Birds without a Nest*, translated by J. G. Hudson (London: Charles J. Thynne, 1904).

5. The 1948 edition was published by the Universidad Nacional del Cuzco. The edition by Fryda Schultz de Mantovani was published in Buenos Aires by Solar/Hachette, 1968. It also contains the essay by Gutiérrez de Quintanillo. The Solar/Hachette edition is the one used for the present study. The Lima: Imprenta del Universo, de Carlos Prince, 1889 edition is at hand for corroboration. Unless otherwise indicated, references made here will be to the Solar/Hachette edition, and page numbers will be given parenthetically in the text.

6. The first of the dissertations is Clifton B. McIntosh, *"Aves sin nido* and the Beginning of Indianism." More recent ones are Ruth C. Crouse, "Clorinda Matto de Turner: An Analysis of Her Role in Peruvian Literature," and George De Mello, "The Writings of Clorinda Matto de Turner." Another dissertation relating to the author and her time is Diane R. Goodrich, "Peruvian Novels of the Nineteenth Century."

7. Antonio Cornejo Polar, Introduction to *Aves sin nido*, pp. vii–xxxv. Many of the points made in Cornejo Polar's analysis accord with the present study, even though the analytical procedures are quite different.

8. Arnold Kettle, "Dickens and the Popular Tradition", in *Marxists on Literature*, ed. David Craig, pp. 214–44.

9. Ibid., p. 214.

10. Ibid, p. 216.

11. *Récit* is used here as defined by Gérard Genette. See his "Le Discours du récit," or references to same in the chapter on Isaac's *María*, in the present volume.

12. Carrillo, *Clorinda Matto*, p. 51.

13. Cornejo Polar, Introduction, pp. xiii–xvi.

14. Jorge Basadre, *Historia de la república del Perú*, IV, 1935.

15. Cornejo Polar, Introduction, p. xvi.

16. Ibid., pp. xxvi–xxvii.

17. Ibid., p. xxv.

18. Kettle, "Dickens," pp. 243–4.

19. Joseph Sommers, "The Indian Oriented Novel in Latin America: New Spirit, New Forms, New Scope," *Journal of Inter-American Studies* 6, no. 2 (April 1964): 162.

CHAPTER EIGHT

1. Gamboa published a volume of short stories, *Del natural*, in 1888; *El evangelista*, a novelette, was published in 1927 (Mexico City: Librería Guadalupana) in the series *La Novela Corta*, Año I, Núm. 6.

2. Alexander C. Hooker, Jr., *La novela de Frederico* [sic] *Gamboa*, pp. 10, 29.

3. A master's thesis (J. O. Theobald, "Naturalism in the Works of Federico Gamboa") has the advantage of having been written during the novelist's lifetime, when the critic was able to correspond with him. The most comprehensive work is Seymour Menton's doctoral dissertation, "The Life and Works of Federico Gamboa." Representative articles on Gamboa (see Bibliography) are: Robert J. Neiss, "Zola's *L'Oeuvre* and *Reconquista* of Gamboa"; A. W. Woolsey, "Some of the Social Problems Considered by Federico Gamboa"; E. R. Moore, "Federico Gamboa: Diplomat and Novelist"; Seymour Menton, "Federico Gamboa: Un análisis estilístico."

4. Emmanuel Carballo, "Diario Público," *El Día* (8 July 1976): 5.

5. See Barzun, *Classic, Romantic, and Modern*, p. 114.

6. For a lucid explanation of this model, see Scholes, *Structuralism*, pp. 23–25. Jakobson's essay "Linguistics and Poetics" may be conveniently found in *The Structuralistics from Marx to Lévi-Strauss*, ed. Richard and Fernande DeGeorge, (Garden City: Doubleday, 1972), as well as in *Style in Language*, ed. Thomas A. Sebeok. My use of "basic anecdote" and "developed plot" corresponds roughly to the Russian formalists' use of *fable* and *sujet*, or Gérard Genette's *histoire* and *récit*.

7. Booth, *The Rhetoric of Fiction*.

8. Hooker, *Gamboa*, p. 7.

9. Carlos González Peña, *Gente mía*. See chapter entitled "Don Federico Gamboa y el don de gentes", pp. 103–10.

10. Federico Gamboa, *Suprema ley* (Paris and Mexico City: Librería de la Vda. de Ch. Bouret, 1896), p. 32. This is the first edition of the novel. Further references to *Suprema ley* will be to this edition and will appear parenthetically within the text of the study.

11. Because of the frequently expository nature of *Suprema ley*, the "implied reader" is similar to the "text reader" defined in Horner's "Text Act Theory."

12. Hooker, *Gamboa*, p. 23.

13. See Horner, "Text Act Theory," for an explanation of "text act reader," especially pp. 93–97. (A brief explanation may be found in chapter 5, footnote 8.)

14. Scholes, *Structuralism*, p. 24.

CHAPTER NINE

1. Gonzalo Picón-Febres, *El sargento Felipe* (Paris: Librería Paul Ollendorf, n.d.). The dedication appears on an unnumbered page immediately preceding the first page of the narrative. This edition, which is not cited in the

Bibliografía de la novela venezolana, was published by the same house that published Picón-Febres' *Nieve y lodo* in 1914. The Paris edition of *El sargento Felipe* will hereafter be referred to by page number, parenthetically, in the text.

2. Dillwyn F. Ratcliff, *Venezuelan Prose Fiction,* p. 85.

3. In addition to Ratcliff, pp. 86–88, see Mariano Picón-Salas, *Literatura venezolana,* p. 156, and Alfred Coester, *The Literary History of Spanish America,* p. 331.

4. Pedro Orgambide and Roberto Yahni, *Enciclopedia de la literatura argentina.* The essay is on pp. 428–35; the specific point is made on p. 432.

5. Ratcliff, *Venezuela Prose Fiction,* pp. 85–86.

6. Northrop Frye, *The Anatomy of Criticism,* pp. 33–34.

7. Schwartz, *Spanish American Fiction,* I, 84.

8. Rafael Di Prisco, *Acerca de los orígenes de la novela venezolana,* pp. 85–86.

9. Picón-Salas, *Literatura venezolana,* p. 156.

10. Coester, *Literary History,* p. 330.

11. Tzvetan Todovov, *Littérature et signification,* p. 53.

12. The diagram of *Les liaisons dangereuses* is on p. 55 of Todorov's *Littérature et signification.*

13. Ibid., pp. 55–56.

14. Ibid., p. 57.

15. Brooks and Warren, *Understanding Fiction,* p. 653.

16. Tzvetan Todorov, *The Poetics of Prose.* The specific reference is to chapter 8, "The Grammar of Narrative," pp. 108–19.

17. Ibid., p. 111.

18. Ibid., pp. 113–16.

Bibliography

1. EDITIONS OF NOVELS ANALYZED

Blest Gana, Alberto. *Martín Rivas*. Santiago: Zig-Zag, 1967.

Gamboa, Federico. *Suprema ley*. Paris and Mexico City: Librería de la Vda. de Ch. Bouret, 1896.

Gómez de Avellaneda, Gertrudis. *Guatimozín*. Mexico City: Imprenta de Juan R. Navarro, 1853.

Isaacs, Jorge, *María*, edited and with introduction by Donald McGrady. Madrid: Editorial Labor, 1970.

Mármol, José. *Amalia*, edited with introduction by Juan Carlos Ghiano. Mexico City: Porrúa, 1971.

Matto de Turner, Clorinda. *Aves sin nido*. Edited by Fryda Schultz de Mantovani. Buenos Aires: Solar/Hachette, 1968.

Meza y Suárez Inclán, Ramón. *Mi tío el empleado*. Havana: Dirección General de Cultura, Ministeriod de Educación, 1960.

Picón-Febres, Gonzalo. *El sargento Felipe*. Paris: Librería Paul Ollendorf, n.d.

2. HISTORY AND CRITICISM

Alegría, Fernando. *Historia de la novela hispanoamericana*. Mexico City: Ediciones de Andrea, 1974.

Anderson Imbert, Enrique. Introduction to *María*, by Jorge Isaacs, Mexico City: Fondo de Cultura Económica, 1951.

_____. "Notas sobre la novela histórica en el siglo xix," in *La novela iberoamericana* (Memorias del Quinto Congreso del Instituto Internacional de Literatura Iberoamericana). Albuquerque, N.M.: University of New Mexico Press, 1952.

Arrom, José Juan. *Esquema generacional de las letras hispanoamericanas*. Bogotá: Instituto Caro y Cuervo, 1976.

Arrufat, Antón. "Ramón Meza y la novela cubana del siglo xix." *Cuba en la UNESCO* 2, no. 4 (December 1961): 184–203.

Basadre, Jorge. *Historia de la república del Perú*, vol. 4. Lima: Ediciones Historia, 1961.

Bibliografía de la novela venezolana. Caracas: Universidad Central de Venezuela, 1963.

Camurati, Mireya. "Blest Gana, Lukacs, y la novela histórica," *Cuadernos Americanos* 197, no. 6 (November–December 1974): 88–99.

Carballo, Emmanuel. "Diario público." *El Día* (8 July 1976): 5.

Carlos, Albert J. "René, Werther y *La Nouvelle Héloise* en la primera novela de la Avellaneda." *Revista Iberoamericana* 31, no. 60 (July–December 1965): 223–38.

Carrillo, Francisco. *Clorinda Matto de Turner y su indigenismo literario.* Lima: Ediciones de la Biblioteca Universitaria, 1967.

Castagnaro, R. Anthony. *The Early Spanish American Novel.* New York: Las Américas, 1971.

Coester, Alfred. *The Literary History of Spanish America.* New York: Macmillan, 1941.

Coll, Edna. *Indice informativo de la novela hispanoamericana: Las Antillas,* vol. I. Universidad de Puerto Rico: Editorial Universitaria, 1974.

Cornejo Polar, Antonio. Introduction to *Aves sin nido,* by Clorida Matto de Turner, Havana: Casa de las Américas, 1974.

Cotarelo y Mori, Emilio. *La Avellaneda y sus obras.* Madrid: Tipografía de Archivos, 1930.

Crouse, Ruth C. "Clorinda Matto de Turner: An Analysis of Her Role in Peruvian Literataure." Ph.D. dissertation, Florida State University, 1964.

Cruz, Mary. "*Sab,* su texto y su contexto," prefatory essay in edition of *Sab,* by Gertrudis Gómez de Avellaneda. Havana: Instituto Cubano del Libro, 1973.

Cuadros E., Manuel E. *Paisaje y obra, mujer e historia.* Cuzco: H. G. Rozas, 1949.

Curcio Altamar, Antonio. *Evolución de la novela en Colombia.* Bogotá: Instituto Caro y Cuervo, 1957.

De Mello, George. "The Writings of Clorinda Matto de Turner." Ph.D. dissertation, University of Colorado, 1968.

Díaz Arrieta, Hernán. *Don Alberto Blest Gana.* Santiago: Nascimento, 1940.

Di Prisco, Rafael. *Acerca de los orígenes de la novela venezolana.* Caracas: Universidad Central de Venezuela, 1969.

Englekirk, John E., and Ramos, Margaret M. *La narrativa uruguaya.* Berkeley: Publications in Modern Philology, 1967.

Finot, Enrique. *Historia de la novela boliviana.* Mexico City: Porrúa, 1943.

Fox, Hugh. "The Novelist as Filter: Naturalism in Latin America." *Southwest Review* 53, no. 3 (Summer 1968): 258–65.

García Vega, Lorenzo. "Prólogo" to *Mi tío el empleado,* by Ramón Meza y Suárez Inclán. Havana: Dirección General de Cultura, Ministerio de Educación, 1960, pp. v–xvii.

Goic, Cedomil. "Brevísima relación de la historia de la novela hispanoamericana," in Vergara, Ricardo, ed., *La novela hispanoamericana: Descubrimiento e invención de América.* Valparaíso: Ediciones Universitarias, 1973.

_____. *La novela chilena.* Santiago: Editorial Universitaria, 1968.

Gómez Tejera, Carmen. *La novela en Puerto Rico.* San Juan: University of Puerto Rico, 1947.

González Peña, Carlos. *Gente mía.* Mexico City: Stylo, 1946.

Goodrich, Diane R. "Peruvian Novels of the Nineteenth Century." Ph.D. dissertation, Indiana University, 1966.

Guerra Cunningham, Lucía. "Panorama crítica de la novela chilena (1843–1949)." Ph.D. dissertation, University of Kansas, 1975.

Gutiérrez de Quintanilla, Emilio. "Juicio crítico," prefatory essay to *Aves sin nido,* by Clorinda Matto de Turner. Buenos Aires: Solar/Hachette, 1968. (Originally published in the Valencia edition of 1889.)

Guzmán, Augusto. *La novela en Bolivia, 1847–1954.* La Paz: Editorial Juventud, 1955.

Herring, Hubert. *A History of Latin America.* New York: Knopf, 1968.

Hooker, Alexander C., Jr. *La novela de Frederico* [sic]*Gamboa.* n.p.: Olympic, 1967.

Iñigo Madrigal, Luis. "La novela naturalista hispanoamericana," in Vergara, Ricardo, ed., *La novela hispanoamericana: Descubrimiento e invención de América.* Valparaíso: Ediciones Universitarias, 1973.

Isaacs, Jorge. *Poesías.* Mexico City: Angel Pola, 1907.

Lazo, Raimundo. *Gertrudis Gómez de Avellaneda: La mujer y la poesía lírica.* Mexico City: Porrúa, 1972.

_____. Introduction to *Facundo, o la civilización y la barbarie,* by Domingo Faustino Sarmiento. Mexico City: Porrúa, 1969, pp. ix–xxxv.

León de Hazera, Lydia de. *La novela de la selva hispanoamericana.* Bogotá: Instituto Caro y Cuervo, 1971.

Lezama Lima, José. *La cantidad hechizada.* Madrid: Ediciones Jucar, 1974.

Lewis, Bartie Lee, Jr. "The Myth and the Moment: A Reappraisal of the Novels of Federico Gamboa." Ph.D. dissertation, University of New Mexico, 1973.

Lichtblau, Myron. *The Argentine Novel In the Nineteenth Century.* New York: Hispanic Institute in the United States, 1959.

Loveluck, Juan. "*De sobremesa,* novela desconocida del modernismo." *Revista Iberoamericana* 31, no. 59 (January–June 1965): 17–32.

Loyola, Hernán. "*Don Guillermo* y *Martín Rivas:* Visión paralela," in Vergara, Ricardo, ed. *La novela hispanoamericana: Descubrimiento e invención de América.* Valparaíso: Ediciones Universitarias, 1973.

Marquina, Rafael. *Gertrudis Gómez de Avellaneda.* Havana: Editorial Trópico, 1939.

McIntosh, Clifton B. "*Aves sin nido* and the Beginning of Indianism." Ph.D. dissertation, University of Virginia, 1932.

Meléndez, Concha. *La novela indianista en Hispanoamérica.* Madrid: Imprenta de la Librería y Casa Editorial Hernando, 1934.

Menton, Seymour. "La estructura dualística de *María.*" *Thesaurus, Boletín del Instituto Caro y Cuevo* 25 (1970): 1–27.

_____. "Federico Gamboa: Un análisis estilístico." *Humanitas* 4 (1963): 311–42.

_____. *Historia crítica de la novela guatemalteca.* Guatemala: Editorial Universitaria, 1960.

_____. "The Life and Works of Federico Gamboa." Ph.D. dissertation, New York University, 1952.

Moore, E. R. "Federico Gamboa: Diplomat and Novelist." *Books Abroad* 14, no. 4 (Fall 1940): 364–67.

Moreno, Daniel. Introduction to *María,* by Jorge Isaacs. Mexico City: Porrúa, 1967.

Navarro, Joaquina. *La novela realista mexicana.* Mexico City: Compañía General de Ediciones, 1955.

Neiss, Robert J. "Zola's *L'Oeuvre* and *Reconquista* of Gamboa." PMLA 61, no. 2 (June 1946): 577–83.

Orgambide, Pedro, and Yahni, Roberto. *Enciclopedia de la literatura argentina.* Buenos Aires: Sudamericana, 1970.

Orjuela, Héctor H. *"De sobremesa" y otros estudios sobre José Asunción Silva.* Bogotá: Instituto Caro y Cuervo, 1976.

Pérez, Trinidad. "Prologo" to *Amalia,* by José Mármol, Havana: Casa de las Américas, 1976, pp. vii–xlvii.

Perús, Francoise. *Literatura y sociedad en América Latina: El modernismo.* Havana: Casa de las Américas, 1972.

Phillips, Allen W. "El arte y el artista en algunas novelas modernistas." *Revista Hispánica Moderna,* 34, no. 3–4 (July–October 1968): 104–10.

Picón-Salas, Mariano. *Literatura venezolana.* Caracas: Editorial "Las Novedades," 1945.

Poblete Varas, Hernán. *Genio y figura de Alberto Blest Gana.* Buenos Aires: Editorial Universitaria, 1968.

Ponsetti, Helena Percas. "Sobre la Avellaneda y su novela, *Sab.*" *Revista Iberoamericana* 28, no. 54 (July–December 1961): 347–57.

Ratcliff, Dillwyn F. *Venezuelan Prose Fiction.* New York: Instituto de las Españas en los Estados Unidos, 1933.

Read, J. Lloyd. *The Mexican Historical Novel, 1826–1910.* New York: Instituto de las Españas en los Estados Unidos, 1939.

Roig de Leuchsenring, Emilio. *La literatura costumbrista cubana de los siglos XVIII y XIX,* vol. 4, *Los escritores.* Havana: Oficina del Historiador de la Ciudad, 1962.

Rojas, Angel F. *La novela ecuatoriana.* Mexico City: Fondo de Cultura Económica, 1948.

Rojas Garcidueñas, José. "La novela en la Nueva España." *Anales del Instituto de Investigaciones Estéticas* 8, no. 30 (1962): 57–78.

Sánchez, Luis Alberto. *Proceso y contenido de la novela hispanoamericana.* Madrid: Gredos, 1953.

Schultz de Mantovani, Fryda. *Apasionados del nuevo mundo.* Buenos Aires: Editorial Raigal, 1952.

————. "Estudio preliminar," introduction to *Aves sin nido,* by Clorinda Matto de Turner. Buenos Aires: Solar/Hachette, 1968.

Schwartz, Kessel. *A New History of Spanish American Fiction,* vol. 1. Coral Gables, Fla.: University of Miami Press, 1972.

Silva Castro, Raúl. *Alberto Blest Gana (1830–1920).* Santiago: Editorial Universitaria, 1941.

————. *Panorama de la novela chilena (1843–1953).* Mexico City: Fondo de Cultura Económica, 1953.

Solera, Rodrigo, "La novela costarricense." Ph.D. dissertation, University of Kansas, 1964.

Sommers, Joseph. "The Indian Oriented Novel in Latin America: New Spirit, New Forms, New Scope." *Journal of Inter-American Studies* 6, no. 2 (April 1964): 149–66.

Souza, Raymond D. *Major Cuban Novelists.* Columbia, Mo.: University of Missouri Press, 1976.

Suárez-Murias, Marguerite. *La novela romántica en Hispanoamérica.* New York: Hispanic Institute in the United States, 1963.

Tapia Olarte, E. "Noticia preliminar," introduction to *Aves sin nido,* by Clorinda Matto de Turner. Cuzco: Universidad Nacional del Cuzco, 1948.

Theobald, J. O. "Naturalism in the Works of Federico Gamboa." Master's thesis, University of Arizona, 1933.

Torres Ríoseco, Arturo. *La novela en la América Hispana.* Berkeley: University of California Press, 1939.

Valledeperes, Manuel. "Evolución de la novela en la República Dominicana." *Cuadernos Hispanoamericanos* 206 (February 1967): 311–25.

Viñas, David. *Literatura argentina y realidad política.* Buenos Aires: Jorge Alvarez Editor, 1964.

Warner, Ralph E. *Historia de la novela mexicana en el siglo XIX.* Mexico City: Robredo, 1953.

Woolsey, A. W. "Some of the Social Problems Considered by Federico Gamboa." *Modern Language Journal* 34, no. 4 (April 1950): 294–97.

Yáñez, Mirta, ed. *La novela romántica latinoamericana.* Havana: Casa de las Américas, 1978.

Yépez Miranda, Alfredo. "Estudio crítico, introduction to *Aves sin nido,* by Clorinda Matto de Turner. Cuzco: Universidad del Cuzco, 1948.

Zum Felde, Alberto. *Indice crítico de la literatura hispanoamericana,* vol 2, *La narrativa.* Mexico City: Guaranía, 1959.

3. THEORY

Aldana, Lorenzo. *La crítica literaria.* Bogotá: Editores Colombia, 1977.

Alter, Robert. *Partial Magic, The Novel as a Self-Conscious Genre.* Berkeley and Los Angeles: University of California Press, 1975.

Arnheim, Rudolf. *Entropy and Art, An Essay on Disorder and Order.* Berkeley and Los Angeles: University of California Press, 1971.

Auerbach, Erich. *Mimesis: The Representation of Reality in Western Literature.* Princeton, N. J. Princeton University Press, 1968.

Bal, Mieke. "Narration et focalisation." *Poétique* 29 (February 1977): 107–27.

Barthes, Roland. *S/Z, An Essay.* New York: Hill and Wang, 1974.

––––––. "Textural Analysis of a Tale by Edgar Poe." *Poe Studies,* 10, no. 1 (June 1977), 1–12.

––––––. *Writing Degree Zero and Elements of Semiology.* Boston: Beacon Press, 1970.

Barzun, Jacque. *Classic, Romantic, and Modern.* Chicago: University of Chicago Press, 1943.

Beck, Mary Ann, et al., eds. *The Analysis of Hispanic Texts: Current Trends in Methodology.* New York: Bilingual Press, 1976.

Booth, Wayne C. *The Rhetoric of Fiction.* Chicago: University of Chicago Press, 1961.

Bourneuf, Roland, and Ouellet, Réal. *La novela.* Barcelona: Editorial Ariel, 1975.

Brooks, Cleanth, and Warren, Robert Penn. *Understanding Fiction.* New York: Appleton-Century-Crofts, 1959.

Campos, Julieta. *Función de la novela.* Mexico City: Editorial Joaquin Mortiz, 1973.

Cirlot, J. E. *A Dictionary of Symbols.* New York: The Philosophical Library, 1962.

Craig, David, ed. *Marxists on Literature, An Anthology.* Harmondsworth, England: Penguin Books, 1975.

Culler, Jonathan. *Structuralist Poetics.* Ithaca, N.Y.: Cornell University Press, 1975.

Davis, Lisa E., and Tarán, Isabel C. eds. *The Analysis of Hispanic Texts: Current Trends in Methodology.* New York: Bilingual Press, 1976.

De George, Fernande M. "From Russian Formalism to French Structuralism." *Comparative Literature Studies* 14, no. 1 (March 1977): 20–9.

De George, Richard T. "Communism and the New Marxists," in *Marxism and Religion in Eastern Europe,* De George and Scanlon, eds., Dordrecht, Holland: D. Reidel, 1976.

De George, Richard and Fernande, eds. *The Structuralists from Marx to Lévi-Strauss.* Garden City, N. Y.: Anchor Books, Doubleday and Company, 1972.

Derrida, Jacques. *Of Grammatology.* Baltimore: The Johns Hopkins University Press, 1974.

Eagleton, Terry. *Marxism and Literary Criticism.* Berkeley and Los Angeles: University of California Press, 1976.

Eliade, Mircea. *The Sacred and the Profane.* New York: Harcourt, Brace and World, 1959.

Fish, Stanley. "Literature in the Reader: Affective Stylistics." *New Literary History* 2, no. 1 (1970–71), 123–62.

Forster, E. M. *Aspects of the Novel.* New York: Harcourt, Brace and World, Inc., 1927.

Freedman, Richard. *The Novel.* New York: Newsweek Books, 1975.

Friedman, Norman. "Point of View in Fiction: The Development of a New Critical Concept." *PMLA* 70, no. 5 (December 1955): 1160–84.

Frye, Northrop. *Anatomy of Criticism, Four Essays.* Princeton, N. J. Princeton University Press, 1957.

García de Aldridge, Adriana. "Two Latin-American Theorists of the Historical Novel." *Clio* 4, no. 2 February 1975): 183–99.

Genette, Gérard. *Figures III.* Paris: Editions du Seuil, 1972.

Gilbert, Allan H. *Literary Criticism: Plato to Dryden.* Detroit: Wayne State University Press, 1962.

Goldmann, Lucien. *Para una sociología de la novela.* Madrid: Editorial Ayuso, 1975.

Guillén, Claudio. *Literature as System.* Princeton, N.J.: Princeton University Press, 1971.

Horner, Winifred Bryan. "Text Act Theory: A Study of Nonficton Texts." Ph.D. dissertation, University of Michigan, 1975.

Jakobson, Roman. "Linguistics and Poetics," in Sebeok, Thomas A., ed., *Style and Language.* Cambridge, Mass.: The MIT Press, 1960.

──────, and Halle, Morris. *Fundamentals of Language.* The Hague: Janua Linguarum, Mouton, 1956.

Jitrik, Noe. *Procedimiento y mensaje en la novela.* Argentina: Universidad Nacional de Córdoba, 1962.

Lemon, Lee T., and Reis, Marion J., eds. *Russian Formalist Criticism: Four Essays.* Lincoln: University of Nebraska Press, 1965.

Lubbock, Percy. *The Craft of Fiction.* New York: The Viking Press, 1957.

Lukács, George. *The Theory of the Novel.* Cambridge, Mass. The MIT Press, 1971.

Marshall, Donald G. "Plot as Trap: Plot as Mediation." *The Bulletin of the Midwest Modern Language Association* 10:, no. 1 (Spring 1979): 11–28.

Martínez Bonati, Félix. *La estructura de la obra literaria.* Barcelona: Editorial Seix Barral, 1972.

Merrell, Floyd. "Structuralism and Beyond: A Critique of Presuppositions." *Diógenes* 92 (1975): 67–103.

Mignolo, Walter. "Aspectos del cambio literario (A propósito de la *Historia de la novela hispanoamericana* de Cedomil Goic)." *Revista Iberoamericana* 42, no. 94 (January–March 1976): 31–49.

Miers, Paul. "Language, Literature, and the Limits of Theory." *The Bulletin of the Midwest Modern Language Association* 10, no. 1 (Spring 1977): 29–37.

Mitchell, Bonner. "The Attack on Gustave Lanson and Literary History, 1908–1914." *University of South Carolina French Literature Series,* vol. 4 (1977): 13–22.

Monteforte Toledo, Mario, et al. *Literatura, idieología y lenguaje.* Mexico City: Grijalbo, 1976.

Morán, Fernando. *Novela y semidesarrollo.* Madrid: Taurus Ediciones, 1971.

Ong, Walter J. "From Mimesis to Irony: The Distancing of Voice." *The Bulletin of the Midwest Modern Language Association* 9, no. 1/2 (Spring/Fall 1976): 1–24.

──────. "The Writer's Audience Is Always a Fiction." *PMLA* 90, no. 1 (January 1975): 9–21.

Piaget, Jean. *Structuralism,* trans. Chaninah Maschler. New York: Basic Books, 1970.

Pizarro, N. *Analisis estructural de la novela.* Madrid: Siglo XXI, 1970.

Prada Oropeza, Renato, *La autonomía literaria.* Veracruz, Mexico: Cuadernos de *Texto Crítico,* 1977.

_____. ed. *Lingüística y literatura*. Xalapa, Mexico: Universidad Vera-cruzana, 1978.

Pratt, Mary Louise. *Toward a Speech Act Theory of Literary Discourse.* Bloomington: Indiana University Press, 1977.

Scholes, Robert. *Structuralism in Literature: An Introduction.* New Haven: Yale University Press, 1974.

_____. "Toward a Semiotics of Literature." *Critical Inquiry* 4, no. 1 (Autumn 1977): 105–20.

_____, and Kellogg, Robert. *The Nature of Narrative.* London, Oxford, New York: Oxford University Press, 1966.

Searle, John R. *Speech Acts: An Essay on the Philosophy of Language.* London: Cambridge University Press, 1969.

Segre, Cesare. "Culture and Modeling Systems." *Critical Inquiry* 4, no. 3 (Spring 1978): 525–37.

"Tel Quel" (ed. dirigée par Philippe Sollers). *Théorie d'ensemble.* Paris: Editions du Seuil, 1968.

Todorov, Tzvetan. *The Fantastic: A Structural Approach to Literary Genre.* Ithaca, N.Y.: Cornell University Press, 1975.

_____. *Littérature et Signification.* Paris: Librairie Larousse, 1967.

_____. *The Poetics of Prose.* Ithaca, N.Y.: Cornell University Press, 1977.

_____. *Poétique de la Prose.* Paris: Editions du Seuil, 1971.

Torre, Guillermo de. *Nuevas direcciones de la crítica literaria.* Madrid: Alianza Editorial, 1970.

Vidal, Hernán. *Literatura hispano-americana e ideología liberal: Surgimiento y crisis.* Buenos Aires: Ediciones Hispamérica, 1976.

Wasiolek, Edward. "Introduction," to Serge Doubrovsky, *The New Criticism in France,* pp. 1–38. Chicago: University of Chicago Press, 1973.

Watt, Ian. *The Rise of the Novel.* Berkeley and Los Angeles: University of California Press, 1957.

Weimann, Robert. *Structure and Society in Literary History.* Charlottesville: University of Virginia Press, 1976.

Wellek, René. *Concepts of Criticism.* New Haven: Yale University Press, 1963.

White, John J. *Mythology in the Modern Novel.* Princeton, N. J.: Princeton University Pres, 1971.

Index